Fritz Hommel, Edmund McClure

The Ancient Hebrew Tradition as Illustrated by the Old Monuments

Fritz Hommel, Edmund McClure

The Ancient Hebrew Tradition as Illustrated by the Old Monuments

ISBN/EAN: 9783337316525

Printed in Europe, USA, Canada, Australia, Japan

Cover: Foto ©ninafisch / pixelio.de

More available books at **www.hansebooks.com**

THE ANCIENT HEBREW TRADITION

As Illustrated by the Monuments

A Protest Against the Modern School of Old Testament Criticism

BY

DR. FRITZ HOMMEL

PROFESSOR OF SEMITIC LANGUAGES AT THE UNIVERSITY OF MUNICH

TRANSLATED FROM THE GERMAN BY
EDMUND McCLURE, M.A., AND LEONARD CROSSLÉ

New York
E. & J. B. YOUNG & CO.
COOPER UNION, FOURTH AVENUE

LONDON
SOCIETY FOR PROMOTING CHRISTIAN KNOWLEDGE
1897

COPYRIGHT, 1897,
BY E. & J. B. YOUNG & CO.

ELECTROTYPED AND PRINTED BY THE
TROW DIRECTORY
PRINTING AND BOOKBINDING COMPANY
NEW YORK

PREFACE TO THE ENGLISH EDITION

IN view of the fact that my Preface to the German edition of the present work contains nothing which does not equally appeal to the English-speaking public, it seems superfluous for me to prefix any special introduction for the benefit of readers on the other side of the Channel or of the Atlantic—more particularly since my *Assyriological Notes* in the *Proceedings* of the Society for Biblical Archæology and my contributions to the *Sunday School Times* have perhaps already made my name familiar to them. I shall merely content myself by referring here to a volume recently published by G. Buchanan Gray, which has only just come into my hands, and which, though in many respects an excellent production, indicates in its main conclusion (see the "late artificial creation of some of the most striking characteristics in the Proper Names[1] of the Priestly Code," cf. the summaries on pp. 194 and 207 *et seq.*) a distinctly retrograde movement when compared with Nestle's work. The investigations recorded in the present volume, based as they are on material obtained from the inscriptions, furnish a sufficient reply to Gray's contention. " External Evidence " must be the banner under which all students of Old Testament Literature are to range themselves in the future.

FRITZ HOMMEL.

Maderno, Lago di Garda,
April 14, 1897.

---

[1] *Studies in Hebrew Proper Names :* London, 1896.

TRANSLATORS' NOTE

THE Proper names—other than Biblical—cited in the text are given, as a rule, in the form adopted by Prof. Hommel, but it has been deemed advisable to substitute for his representative of the letter *Tsade*, the more familiar *ts*, and for the *Kheth*, "Kh" instead of "Ch." Biblical Proper names are given for the most part in the form they assume in the Revised Version of the Old Testament, but the Hebrew *yod* is rendered by *y* and not *j*, (as in "Yahveh"), except in a few instances where common usage has secured the permanence of the latter letter.

PREFACE

FOR years past, I have been convinced that the question of the authenticity of the Ancient Hebrew tradition could not be finally decided, until the Hebrew personal names found in the Old Testament had first been exhaustively compared with other contemporary names of similar formation, and carefully checked by them; and that all that was needed was the hand of an expert to disclose the treasures hitherto concealed in them, and to set forth the evidence they contain in such clear and convincing fashion as to render all further discussion impossible. Twenty-one years ago, Eberhard Nestle,[1] in a valuable work which still retains its place in the estimation of scholars, endeavoured to use the personal names of the Old Testament as a touch-stone by which to test the authority of Hebrew tradition. Nestle correctly divided Hebrew personal names into three main groups, corresponding to the three stages of evolution observable in the religion of the Old Testament. In the first, he placed names compounded with El (God); in the second those belonging to the period between Joshua and Solomon (or

[1] *Die israelitischen Eigennamen nach ihrer religions-geschichtlichen Bedeutung*, Haarlem 1876.

Elijah), in which the divine name Yahveh comes to occupy a favoured place beside El, the name of the Canaanite deity Baal (Lord) being subsequently added, and lastly, the names of the monarchical period, containing almost without exception the element Yahveh (Yo, Yahu or Yah), and thus bearing witness to the permanent victory of Yahveh over Baal. Moreover, in his explanation of the ancient Hebrew equivalents of the divine name El, viz. *Abi* = my father, *Ammi* = my uncle, Nestle was not far wide of the mark.[1] Indeed, this attempt of Nestle's might have found acceptance, as a solution of the Pentateuch problem, had not Wellhausen roundly asserted that the personal names of the Mosaic period to be found in the Priestly Code, had been deliberately manufactured in later times after an earlier pattern, and that their testimony was consequently worthless. The question was thus left in very much the same position as before.

One of the main objects, therefore, which I have kept before me in writing the present book, has been to adduce external evidence (*i.e.* from contemporary inscriptions) to show that even from the time of Abraham onwards personal names of the characteristically Mosaic type were in actual use among a section of the Semites of Western Asia, and that it is consequently useless to talk any longer of a later postexilic invention. On the contrary, the theory of their evolution put forward by Nestle is confirmed and corroborated in every direction. The great im-

[1] Cf. more especially pp. 182 *et seq.* (particularly p. 187, note 3, contrasted with p. 50) of Nestle's book.

portance of its subject-matter must be my excuse for entering, in Chapter III., into what may at first sight seem excessive detail. This chapter supplies the basis of my whole argument, and it was therefore necessary to examine the material contained in it from as many different points of view as possible. Just as in Chapter II. (the History of Palestine before the time of Abraham) I had to prepare the way for the later historical chapters (the 4th and subsequent chapters), in order to help the reader to a proper understanding of that part of the history of Israel which begins with Abraham, so too, in Chapter III., it was necessary to explain as fully as possible the peculiar system of name-formation in vogue among the earliest Arabs—to which race the Hebrews of that time belonged—and to emphasize the important lessons which it has to teach the student of religious history. On the other hand, this chapter afforded me an opportunity, which I could not allow to pass, of completing the evidence in support of a fact of the utmost historical importance, namely, the Arabian origin of the dynasty which occupied the throne of Babylon in the time of Abraham. Before going any farther, therefore, I must ask my readers not to allow themselves to be deterred by the array of personal names — to each of which I have been careful to add a translation—which they will find in Chapter III., but rather to peruse it with particular attention before proceeding farther. Even those who are not acquainted with Hebrew will be able to understand it, notwithstanding the fact that the present volume is primarily addressed to the theologian and the archaeologist; these latter will find themselves on what has long been familiar ground to them, in the company of old acquaintances, such as Khammurabi and other similar personages. I look forward to the time when every enlightened reader of the Bible will also be something of an archaeologist: in England and America this is much more generally the case than in Germany, a fact which is proved by the large circulation attained by popular scientific works on Assyriology and the literature of the Old Testament, such as those of Sayce and Maspero, etc.

For the rest, the Table of Contents appended below (p. xiii.) will convey the best idea of the subjects dealt with in this volume. In addition to those portions which bear on the criticism of the Pentateuch, this work contains such a mass of evidence from the inscriptions—throwing new light on the history of religion and on sacred archaeology—that even those who may consider that I have failed in my main purpose, will still find plenty of material which they cannot afford to treat with indifference, or explain away. But truth must in the end prevail. The monuments speak with no faltering tongue, and already I seem to see signs of the approach of a new era in which men will be able to brush aside the cobweb theories of the so-called "higher critics" of the Pentateuch, and, leaving such old-fashioned errors behind them, attain to a clearer perception of the real facts. The gales of spring are already beginning to sweep across the fields that have so long lain ice-bound. I seem to trace their influence in the effect produced on every unprejudiced mind by that marvellous book of James Robertson's on the pre-prophetic religion of Israel,[1] of which no less a personage than the late August Dillmann declared that it hit the nail right on the head. In the same category I would place a paper from the pen of the Swedish scholar S. A. Fries, which has only just come under my notice, entitled, "Were the Israelites ever in Egypt?"[2] in which he puts forward the view set forth in the present volume. He holds that certain of the tribes of Israel had already settled in Palestine before the time of Moses; that the land of Goshen included also the southern portion of Judah; that Moses ("influenced, as he is inclined to think, by the speculative ideas of the Egyptian priests") transformed the ancient divine name Yo or Yahu into Yahveh; that Hebron, which had from time immemorial been connected with Tanis by community of interests (cf. the well-known passage in Num. xiii. 22), owed its new name to the Khabiri (prior to this it was known as Kirjath Arba); and finally, that the 49th chapter of Genesis, even if it were not composed by Jacob himself, must at any rate be of pre-Mosaic origin.[3] Neither has Fries failed to note W. Max Müller's contention that the

[1] *The Early Religion of Israel*, Edinburgh and London, 1890.
[2] In the Egyptological journal the *Sphinx*, vol. 1 pt. 4 (Upsala 1897), pp. 207—221; this did not appear until the index of the present volume was ready for press.
[3] Fries draws attention to a very important point which I had overlooked, viz. that in 1 Chron. vii. 20, we have an ancient pre-Mosaic tradition dealing with a predatory raid made by the Ephraimites into Palestine (and therefore from the Land of Goshen).

tribe of Asser (Asher) must have been installed in the territory ascribed to it in later times as far back as the time of Seti I.; he will be, therefore, all the more likely to agree with what I have said of Heber and Malki-el (end of Chap. VII.), and of the Land of Ashur in southern Palestine (Chap. VIII.).

Many of the conclusions at which I have arrived are of even wider importance than I had supposed when I first put them on paper; *e.g.* the fact on which I have so frequently laid stress, that the Israelites in the time of Abraham to Joshua spoke a dialect of Arabic, and that it was not till after the conquest of the region west of Jordan that they adopted the Canaanite tongue. In connection with it stands my other conclusion that the earliest Israelite traditions, and undoubtedly the Mosaic law as well, must originally have been set down in the Minaean script (or at any rate in characters more nearly related to the latter than to the Canaanite alphabet). This assumption (in regard to the Arabic character of the earliest Hebrew), which is a necessary corollary to my researches in regard to the early personal names, clears up more than one doubtful point in the history of the Hebrew language; it throws a fresh light on the much-discussed alternative forms of the word "*anoki*" and "*ani*" [= I], the first of these being the Canaanite form, while the second (which belongs for the most part to the Priestly Code) is the ancient Hebrew equivalent of the pronoun (cf. Arab-Aram. *ana* = I).[1]

[1] And here the word must have been borrowed from Babylonian, cf. Babyl. *anaku* = I ; all the Western Semitic races must originally have

I take this opportunity of urging the younger school of Old Testament theologians to abandon their barren speculations in regard to the source of this or that fraction of a verse, and rather to devote their youthful energies to the far more profitable study of the Assyro-Babylonian and South Arabian inscriptions, in order that they may be able, at first hand, to place the output of these absolutely inexhaustible mines of knowledge at the service of Biblical students; nothing can be more deplorable than to find a scholar persistently devoting his most important labours to second-hand sources of information. There are hundreds of contract tablets of the time of Abraham, any one of which may contain some interesting find—such as the name Ai-kalabu (*v. infra* pp. 110 *et seq.*) or Jacob-el (Ya'kubu-ilu, *v.* p. 294),—which lie still unedited in the museums of Europe; and the importance of the Minaeo-Sabaean inscriptions to the study of the Old Testament is shown—apart from the numerous examples adduced in this volume—by the fact that expressions in the Priestly Code, such as *bara'* = to create (Gen. i. 1), or religious terms such as *berith*[1] = covenant, agreement, find their closest parallels—not in the later Aramaic, but in South Arabian. I earnestly hope that Eduard Glaser, the indefatigable explorer of the "Arabian Empire," will not oblige us to wait

used the word *ana* for " I " (an abbreviation from the primitive Semitic *anaku-ya*, cf. the plural *anakh-na*).

[1] Cf. the Sabaean *bara'a* = to build, lay the foundations of, and *berît*, Æthiopian (*i.e.* originally Hadramautic, Z.D.M.G. xlvi. pp. 536 *et seq.*), *ebrêt* = alternating service or function.

much longer before he consents to open his treasure-chambers. He was the first to assign to the Minaeans their true place in history, and thus reinforced Sayce in his epoch-making identification of the name of the Babylonian king Ammi-zaduga with the Minaean Ammi-tsaduka; he is, however, very chary of his inscriptions (apart from the originals which he brought back with him to Europe), and only allows us to examine them piece-meal.[1] And yet no further addition of any real value can be made to our knowledge of South Arabian antiquity until the material so far available has been made better known. Glaser's inscriptions consist of hundreds of casts and numerous copies, but they are unfortunately inaccessible to all so long as they remain buried in his cases. A great benefit would be conferred on science, and on the study of the Old Testament in particular, if these documents, which no one but a Glaser could have ferreted out and procured, were to be placed in some museum where they would be available for general use.

[1] Cf. certain later Sabaean inscriptions, edited and annotated in a most masterly manner by Glaser in his recent work, *Die Abessinier in Arabien und Afrika*, Munich, 1895.

TABLE OF CONTENTS

CHAPTER I

INTRODUCTION..................................Page 1

The view of the Evolution of the History of Israel presented (1) by tradition, (2) by the "higher critics"—The "sources" of the Old Testament—Deuteronomy quoted by Hosea—The late date assigned by Wellhausen to Deuteronomy and the "Priestly Code"—Amos v. 25—Obsolete expressions found in the "Priestly Code"—Green and Sayce—Application of the Critical methods formulated by Meyer to the "Priestly Code."

CHAPTER II

THE EARLY HISTORY OF PALESTINE................Page 28

Assyriology and Egyptology—Tel el-Amarna—Gudea's [1] relations with the "Countries of the West"—The Nimrod Epos and Arabia—The later kings of Ur and the *Nûr Bel*—Elam and Arabia—The kings of Larsa—The Arabian dynasty of Khammurabi, its conquest of Larsa and Elam and its supremacy over Palestine—The Pharaohs of the Pyramid Period and the Sinaitic Peninsula—Campaign against the Heru-sha—The "Middle Empire"—Adventures of Sinûhît—The 37 Asiatics on the Tomb of Khnûmhotpû—Babylonians and Western Semites.

CHAPTER III

THE ARABS IN BABYLONIA BEFORE AND IN THE TIME OF ABRAHAM....................................Page 56

The *Nûr Bel* and Martu—Arab personal names under the Khammurabi Dynasty—Babylonian Nomenclature—The Baby-

---

[1] Evidence has now been obtained from contemporary inscriptions to prove that even the early kings of Agadi (Akkad), Sargon and Naram-Sin (c. 3500 B.C.) made expeditions not only to Arabia (Magan), but to Martu as well.

Ionian Pantheon—The South Arabian Inscriptions—The Arabian Pantheon—South Arabian Nomenclature—Religious significance of both Babylonian and South Arabian personal names—Arabian origin of the Khammurabi Dynasty, Pognon, Sayce, etc.—Conclusive evidence of the Arabian form of all the names of the kings—Arabian names of private individuals under the Khammurabi Dynasty—Shem and Yahveh—Shaddi—Aī or Ya—Yah.

CHAPTER IV

CHRONOLOGY OF THE TIME OF ABRAHAM..........Page 118

Previous attempts to fix the date of the Khammurabi Dynasty—The small tablet containing lists of the two first Dynasties—The List of Kings—Dynasties A and B contemporaneous—The Biblical Chronology—Apocryphal Character of Dynasty B—Its founder Ilû-ma alone historical—Gulkishar—The Biblical Chronology again—Pieser's Theory—Arabian Origin of the Assyrian Nation.

CHAPTER V

ABRAHAM AND KHAMMURABI.....................Page 146

The narrative in Gen. xiv. — The Melchizedek Episode — Quoted in the Epistle to the Hebrews—'Abd-khiba of Jerusalem—Proposed emendation of Gen. xiv. 17—24—The political background in Gen. xiv.—View taken of it by the "higher critics"—Inscriptions of Kudur-Mabug and Eri-aku—Conquest of Erech and Nisin—Yamutbal (Elam) and Martu—Khammurabi's letter to Sin-idinam in reference to Kudur-luggamar—Khammurabi's victory over Eri-Aku and conquest of Yamutbal—The Babylonian Epos in regard to Kudur-lugmal's devastation of Babylon and Borsippa—Conclusions which we may draw from it—The Ancient Babylonian cuneiform original of Gen. xiv.—The City of Malgî and Assur-bel-kala's Ebir-nâri Inscription (K. 3500).

CHAPTER VI

JACOB THE ARAMAEAN ....Page 201

Dillman's view—Aramaic and Arabic—The Achlami—Padan—The land of Kir and the Aramaean tribes of Babylonia—Ur-Kasdim and the Chaldaeans.

CHAPTER VII

PALESTINE IN THE TEL EL-AMARNA PERIOD...... Page 213

The Canaanite language in 1400 B.C.—Canaanite and Phoenician personal names—Arabic names in South Palestine—The Canaanite religion in 1400 B.C.—Hebrew personal names—The Land of Goshen—The Israelites did not lead a mere nomadic existence there—The Khabiri—Heber and Malki-el—Hebron.

CHAPTER VIII

THE LAND OF SHÛR AND THE MINAEANS..........Page 235

The tribe of Asser (Asher) and its territory in Goshen in Southern Palestine—Ashurim and Dedan—Shûr an abbreviation of Ashûr—The Southern Geshur an abbreviation of Gê-Ashûr—Ashûr and 'Eber in Balaam's " Parables "—The invasion of the " Peoples of the Sea" foretold—The Minaean Inscription Hal. 535 (= Gl. 1115) and the date at which it was composed—The term 'Ibr naharân—Ebir-nâri—Eber ha-nahar (cf. Appendix)—The Epri of the Egyptian Inscriptions—The land of Eshru—The land of Gari in the Tel el-Amarna Inscriptions—Char or Chor—Ashur in Hosea ix. 3 (quotation from Deut.) a part of Goshen—The Mînephtah Inscription in which Israel is referred to—Levi and Simeon.

CHAPTER IX

THE TIME OF MOSES..........................Page 268

Commerce of the Minaeans and Midianites—Midian and Ma'ân Mutsrân synonymous terms—South Arabian place-names in the region east of Jordan—The spelling of the Mesa Inscription and of Hebrew based on Minaean influence—Conclusion to be drawn therefrom in regard to the earliest Hebrew script—Jethro, Priest of Midian—Ancient Arabic expressions in the " Priestly Code "—Egyptian original of the High Priest's Breast-plate or *khoshen*—The Levites in the " Priestly Code," in Deuteronomy and in Ezekiel—The " Priestly Code," in the time of the Judges and of the Kings—Egyptian loan-words in the Old Testament—Arpakeshad and Ur-Kasdim—Personal names in the Book of Numbers.

CHAPTER X

FROM JOSHUA TO DAVID — RETROSPECT AND CONCLUSION .... Page 302

Distinction between the Names of the time of the Judges and those of the Mosaic Period—The Primitive History in the Bible not of Canaanite origin—The Hebrew Metrical system a legacy from Ancient Babylonia—The story of the Fall.

APPENDICES .... Pages 317–326

(a) *The land of Yadi'a-ab.*
(b) *The Divine Name Tsûr* in the South Arabian Inscriptions—Purification and sin-offerings prescribed in them.
(c) *The land of Eber* and the geographical term Ebir Nâri, (Eber ha-nahar, 'Ibr naharân) originally Ur-Kasdim.

INDEX .... Page 327

LIST OF AUTHORS REFERRED TO .... Page 347

LIST OF BIBLICAL PASSAGES REFERRED TO .... Page 349

THE ANCIENT HEBREW TRADITION

CHAPTER I

INTRODUCTION

No nation of early times has had two such widely different versions of its history presented to modern readers as that of Israel. If we may accept the almost unanimous verdict of late, not to say the latest, criticism, certain Hebrew tribes, who were soon joined by others, started out, it is alleged, from the Sinaitic peninsula about the year 1200 B.C., and after long wanderings in the desert, at length arrived in the region east of Jordan, under the leadership of their prophet Moses. After his death they crossed the Jordan under Joshua, and succeeded after a series of protracted conflicts in subduing or exterminating the Amorite and Canaanite settlers on its western banks. As the Canaanites were, so the critics tell us, in possession of a higher culture, the Israelites, who are represented as having been at that time a race of semi-barbarous nomads, were really conquered by the more advanced civilization of their foes, a nemesis which frequently dogs the footsteps of the victorious barbarian, if we may credit the lessons of history. The new-comers, as we are informed by the critics, appropriated the holy places of the Canaanitish heroes, such as that of Abraham at Hebron, or that of Jacob at Bethel, and came in the course of centuries to regard them as so entirely their own, that later on it became a firmly established article of popular belief that Abraham, Isaac, and Jacob were the earliest ancestors of the Hebrew race. The laws traditionally ascribed to Moses, it is contended, first came into existence either during or after the monarchical period, while of the prophets only a certain number, such as Amos, Hosea, Isaiah, Jeremiah, and Ezekiel, are allowed by the critics to retain the place so long accorded to them.

This is a brief account of the evolution of the history of the Israelites during the past two decades, according to the results of investigations associated with the name of Wellhausen and others, and put forward in Stade's[1] well-known work on the subject. The representatives of the orthodox opponents of this school are being gradually reduced to a minority, and the new views, especially among the younger disciples, are so triumphantly pressed home, that an attempt to return to the old line seems, especially to the lay mind, as only worthy of a pitying smile in the face of the assured position of the critics. To realize the present position we have but to listen to the words of one of the most strenuous defenders of the so-called "modern" critics of the Pentateuch, Professor C. H. Cornill of Königsberg, in the prospectus of his *Der Israelitische Prophetismus* (a little volume intended for the general Reader)—words which I

---

[1] *Geschichte des Volkes Israel*, 2nd ed.: Berlin, Grote.

purposely transcribe in full: " Scarcely any branch of scientific study has, during the last few generations, undergone such a revolution as that dealing with the Old Testament. A rigidly critical attitude has taken the place of the traditional view of the history of the Hebrew religion. Its various stages are now regarded as steps in a process of organic evolution. Individual facts are assigned their true place in the general scheme, and receive their proper meaning and explanation in connection therewith. This organic view of the Old Testament was at first received with distrust and aversion, even by experts, for it is no easy matter to make up one's mind to abandon beliefs which have been accepted without question for two thousand years: gradually, however, owing to the persuasive power of its inherent truth, it has succeeded in gaining headway; and, especially since the appearance, in 1878, of Wellhausen's brilliant and convincing exposition of his views,[1] has entered upon a course of uninterrupted triumph." So far Professor Cornill, and many other utterances to the same effect might be adduced in support of his position.

It would seem to follow, then, that we must no longer date the commencement of the history of Israel from the migration into Canaan of the pious and God-fearing patriarch Abraham from Ur of the Chaldees, nor give credence to the story of the sojourn of the children of Israel in Egypt, and of their wonderful exodus from that land of bondage—for all this, according to the critics, is pure myth, the poetic

[1] *Geschichte Israels*, vol. i., Prolegomena.

invention of a later period. The true beginning, it is alleged, was the time of the "Heroic Legend," which includes not only the period of the Judges, but a part of the time of Samuel, and the early life of David. According to the critics, it is only when we come to Solomon and his successors that we find ourselves on firm historical ground, and even then they would have us believe that the narrative in the Books of the Kings has been subjected to a biassed revision. The Bible narrative tells us, for example, that in the reign of Josiah, one of the last kings of Judah, the so-called "Second giving of the Law" (Deuteronomy), which has come down to us as the Fifth Book of Moses, was discovered during the rebuilding of the Temple. In no other part of the Biblical code do we find so marked an insistance on the necessity for a single centre of worship (meaning, of course, Jerusalem), and on the observance of moral obligations, as in this "recapitulation" of the Law of God given by Moses in the land of Moab. Now, as far back as 1878, Wellhausen declared in the most emphatic terms, "that in all centres where scientific results may hope for recognition, it is admitted that it (Deuteronomy) was written at the time in which it was discovered, and was employed as a basis for the reforms introduced by King Josiah." In other words, however pious the intention may have been, a downright forgery on a grand scale had been carried out. When, therefore, we come upon traces of the influence of this Deuteronomic code in the Books of the Kings prior to the time of Josiah, we have merely to assume that the passages in question have been subjected to a so-called Deuteronomistic revision. According to Wellhausen, the whole of these passages have been re-edited to bring them into harmony with Deuteronomy.

This view of the origin of Deuteronomy has been very variously received. It is significant to note, that the primary effect of these conclusions was to produce wide dissension among theologians themselves, the official guardians and expounders of the sacred records of the Bible, dissensions all the more serious, since the post-dating of Deuteronomy necessarily involved, as we shall learn further on, the ascription of a still later date to other parts of the Pentateuch. The orthodox or conservative party naturally regarded an acceptance of the new theories as equivalent to admitting that the Old Testament is nothing more, from beginning to end, than a tissue of pious deceptions, an admission which, of course, was entirely opposed to their conception of its inspired character. Others, while reverently adhering to their belief in the divine administration, even under the Old Covenant, felt, at the same time, that they could not entirely ignore the main points of Wellhausen's arguments, and took refuge in the assumption that, in so far as the words which were put into the mouths of the earlier authorities are concerned, the idea of a code of literary ethics was as foreign to Old Testament writers as it was to the rest of antiquity; and that, provided they had warrant for believing that the matter they set down was in harmony with the meaning and spirit of those earlier authorities, and that it was to the advantage of the people that it should be handed down to them, they were justified in speaking in their names (or, as in the present instance, in the name of Moses). Lastly, there were those who possessed no sort of respect for tradition, or who felt nothing but scorn and contempt for anything supernatural, and took a cynical delight in pressing Wellhausen's conclusions to their ultimate consequences. It is interesting to note, in this respect, the opinion expressed by a scholar who stands entirely outside the clique of higher critics, an Orientalist whose work lies in a totally different province, Ferdinand Justi of Marburg. In his popular *History of the Oriental Peoples of Antiquity*, published in 1884 by Grote of Berlin, we find on page 352 the following remarks on the period immediately subsequent to the Babylonian Captivity (586—538 B.C.):

"Sacred and profane tradition had already undergone more than one transformation to meet changes in religious views or in the political situation, but now, in order to confer some show of authority on the poor remnant of an executive that had survived the Captivity, the falsification of ancient tradition was undertaken on a more extensive scale than ever before. A fiction was set on foot to the effect that the Priestly Code had long ago been delivered to the people by Moses, either as a law to be immediately followed by them, or as a rule for their future guidance under new conditions which Moses, in his capacity as prophet, must have been able to foresee. A wholesale perversion of history was the result; the whole body of tradition was revised on theocratic lines with a view to prove that the Levitical priesthood and priestly office had existed prior to the time of the kings, and even during the wanderings in the desert; even the history of primitive times, which teems with mythical (polytheistic) associations, was distorted in the interests of the new code, and employed to strengthen the arguments in favour of its pre-existence. The forgers carried out their work without the slightest regard for historical accuracy, and did not hesitate to asperse the memory of men who had raised the nation to greatness,[1] while they glorified tyrants and weaklings who had allowed themselves to be ruled by the priests. The forgery was too clumsy to escape detection under the searching eye of the modern critic, yet sufficiently well done to have misled mankind for centuries, and to have induced them to accept, as divine ordinances, inventions devised by Jewish Rabbis of the sixth and following centuries before Christ in order to strengthen their own influence. It was not until modern times that certain Protestant theologians, such as Ewald, Hupfeld, Vatke, de Wette, Bleek, Kuenen, Graf, Reuss, Nöldeke, Wellhausen,[2] and many others, discovered the true condition of affairs, to which only the narrow-minded or those who are misled by class interests can shut their eyes."

[1] Evidently Justi here refers to Israelitish kings such as Ahab and Joram, the "tyrants and weaklings" being the so called righteous kings of Judah.
[2] The order in which the names are given is misleading. They should properly run as follows : de Wette, Vatke, Georges, Reuss, Graf, Kuenen, Nöldeke, Wellhausen, Stade, etc.

Professor Justi does not mince matters, but his attitude is a far more honest one than that of the temporizing theologian who strives to throw dust either in the eyes of the public or in his own. For, after all, black is black, however much we may desire, on opportunist grounds, to prove it to be white.

And now, many of my readers may ask with astonishment, how, in the absence of any distinct new documents, it was possible, within the space of a few decades, for so radical a change to take place in the attitude of critics towards the Old Testament and the evolution of the Hebrew religion? Assuredly, it was not brought about by the discovery of any new monuments, either inscriptions or MSS., and yet a certain class of documents, arranged under a new system and considered in a new light, was largely responsible for the development of the theories which have now become fashionable. I refer to what are known as the "sources" of the Hexateuch (or five Books of Moses and Book of Joshua), which have been submitted of late to increasingly strict scientific scrutiny. Attention was first called to them in the last century by a French physician named Astruc; and at the present time students of the Old Testament writings are almost unanimous in recognizing the existence of four different main "sources." There is, first of all, the so-called Priestly Code, which includes the greater part of the law in Leviticus and Numbers, and the detailed description of the Tabernacle in Exodus; it is also traceable here and there in the Book of Genesis—the account of the creation in Gen. i., the genealogies in Gen. v., and several passages in the history of the patriarchs, etc., etc. being generally assigned to it. The name employed in this source to designate the Supreme Being up to Exodus vi. is not "Yahveh," but "Elohim," *i.e.* simply "God." Two other sources of a more popular nature are also readily distinguishable: One of these is the so-called "Jehovistic," in which God is always called Yahveh (Jehovah is a later and corrupt form); to this belongs the account of the creation in Gen. ii., the story of Paradise and the Fall, that of the Tower of Babel, etc. etc., in short, everything in the nature of popular narrative. It is characterized by a certain primitive freshness and vivacity which distinguish it from the didactic and often almost jejune formalism of the narrative passages in the Priestly Code. The other source of a popular character runs parallel with the Jehovistic, from the time of the Patriarchs up to the history of the Exodus and the Conquest of Canaan, and is in many respects similar to it, at any rate in its treatment of the more important incidents. This is the *Elohistic*, which seems to have owed its existence to members of the Ephraimite priesthood,[1] and follows the Priestly

[1] It is no mere coincidence that the two sources which bear traces of priestly origin should both employ, by preference, the older form "Elohim" for the divine Name. Moreover (thanks mainly to the researches of Klostermann), the theory becomes daily more probable, that the narrative portions of the so-called Priestly Code did not originally form part of an independent record, but are the works of a compiler, who took various portions, until lately regarded as peculiar to himself, from the Elohist (and this from Gen. i. onwards), but only in a revised and partly amplified form.

Code in its avoidance of the name Jahveh throughout the pre-Mosaic period. As this source was amalgamated with the Jehovistic before the introduction of both into the Priestly Code, it is in many cases no longer possible to distinguish the one from the other. Finally, the fourth source is Deuteronomy (or fifth Book of Moses), of which mention has already been made. In addition to these there is a special legal division within the Priestly Code itself known as "the Law of Holiness" (Levit. xvii.—xxii.), and in JE (a convenient symbol used to indicate the united Jehovistic and Elohistic narratives) there is a further division called "The Book of the Covenant" (Ex. xxi.—xxiii.).

It has yet to be proved, however, that we have any right to assume that Deuteronomy first came into existence at the time in which it was discovered, *i.e.*, in the latter half of the seventh century B.C., or, in other words, some 650 years after the death of Moses. And yet it is on this very assumption that Wellhausen bases one of the main pillars of his system; "in all centres where scientific results may hope for recognition" this is admitted, says Wellhausen in the Introduction to his Prolegomena. Yet Professor Klostermann has recently shown most conclusively that the narrative of the discovery of a legal code in the time of Josiah, which is rightly taken to refer to Deuteronomy, bears the impress of absolute credibility, and consequently excludes the possibility of any such subtle deception as that predicated by critics of the modern school.[1] From a single in-

[1] *Der Pentateuch* (Leipzig, 1893), pp. 92—100.

stance, viz. the passage in Deut. xxviii. 68, I am able to prove that Deuteronomy must have been known to the prophets at least as early as the time of Jotham and Menahem, about 740 B.C., and was not lost until later on during the long reign of the idolatrous king Manasseh. In this verse there is a threat that "the Lord shall bring thee into Egypt again with ships." This passage is twice quoted by Hosea, viz. Ephraim "shall return to Egypt" (viii. 13), immediately followed by (ix. 3), "and they shall eat unclean food in Assyria," a threat more in harmony with the apprehensions of the time when the cloud on the horizon was no longer Egypt but Assyria. The only possible deduction from this is that Deuteronomy must have been in existence at least long before Hosea. For, in the first place, it is evidently Hosea who has Deut. xxviii. 68 in his mind, and not Wellhausen's supposed compiler of Deuteronomy—writing in the time of Josiah—who is thinking of Hosea viii. 13; and secondly, we note that the prophet, writing under Tiglathpileser, finds the quotation inadequate, and not sufficiently appropriate to the circumstances of the time: he therefore supplements it in Hosea ix. 3 (and, indeed, according to the LXX., in Hosea viii. 13 also) by a reference to Assyria.

Another assertion of the Wellhausen school which also remains to be proved, is the statement that, prior to the conquest of the territory west of the Jordan, the Israelites were a semi-barbarous nomadic race. The same remark applies to the collateral hypothesis that the Israelites in the course of time derived the cult of the patriarchs and the heroic legends connected therewith from the Canaanites. In the present volume I propose to show, by a careful examination of the personal names which occur in the inscriptions, the high degree of development which religious ideas had attained among the Arabs, Midianites, Kenites, and kindred peoples by the middle of the second millennium before Christ. Moreover, as will be demonstrated later on, the inscriptions throw a totally new light on the relatively high degree of civilization possessed by these " nomadic " Semitic peoples.

As a general rule, the "sources" mentioned above can be readily distinguished one from another by the name which is applied in each to the Supreme Being, and by their style and language, so that it is often possible to assign with certainty a whole chapter, or at any rate large portions of a chapter, to one or other of them. Often, however (as, for instance, in the story of the Flood), the task of analysis is more difficult, owing to the intimate fusion which has taken place. In many cases, indeed, it is a pure fantasy to imagine that science possesses any solvent capable of reducing the compound to its primary elements. We too readily lose sight of the fact, sufficiently proved by the evidence of the early translations, that even after the amalgamation of the various sources, the Old Testament text underwent many modifications at the hands of officiating priests and copyists before it assumed the form in which we now possess it. The oldest known MSS. of the Hebrew Bible do not, we must remember, go further back than the eighth century A.D.[1]

So long as men were content to regard these sources as nearly contemporaneous documents, and —though originating from different quarters, and not having perhaps received their final redaction before the time of the Kings — as based on a trustworthy Mosaic tradition, it was impossible for a theory of the events of Hebrew history and of the evolution of the Hebrew religion, such as that indicated above in the passages quoted from Cornill and Justi, to gain currency.

Julius Wellhausen, following in the steps of Reuss, Vatke, and Graf, and on the strength of ingenious but misleading arguments, was the first to allot the different sources, according to their fancied origin, to various dates, far apart from one another, and all distant from the time of Moses. He not only assigned Deuteronomy to the time of Josiah (*vide supra*), but, following up his misleading theory, placed the source which contains the greater part of the Law (*i.e.* the Priestly Code) last of all—in the late post-exilic period. It is only since Wellhausen that a theory in regard to the events of sacred history, has assumed a shape which is diametrically opposed to Biblical tradition, and especially to the narrative part of the Priestly Code.

[1] Great credit is due to Aug. Klostermann for drawing special attention to this weak side of the methods employed in distinguishing between the various sources, as he has done in his book *Der Pentateuch, Beiträge zu seinem Verständniss und seiner Entstehungsgeschichte.* Leipzig, 1893.

The main reasons which led Wellhausen and his predecessors to refer the Books of Moses to such late dates are to be found in certain contradictions —the existence of which cannot be altogether denied—between the demands of what had previously been regarded as the priestly law of Moses, and the actual conditions of life in the time of the Judges, Samuel, and the Kings. The law given in the desert, with its one central Holy of Holies in the Tabernacle, its complicated system of sacrificial rules and other ceremonial observances, its hosts of religious officials (Priests and Levites), seems in after-times to have remained, in many respects, little better than a dead letter, until, about one hundred years after the return from exile, when the prophet Ezra, who was born and had grown up at Babylon, insisted on its proper observance, and by so doing founded the Jewish Church.

If we add to this that in 760 B.C. the prophet Amos, speaking in the name of God, asks the Israelites, " Did ye bring unto Me sacrifices and offerings in the wilderness forty years?" (Amos v. 25), and that Jeremiah in 608 B.C. (some years after the discovery of Deuteronomy in 621 B.C.), in speaking of God, declares that He gave the Israelites, when He brought them out of Egypt, no commands in regard to burnt-offerings and meat-offerings, but only enjoined that they should hearken to His commandments and walk in His way; then indeed it would almost seem as though the latter prophet either did not know of the Priestly Code, or at any rate did not regard the numerous sacrificial and ritual laws inserted in it as emanating from Moses.

The different interpretations, however, which have been given of the passage just quoted (Amos v. 25 *et seq.*), prove that it is not safe to base deductions on sentences thus torn from their context. Kautzsch[1] thus translates it: " Did ye bring unto Me for forty years in the desert sacrifices and offerings, O ye Israelites? Therefore shall ye now take [upon your necks] Sikkut your king, and the star your god, the Kevan, your images, which ye have made for yourselves, and I will lead you out into captivity beyond Damascus, saith the Lord." Dillmann, on the other hand,[2] renders the passage more freely, and, it seems to me, far more correctly, as follows: " Have ye then offered Me sacrifice for forty years, and at the same time borne your star-gods about with you (both of which things ye now do)?" Finally, the Greek translation (which is followed by S. Stephen, *Acts* vii. 42 *et seq.*), runs thus: Did ye offer unto Me slain beasts and sacrifices forty years in the wilderness, O house of Israel? And (=No, but) ye took up the tabernacle of Moloch, and the star of the god Raiphan (A. V. Remphan), the figures which ye made, to worship them. And I (= but I) will carry you away beyond Damascus (A. V. Babylon)." In regard to the second passage (Jeremiah vii. 22 *et seq.*), Baxter[3] has recently drawn attention to its analogy

---

[1] Or rather Hermann Guthe, who is responsible for the translation of Amos in Kautzsch's work on the Bible.
[2] *Handbuch der Alttest. Theologie* (Leipzig, 1895), p. 56.
[3] *Sanctuary and Sacrifice* (London, 1895), p. 194.

with the declaration of the Apostle St. Paul in 1 Cor. i. 17: "Christ sent me not to baptize, but to preach the gospel"; just as the words of the Apostle cannot be taken to imply that he was ignorant of the institution of the Christian rite of Baptism, so the rhetorical expression employed by Jeremiah ought not to be construed as a denial of the existence of sacrificial laws in the time of Moses: he merely intended to show that they are of secondary consequence to the people as compared with the far more important moral laws.

Moreover, it is precisely the *legal* portion of the Priestly Code, to the pre-prophetic written existence of which Hosea (viii. 12 *et seq.*) refers in such unmistakable terms,[1] which gives one, in places, an impression of extreme antiquity. The language is excessively formal and characteristic, and there is absolutely nothing to suggest that it belongs to the exilic or post-exilic period. In this latter event we should expect it to contain a large number of Babylonian and Aramaic loan-words, and it is, in fact, the absence of these which, in my opinion, constitutes the chief argument in favour of referring the Priestly Code to a far earlier date. There are, it is true, a whole host of words in the ritual language of the Old Testament which can be satisfactorily explained only by a reference to Babylonian. But

---

[1] "Though I write for him my law in ten thousand precepts (*i.e.* countless times oftener than I have already done), they (these myriads of laws) are counted as a strange thing. As for the sacrifices of mine offerings, they sacrifice flesh and eat it; but the Lord accepteth them not; now will He remember their iniquity and visit their sins."

these terms¹ date back to the early Babylonian period, and belong therefore to a totally different category from the Neo-Babylonian words which occur in Ezekiel, and which can be recognized at a glance as more recent appropriations. On the other hand, there are many ritual *termini technici* such as *tamîd*, " perpetual burnt-offering," or rather " everlasting sacrifice," which can only be explained through the Arabic (Arab. *ta'mîd*, " fixed appointment," *amad*, " End, Eternity "), the obvious source of them being traceable, as will be more fully explained hereafter, to the ancient relations between Israel and Midian (Moses and Jethro).

To assume that the inconsistencies—which are often enough merely superficial—between the Priestly Code and the state of affairs in the time of the Judges afford sufficient reason for proclaiming the whole Priestly Code a post-exilic fabrication, and as having no existence in the time of the Prophets, and for regarding every indication to the contrary as due to a recension made with a special purpose, is indeed a drastic remedy. True, it explains everything, but at the same time it compels us to assume, in defiance of all psychological probability, such a monstrous falsification of tradition during the relatively short period between Ezekiel (*i.e.* the commencement of the Captivity) and Ezra, as is absolutely incompati-

¹ There are, no doubt, a number of direct loan-words among these, *e.g.* Hebr. *kohen*, " Priest," Babyl. *mushkînu* (from *mushkahînu*), " votive," " offering homage to the Deity "; or *terûmah*, " heave-offering," Babyl. *tarîmtu*, " offering-cup "; or Hebr. *torah*, " law, commandment," Babyl. *urtu* and *têrtu*.

ble with everything we know of the national character of the Israelites from their previous history. We must seek, therefore, for other solutions of the enigma more in harmony with tradition.

The simplest course to meet the difficulty would, no doubt, be to endeavour to make good the contentions of the learned Professor of Old Testament Literature at the American University of Princeton, W. H. Green, who has recently written a comprehensive volume,[1] with the aim of entirely disproving the alleged existence of different sources in the Pentateuch; a course which is in some measure commended by the attitude of the English Assyriologist, A. H. Sayce, who not long ago opened a bold and destructive fire, from an archæological standpoint, upon the whole method of the so-called "Higher Critics" of the Bible.[2] It is unquestionable that the higher critics have gone virtually bankrupt in their attempt to unravel, not only chapter by chapter, but verse by verse, and clause by clause, the web in which the different sources are entangled, arguing frequently from premises which are entirely false.

The numerous weak points to which Professor Green calls attention with pitiless logic, are merely fresh proof of what Klostermann has described by such terms as "hair-splitting" and "atom-dividing" on the part of the modern critics of the Pentateuch. On the other hand, the denial of the existence of

---

[1] *The Unity of the Book of Genesis*, New York, 1895.
[2] *The Higher Criticism and the Verdict of the Monuments*, 5th ed.: London, 1895 (1st ed., 1894).

different sources is another equally drastic remedy. It would give us back, it is true, the Mosaic writings of former times in their indissoluble unity—a procedure, however, which, in the face of all that the study of the Old Testament has revealed during the last hundred years, would carry us distinctly too far, and would be equivalent to cutting the Gordian knot in place of untying it. While Klostermann is not disposed to dispute the existence of the main sources of the Pentateuch, yet he protests against the narrative portions of the Priestly Code being regarded as a separate source, and would attribute them rather to the compiler himself.

That several sources really did exist is shown by the mere fact of the double narrative, quite apart from the various forms of the Divine name and certain differences in style, upon which it is hardly safe to put very much dependence. The existence of this double narrative has been questioned, it is true, by many learned apologists, Professor Green being among the number, but without sufficient reason. Such an attitude was due to a natural reaction from the unfair use made of these duplicated passages by modern critics of the Pentateuch, in their efforts to discredit the historical credibility of the whole. For my part, I consider that we have a right to draw from them an exactly opposite inference. The more numerous the discrepancies in unimportant details between two independent accounts of an event, so much the higher is the probability that the event itself is historically true. The justice of this contention receives daily confirmation from the chronicles of events in our newspapers, and we need not, therefore, because of a few trifling discrepancies, dismiss the narratives in question as mere legends with only a certain nucleus of historical truth at their base. As a matter of fact, the theory of double recensions may be easily carried too far; for instance, the so-called "Jehovistic Decalogue" in Exodus xxxiv. is a mere creation of the modern critic's imagination. In reality we have here only the beginning of the Decalogue (xxxiv. 14—17) amplified by a duplicate passage at the end of the Book of the Covenant (xxxiv. 18—26 = xxiii. 14—19).

Unfortunately, in spite of the amply rewarded attempts by Klostermann and others to drive the hair-splitting philology of the source-investigators to a *reductio ad absurdum*, many people still accept the conclusions of the latter as gospel. The late August Dillmann[1] was the only scholar of modern times who attacked the subject from the actual position of these critics, and yet came to regard the Priestly Code as a pre-exilic document. Realizing that God had revealed Himself even in the days of the Patriarchs, he arrived at the conclusion that the groundwork, at any rate, of the tradition contained in the sources of the Pentateuch is of Mosaic origin.

But Dillmann stands almost alone, and, in spite of our high appreciation of his profound learning and carefully discriminating judgment, it has come to be

---

[1] Cf., in addition to his Commentaries, the *Handbuch der alttest. Theologie*, Leipzig, 1895, compiled by Kittel from his literary remains.

the fashion in Germany to regard his protests against the hypothesis of Graf and Wellhausen as misdirected, or at any rate unconvincing.[1]

Even such a moderate and earnest theologian as Professor Kautzsch of Halle, at the end of the appendices to his translation of the Old Testament, includes Wellhausen's theory among the "verdicts which no exegetical skill can now hope to reverse." This is equivalent to an open confession, that, if our study of the Old Testament is to be confined to methods of purely literary criticism, we must accept the conclusions of modern criticism of the Pentateuch as decisive, however revolutionary it may be in its character.

The question, however, arises, whether by attacking the matter from an entirely different side, and with totally new weapons, it may not be possible to discover some proof that the Hebrew tradition, especially that part of it which deals with the period of the Patriarchs and the time of Moses, is not so untrustworthy as the present prevailing theory would make it out to be. Tradition associates the history of Abraham with *Babylonia*, that of Jacob and Joseph with *Egypt*, and that of Moses with Egypt and *Arabia*. Now, if it were possible to adduce evidence from the inscriptions which would prove even a part of the Hebrew tradition, at present rejected as spurious, to be of the highest antiquity and thus far trustworthy, the ground would be effectively cut

[1] Cf. the section in H. Holzinger's *Einleitung in den Hexateuch* (Freiburg, 1893), pp. 466-73, on "Dillmann's position in regard to Graf's hypothesis."

away from beneath the feet of modern critics of the Pentateuch.

It is from *external evidence*, therefore, that the final decision must come.

Before I endeavour, in the following chapters, to bring forward this evidence in detail, I should like to cite some pertinent observations on the subject of critical methods—to which I attach all the more importance because they have been formulated, not by myself, but by Eduard Meyer of Halle, a historian who is well known to be one of the most radical investigators in the field of Old Testament criticism.

His *History of Antiquity*,[1] a work distinguished by its breadth of view as well as by its execution, gained him on the one hand a high reputation, while on the other it brought him into disrepute because of the almost fanatical antipathy he displayed against the recognition of any positive religious movements among the ancient Semitic races, and especially among the Israelites.[2] Within the last few months he published a work on *The Origin of Judaism*

[1] Vol. i., *Geschichte des Orients bis zur Begründung des Perserreiches* (Stuttgart, 1884); vol. ii., *Geschichte des Abendlandes bis auf die Perserkriege* (Stuttgart, 1893).

[2] On pp. 262-4 of my *History of Babylonia and Assyria*, I have drawn attention to some of the more striking instances of this kind, and have quoted them at length. Compare *e. g.* the statement of Meyer's book, p. 208, note 1, " The same remarkable poverty [of religious conceptions] which pervades the Koran lies also at the root of the human sacrifices of the Canaanites, of the religious phrases of the Assyrians, and of the worship of Jahveh also: the Aryan finds it intolerable to give them even a passing attention." This last admission is especially significant.

(Halle, 1896, issued in October, 1896), in which he shows that the various letters and lists which occur in the Books of Ezra and Nehemiah (*e.g.* the correspondence with the Persian court in Ezra iv.—vi., which is by many considered to be spurious) must be regarded as absolutely genuine documents, and supports his contention mainly by external evidence, adducing for his purpose other genuine documents of the time of the Achæmenides.

In the introduction to this book Meyer refers to the furious assault made some years ago by the Dutch critic Kosters against the whole Biblical tradition of the time of Ezra and Nehemiah. These and similar researches are based (I purposely quote Meyer word for word) "on the extraneous information which we possess regarding Jewish history: from this they endeavour to formulate a theory of what actually took place: if the documents fail to support this theory, the documents must be spurious." This Meyer rightly characterizes as "a very hazardous proceeding on the part of an historian." "For a document," he goes on to say, "is, *if genuine, a witness which defies contradiction;* should there arise within the field covered by a document a contradiction between the document itself and other historical narrative, the latter must give way" (*op. cit.* p. 3). And on p. 4 he writes: "*It matters not how ingenious an historical theory may be, it must collapse irretrievably if it is found to be in contradiction with a genuine document.*[1] A document can only be rejected

---

[1] The italics are mine; in Meyer's book the words are printed in ordinary type.

as spurious after a most searching and unbiassed examination, and this is just what the documents in Ezra iv.—vii. have, so far, failed to obtain. The authenticity of a document once proved, the ground would be cleared for fresh structures for which there would be otherwise no foundation. For the historian must not attempt to dominate facts by hypotheses and theories, but, on the contrary, seek first of all for trustworthy facts, *entirely uninfluenced by any theory which he may in any way have deduced from events*.[1] It is only after he has obtained his facts that he is able to clear up uncertainties, to fill up the gaps in tradition, and to arrive at a consistent theory of development." I trust I may be pardoned if I make one more quotation from the close of the Introduction (pp. 6 *et seq.*): "If we succeed . . . in showing that a document . . . is perfectly intelligible in relation to the circumstances of its time; if it be possible, by a careful analysis, to penetrate more deeply into its meaning, . . . and to demonstrate that it cannot have been tampered with by the compiler of the chronicle; . . . *and further, if it be possible to adduce in evidence documents of undoubted authenticity obtained perhaps from distant countries with which the author of the tradition was unacquainted*[1] (such, for instance, as the Gadatas Inscription, an edict of the Persian monarch Darius I. to his satrap Gadatas, which is the instance that Meyer has here in view), then the defence is as complete as it can well be made."

In immediate connection with this, Meyer contrasts

[1] The italics are mine.

the traditions of Jewish history in the Persian epoch with those of the earlier history of the Israelites. With regard to the tradition of post-exilic history, while maintaining that there is "firm historical ground" to go upon, and that the historical inaccuracy of many portions of this tradition (not, be it remarked, the historical accuracy of the remainder) still remains to be proved, yet when we come to a period, he says, "for which no authentic historical tradition exists, and have to deal with oral tradition which has been worked up into a coherent narrative by a number of later writers acting in combination with one another,[1] . . . then, we must first prove that the narrative is historically true, or at any rate contains a modicum of historical truth;" until such proof be forthcoming the tradition must be taken for what it is, that is to say, as legend and not history.

In the following chapters it will be shown that those very traditions concerning the early history of Israel, especially those preserved in the so-called Priestly Code (which is notoriously regarded by the Wellhausen school as a post-exilic forgery), contain a whole host of *records*, the antiquity and genuineness of which are vouched for by external evidence. These include, in the first place, the lists of names in the Book of Numbers, and personal names generally from the time of Moses down to Solomon. They also include the Song of Deborah (which even modern critics of the Pentateuch admit to be a fairly un-

[1] It is evident from the antithesis, that Meyer here refers to the early history of Israel, and probably to a large part of the monarchical period, though he does not say so in so many words.

modified document of the time of the Judges), as well as various lyrical passages, such as the prophesyings of Balaam,[1] the blessings pronounced by Jacob, etc. Then we have the mention of various nations (including for example, those very portions of the ethnological table which Wellhausen attributes to the Priestly Code), and legal enactments, the various versions of which only differ from one another in minor details (*e.g.* the decalogue), or which contain historical allusions applicable only to a definite period. And lastly, there are all those passages which afford internal evidence of antiquity, from the occurrence of expressions which in later times had become either unintelligible or obsolete.

Now everything that Meyer has so emphatically affirmed in the passages quoted above, with regard to the documents and lists of names in the Books of Ezra and Nehemiah, applies with immediate and startling force to a great many of the most important and characteristic sections of the Priestly Code. According to the principles put forward by Meyer in his historical capacity, the theory of the history of Israel which Reuss, Graf, and Wellhausen have built up with such wonderful ingenuity "must collapse" inevitably and "irretrievably": a deduction which, though altogether contrary to Meyer's intention, is none the less amply warranted if we apply the historical methods which he advocates. For the Graf-

---

[1] Later on I hope to prove, from the political setting in which it occurs, that one of these could only have originated shortly before the conquest of the Holy Land. The same remark applies to a part of Jacob's blessing, as will also be shown later on.

Wellhausen theory is contradicted in various particulars by evidence of the most direct kind, which, to use Meyer's own expression, "defies contradiction." This evidence does not rest on any later forgery, but on documents whose authenticity is confirmed by contemporary inscriptions which are found in distant regions.

The higher critics, therefore, here play the part of Balaam, however little they may have foreseen or desired the issue. Called in to curse, they have been constrained to bless the Israelites.

CHAPTER II

THE EARLY HISTORY OF PALESTINE

It is a cardinal article of belief among modern critics of the Pentateuch, that the Hebrews of pre-Mosaic times were uncivilized nomads, whose religion consisted in the worship of ancestral heroes and the adoration of stones, trees, springs and animals, in other words, of a mixture of Fetishism and Totemism. This view of the early beginnings of the Hebrew faith is one of the most vital factors in Wellhausen's system; it is at once the necessary conclusion to which his theories lead, and the actual basis and assumption on which they rest. Viewed, however, from the stand-point of profane history alone, its extreme improbability is sufficiently proved by a single glance at the nations who lived in and around Palestine during the earliest ages, and at the facts recorded concerning them.

It is perfectly true that traces of such ancestor-worship and fetishism have in all ages been found among the Israelites, especially among those of the northern kingdom; this is abundantly proved by various passages in the Old Testament literature, but it is no more an argument against the concurrent existence of a higher conception of the Deity, than the numerous superstitious customs and ideas still prevalent among the lower orders of almost every civilized country of the present day are arguments against the existence and practical results of Christianity. The Semites, partly settled, partly nomadic, who inhabited the vast territory lying between the two great centres of primitive civilization, Egypt and Babylonia, were exposed from at least about 3000 B.C., as the evidence of the inscriptions proves more and more clearly every day, to influences of the most varied kind both from the Nile and the Euphrates. Even the nomads among them had by that time emerged from that state of uncivilized barbarism, which modern critics of the Old Testament would have us believe to have been the condition of the Hebrews shortly before the time of David.

It has been the ill fortune of the higher critics to elaborate and perfect their historical theories without paying any serious attention to the results brought to light by Assyriologists and Egyptologists. Let us in the first place review for a moment the discoveries made by Assyriologists in the highly interesting branches of historical and philological research, with a special eye to the information that can be gleaned from them in regard to *Palestine and the other surrounding countries prior to the time of Abraham*. It is necessary here to remark, that the application of the term "Assyriology," as it is now generally used, to the study of the cuneiform inscriptions, is not quite correct; indeed it is actually misleading. It is true that the study of these inscriptions first began in connection with the *Assyrian* royal inscriptions, which for some ten years monopolized the public interest, and proper names, most of which were already familiar to readers of the Bible, such as Tiglathpileser, Shalmaneser, Sargon, Sennacherib, Esarhaddon, and Sardanapalus, became, thanks to the decipherment of the cuneiform inscriptions, as much household words as those of Alexander or Cæsar. But when the celebrated Clay Tablets of Assurbanipal's (or Sardanapalus') library were discovered and closely examined, it became more and more clear that the literary treasures it contained belonged to an epoch far earlier than that of the Assyrian monarchy, namely, to that which is now known as the *early Babylonian* period. Original monuments of that remote era having been discovered in increasing numbers, it now grows daily more apparent that in it are to be found the sources, not only of early Asiatic civilization (including that of primitive Egypt), but also of western culture, *i.e.* of classical antiquity, with which our own is bound up.

While to the lay mind Babylonia and Assyria are nearly synonymous terms, they are, in fact, quite distinct geographically. Babylonia is the shallow depression between the lower reaches of the Tigris and Euphrates, and owes its distinctive features and characteristics to the latter river. Assyria, on the other hand, is the region to the east of the middle Tigris, quite one-half its area being mountainous. There is, furthermore, an even greater difference between them from an historical point of view, especially in so far as the evolution of their civilization is concerned. Babylonia is the cradle of the earliest civilization, and could look back to a history covering several thousands of years at a time (about 1900 B.C.) when the history of Assyria was in its infancy; it is for this reason that the Assyrian civilization (its language, script, and religion) is, in the main, merely an offshoot of the Babylonian. It is absurd, therefore, to speak of an independent Assyrian literature; unless, of course, we are prepared to regard the inscriptions of the Assyrian kings as a separate school of literature by itself. The material which Sardanapalus placed in his library consisted, however, with unimportant exceptions, of mere copies of earlier Babylonian texts.

As I have already pointed out, the study of the cuneiform inscriptions first began with the investigation of Assyrian monuments, and for this reason received the not altogether appropriate name of Assyriology. If, however, we go back to the first beginnings of the deciphering, we find ourselves again face to face with Babylonia, though, it is true, at a very late stage of its development; for it was a Babylonian translation of the early Persian Achæmenid texts—the inscriptions of Cyrus, Darius, and Xerxes—which first led to the unravelling of the tangled web of Semitic cuneiform writing.

I mention this merely to clear away any misapprehension which may exist in regard to the name of a science which is of such supreme importance to biblical students.

As a rule, the early history of a state moves within narrow limits; the more important political complications do not arise till much later. The great victories of the Egyptian Pharaohs did not occur until the time of the so-called Later Empire; the preceding epoch was, by comparison, peaceful and patriarchal, yet even then (in the time of the Later Empire, about 1500 B.C.) the might of Egyptian arms did not extend beyond Syria and Mesopotamia, for Babylon and the growing power of Assyria were conciliated by gifts. We find a precisely similar state of things in Assyria; for nearly a thousand years the Assyrian kings thought themselves lucky if they were able to secure and retain a firm foothold even in Mesopotamia, and steal a march now and then on the Babylonians; and it was only gradually that they were fired with the ambition to found a universal Empire. In this they succeeded to some extent; but their successors, the late Babylonian kings and the Persians, came still nearer to the goal, which was only eventually attained by Alexander the Great and the Romans.

It would be a mistake, however, to argue from these analogies that the early history of Babylonia was a period of tranquil and peaceful development, disturbed only now and then by little differences with their next-door neighbours (especially with the Elamites, and later on also with the Assyrians and others).

The remarkable discovery made a few years ago at Tel-el-Amarna, which has given us on cuneiform tablets the correspondence between the kings and princes of Babylonia, Assyria, Mesopotamia, and Palestine with the Pharaohs, Amenothes III. and IV. (about 1400 B.C), has led to a considerable modification of our former views on this point. The fact that Babylonian, and not Assyrian, was the official language of diplomatic intercourse throughout the whole of Western Asia towards the end of the fifteenth century B.C., can only be explained or made intelligible by assuming that *for a prolonged period—of several centuries at least—Babylon must have exercised a civilizing influence of the most marked description on Syria and Palestine*, an influence which can only be satisfactorily accounted for on the assumption that the " countries of the West " were at one time politically dependent on Babylon, and that consequently there had been a previous Babylonian invasion.

It will be necessary to examine the early Babylonian cuneiform monuments somewhat more closely for evidence on this point, and, to carry our investigations back to a *very early* (perhaps even to the very earliest) *period of Babylonian history*—to a time when the metropolitan kingdom of Babylon was not yet in existence, and when there were still independent Sumerian (non-Semitic) as well as Semitic kings in Southern Babylonia, who had their successive seats of government at Sirgulla, Ur, and Nisin, then again at Ur and at Larsa—in round numbers, to a period between 3000 and 2000 B.C. There were in the north, at the same period, kings of Akkad (Agadê) and of Kish or Kishar who were more or less dependent on the South.

We come in the beginning of our investigation upon the mighty " Priest-king " Gudêa of Sirgulla, who reigned at the beginning of the third millennium before Christ. We learn from certain inscriptions of his, written in pure Sumerian, and discovered by the French Consul, M. de Sarzec, that he had procured for his building operations cedar and boxwood from the forests of Mount Amanus, building stone from Subsalla, a mountain in the " countries of the West " ;[1] alabaster from Tidanum (Dedan), another mountain in the "countries of the West" close to Moab; and cedars, plane-trees, and other precious woods from Ursu, a mountain of Ibla (Lebanon ?). In addition to the West there was another region which owned the sway of Gudêa, or at any rate belonged to the confederacy of which he was the head; this was the great Arabian peninsula which served as a buffer between Babylonia and Africa. From this land also he levied materials for his undertakings. From the " Gate of Ancestors," a mountain of Ki-Mashu (afterwards abbreviated to Mashu), he obtained copper; from Melukhkha, or North-western Arabia, " ushu " wood and iron; from Khâkhum, a mountainous district near Medina, and from the same Melukhkha, gold-dust; and from Magan (in Eastern Arabia) diorite. Apparently the date palm was imported into Babylonia from this latter region long before the time of Gudêa.

A reference to the map will show us the wide extent of country which was either subject to Gudêa, or made accessible, by his alliances, to his ships and caravans. It reached northwards as far as the boundaries of Armenia and Cilicia; on the west it

---

[1] *I.e.* Martu, properly, the country of the Amorites, whence we get Amurrî = "Amorites" and "western."

included the whole of Mesopotamia (Borsippa near Carchemish being mentioned as one of his ports of call) as far as Lebanon and the Dead Sea ; and lastly Arabia, at any rate as far as the two mountains Aga and Salma (the "Gate of his Ancestor" Nimrod), and Medina. Indeed, if Amiaud, the French Assyriologist, be right in his conjecture with regard to Gubin, the place from which Gudêa obtained the timber (chalup-wood) for his ships, his sphere of influence must have extended as far as Koptos, near Thebes, in Upper Egypt, in which case we may be right in identifying the chalup-tree with the Persea or Lebbakh, which is found growing in Egypt, and is now called by the Syrians "khalûpa."

From what has been said, we can now understand the part played by Arabia in the ancient Babylonian epic of Nimrod or Gisdubar, which we possess in a form dating from about 2000 B.C. In the ninth canto we are told how Gisdubar set out for the land of Mâshu (*i.e.* Central Arabia), the gate of which (*i.e.* the rocky pass formed by the cliffs of Aga and Salma) was guarded by legendary scorpion-men. For twelve miles the hero had to make his way through dense darkness;[1] at length he came to an enclosed space by the sea-shore where dwelt the virgin goddess Sabîtu[2] ; from thence he had to travel by sea for forty-five days—though the return voyage only oc-

[1] Hence we may probably see why Arabia was called "the land of darkness" (an expression found as early as the time of Abraham, in the signature of a deed of sale).

[2] *I.e.* "she of Mount Sabu," a mountain evidently situated somewhere in Arabia.

cupied three days—till he arrived at the Waters of Death (Bab-el-Mandeb?) and at the Isle of the Blest (Sokotra?), where his great-grandfather Shamash-Napishtim dwelt.

The "Priest-kings" of Sirgulla were succeeded in the hegemony over Babylonia by the "kings of Ur," who styled themselves by the supplementary title of "kings of Ingi and of Akkad." Ingi (otherwise Imgi, originally Imi-gur), or Sumer, was the name of the southernmost portion of Babylonia, afterwards more distinctively known as Chaldæa. It included Ur and the strip of Babylonia bordering on Arabia, while Akkad, on the other hand, comprised Northern Babylonia. After these came, somewhere about 2500 B.C., the Semitic kings of Nisin, a town of Central Babylonia, who appear to have ruled for several centuries, and to have also styled themselves kings of Ingi and Akkad. They were succeeded by another Semitic dynasty, the "kings of Ur," so called from the fact that Ur was their capital, but it is evident that they only held sway over a smaller part of Babylonia; they no longer possessed Ingi, and had lost Akkad as well, another dynasty having meanwhile established itself there. They made up for this loss, however, by extending their rule over Elam, Arabia, and the countries of the West, and for this reason described themselves by the proud title of "kings of the four cardinal points." This extension of empire took place somewhere about the middle of the twenty-third century B.C., or at any rate not later than the year 2000 B.C. We possess an extremely interesting historical document dealing with this period, in the shape of an astrological work, of which extracts and important fragments were preserved to us in the library of Sardanapalus. It is called the *Nûr Bel* (or "Light of the god Bel"). According to this work, the historical importance of which I was one of the first to recognize, the list of constellations appearing on the political horizon at that time embraced the following. In Northern Babylonia there were the kings of Akkad or (as they also styled themselves) of Kishar; in Ur, the kings already mentioned (Ini-Sin, Bur-Sin, Gimil-Sin, and probably a number of others as well), who exercised an intermittent rule over part of Elam in addition to all the "countries of the West"; then there were their neighbours the still independent kings of Ingi (the so-called "country of the Sea" on the Persian Gulf and confines of Arabia), those of Anshan (in Elam), the rulers of Khâtu (part of the Hittite country in Northern Syria), and many others. Moreover, a large number of Babylonian Sacrifice-lists recently discovered are dated from events which had taken place under the rule of these kings of Ur. They supplement in a most remarkable manner the data obtained from the astrological work referred to above. Thus, we learn from them that daughters of king Ini-Sin were given in marriage to the Priest-kings (patesi) of Anshan (in Elam), of Zapshali (= Zapsha of the Van inscriptions, and therefore probably situated in Cilicia or Armenia), and of Markhashi (Mar'ash in Northern Syria). We are further informed that this same king Ini-Sin (who, by the way, is also mentioned by name in the *Nûr Bel* previously referred to) subdued Kimash (in Central Arabia) and Simurru (Simyra in Phœnicia, between Arvad and Tripoli?); Sâbu (in Central Arabia) is also mentioned as a place which paid tribute to him.[1] If we could only obtain more precise information in regard to this remote period, it would undoubtedly prove to be one of the most interesting epochs of Babylonian history. We have good reason to be grateful, however, even for the meagre data supplied by the *Nûr Bel* and the Sacrifice-lists, since they enable us to establish the one important fact, that even then—*i. e.* before the time of Abraham—the whole of Syria, Phœnicia, and a great part of Arabia were under the direct influence of Babylonian civilization, an influence the permanent effect of which can hardly be over-estimated, and from which the nomadic and semi-nomadic elements therein were certainly not exempt.

There is no mention made of Egypt in the documents referred to above. On the other hand, the Egyptian records furnish us with an important piece of ethnological evidence which has a direct bearing on the question before us. From the time of the twelfth dynasty (*circa* 2200 B.C. ?) onwards a new race makes its appearance on the Egyptian horizon, viz. the Kashi in Nubia. Dr. E. Glaser, the Arabian explorer, in his learned and epoch-making work, *A Sketch of the History and Geography of Arabia*[2] (vol. ii.), draws attention to the fact that this name was

---

[1] For the publication of these most interesting texts we are indebted to Père Scheil (*Recueil*, vol. xvii.) and Professor Hilprecht.

[2] *Skizze der Geschichte und Geographie Arabiens.*

originally applied to Elam (Babyl. "Kashu"; cf. the
Κίσσιοι of Herodotus), and, according to the Hebrew tradition, was afterwards given to various
parts of Central and Southern Arabia: from this he
argues that in very early times—prior to the second
millennium before Christ—North-East Africa must
have been colonized by the Elamites, who had, naturally, to pass across Arabia on their way thither.
This theory is supported by the fact that in the socalled Kushite languages of North-East Africa, such
as the Galla, Somali, Bedsha, and other allied dialects, we find grammatical principles analogous to
those of the Early Egyptian and Semitic tongues
combined with a totally dissimilar syntax presenting no analogy with that of the Semites or with any
Negro tongue in Africa, but resembling closely the
syntax of the Ural-altaic languages of Asia, to which,
at any rate in so far as syntax is concerned, the Elamite language belongs. According to this view, the
much-discussed Kushites (the Æthiopians of Homer
and Herodotus) must originally have been Elamitic
Kassites, who were scattered over Arabia, and found
their way to Africa. It is interesting to note that
the Bible calls Nimrod a son of Kush, and that the
cuneiform alternative for Nimrod [Gisdubar], viz.
Gibilgamis (originally Gibil-gab), shows an Elamitic termination. What the Nimrod epic tells us
of Nimrod's wanderings across Arabia must therefore be regarded as a legendary version of the
historical migration of the Kassites from Elam into
East Africa: Nimrod is merely a personification of
that Elamitic race-element of which traces are still

to be found both in Arabia and in Nubia. The fact that the poet claims Gisdubar as a national hero of Babylonia, and as conqueror of the Elamite king Khumbaba, is in no way opposed to this view; the Elamitic origin of Gisdubar came in course of time to be forgotten even in Babylon itself; moreover, the Gisdubar-Nimrod of the epic possessed originally an affinity with Nabu-Nusku, the fire-demon and planet-god, into which it is outside our present purpose to enter.

After this digression we may now continue to trace the course of early Babylonian history in so far as Arabia and the "countries of the West" are concerned. The Semitic kings of Ur were followed by those of Larsa (Nûr-Rammân, Sin-idinna, etc.). While Nûr-Rammân, the former of these, merely describes himself as "Shepherd of Ur, king of Larsa," his son Sin-idinnam having succeeded in winning back the supremacy over Ingi (Sumer) and over Akkad, made himself thus master of the greater part of Babylonia. After an interval of somewhat doubtful duration, an Elamite named Eri-Aku [Arioch] succeeded to the throne of Larsa, Sumer, and Akkad about 1900 B.C.; he is also mentioned by the Semitic name Arad-Sin, and by the half-Semitic, half-Sumerian name of Rim-Sin. We shall hear more fully about him later on. His father bore the purely Elamite name of Kudur-Mabug, and is described, in one place, as king of Martu (*i.e.* of the countries of the West), in another as prince of Ya-mutbal; Elam itself was ruled by king Kudur-Lagamar (Chedor-Laomer), whose vassal Eri-Aku was.

Meanwhile, however, an *Arabian* dynasty[1] had managed to establish itself in Northern Babylonia, fully one hundred years before the reign of Eri-Aku; these aliens soon learnt to assimilate themselves completely with the Babylonians, and from their ranks sprang a king who was destined to go down to posterity as the greatest ruler ever known in Babylon, Khammurabi, or, to give him his Babylonian name, Khammu-rapaltu. He overcame Kudur-Lagamar — who had devastated Northern Babylonia — as well as Eri-Aku of Larsa, and the father of the latter Kudur-Mabug, who shared the throne with him, and succeeded in bringing about such complete union between North and South Babylonia, that from his time onwards, with scarcely an interruption worth mentioning, the city of Babylon remained for fifteen hundred years the political centre of Babylonia.

These are assuredly most singular and remarkable facts, which have so far never been clearly explained by any historian or Assyriologist, simply because the *Arabian* origin of what is known as the first dynasty of the metropolitan rulers of Babylon had not been hitherto recognized. Babylonia was then at the close of a long period of development; from henceforward we are confronted, in so far as Babylonian

---

[1] The *Arabian* origin of a part of this dynasty was first recognized a few years ago by Professor Sayce of Oxford; but I have recently been able to prove conclusively that the whole dynasty is Arabian (cf. Hilprecht's *Recent Research in Bible Lands* (Philadelphia, 1896), pp. 131—144, and the *Zeitschrift der Deutsch. Morgenl. Gesellsch.*, vol. xlix., pp. 524—28 : Leipzig, 1895).

civilization is concerned, by a spirit of conservatism which, in some respects, tended towards fossilization; a precisely similar state of things is observable in the history of Egypt. With the Arabs, however, came a current of new life-giving elements to the rescue of the already effete civilization of Babylonia. It was not long before they succeeded in bringing about the first real unification of the empire. No doubt this had also been the aim of the other alien races in the south, such as the Elamites, Eri-Aku, and Kudur-Mabug; unfortunately the Elamite civilization belonged to the same stock as the Babylonian, and therefore suffered from the same defects; consequently, in the long run, they were unable to make head against the youthful vigour of the Arabs. We must not run away with the idea, however, that these latter were nothing more than mere nomads, absolutely innocent of any trace of culture. East Arabia—and it was from thence Khammurabi's dynasty took its origin—had been, as we have seen above, for nearly one thousand years in intimate contact both with Sumerians and Elamites. The beginnings of Arab civilization which confront us on all sides in South Arabia, from the middle of the second millennium B.C. onwards, represented by traces of mighty buildings and by numerous inscriptions, must, in Khammurabi's time, have already begun to develop. Throughout Northern Arabia, too, both in the East (Magan) and in the West (Melukhkha), civilization must have made great progress just then. For at this very time occurs the memorable period of the Shepherd Kings or Hyksôs in Egypt, whose Arabian origin, in the face of the unanimous testimony of both native and Greek tradition, can hardly be disputed. Thus we see the two most ancient civilized states of the world simultaneously fall a prey to the Arabs, while these latter were as yet a semi-nomadic people. In both cases the strangers were not long in becoming assimilated to the ancient countries they had conquered: the Hyksôs to the Egyptians, the Arabs who had forced their way into Northern Babylonia to the Babylonians.

As to the Elamite princes, Eri-Aku of Larsa and his father Kudur-Mabug, besides the fact that the former was dethroned by Khammurabi, we gather from a number of original inscriptions, two further items of information, of a totally unlooked-for and yet mutually confirmatory character. In the first place, we learn from what is manifestly an extremely ancient Hebrew tradition, in Gen. xiv., that the kings of Sodom and Gomorrha (who were, of course, Amorites) had for twelve years been vassals of a certain king Chedor-Laomer of Elam; in the thirteenth year they rebelled, and in the fourteenth, Chedor-Laomer took the field against them with his allies, king Amraphel of Shinar (Northern Babylonia), king Arioch of Ellasar, and king Tidal of Goi [Goiim, R. V.]. Further, a tablet discovered in London, by Mr. Pinches, only a part of which has, unfortunately, been preserved, tells of a victory obtained over Elam by the Babylonian king Khammurabi; on the back of the tablet his adversaries are mentioned by name, viz. Kudur-dugmal, Eri-Aku, and Tudghul (or Tudkhul). Although, therefore, the event referred to is totally distinct from that mentioned in Gen. xiv., the names of the parties concerned are the same, viz. Khammurabi = Amraphel, Eri-Aku = Arioch, Tudghul = Tidal, and Kudur-dugmal = Chedor-Laomer. In connection herewith it should be noted that Lagamar (or Lagamal) is the name of an Elamite goddess mentioned in the cuneiform inscriptions, and that Larsa and Ellasar are the same name (a fact which had been recognized before). In conclusion, Scheil has recently discovered among the early Babylonian documents a letter from Khammurabi to a certain Sin-iddinam of Yamutbal, in which mention is made of the overthrow of Kudur-lagamar. The only point which remains to be settled is the precise relationship between Kudur-Mabug, prince of Yamutbal (a part of Elam), and Kudur-Lagamar (or -Lagmal, or -Dugmal); probably they were brothers, or, at any rate, nearly related, for the title "Prince of Martu" (*i.e.* of Palestine) occasionally assumed by Kudur-Mabug, and the fact that Martu was subjugated by Kudur-Lagamar (which we gather from Gen. xiv.), must, naturally, have some connection with one another. The theory of modern critics of the Bible, that Gen. xiv. was not written till the time of the Babylonian Captivity, and is merely a free reproduction of a cuneiform record by some learned Rabbi, must be absolutely rejected.

It may now be asked, what historical deductions are to be drawn from all these records of the time of Khammurabi and Eri-Aku—records which, owing to their fundamental importance to students of the Pentateuch, it is intended to deal with more fully later on? They are briefly as follows: the Elamites and their kinsfolk, the kings of Larsa, had succeeded in subjugating the "countries of the West," as the kings of Ur had done before them. It is at this juncture that the Hebrew tradition fixes the migration of Abraham from Ur of the Chaldees, through Haran, into Palestine. When, however, the Arab dynasty of Northern Babylonia under Khammurabi drove the Elamites out of the land, the supremacy over the "countries of the West" naturally fell into the hands of the Babylonians, and, as a matter of fact, inscriptions have now been discovered in which Khammurabi and one of his successors expressly add after the title "king of Babylon," the further title "king of Martu." It was not till long afterwards that this Babylonian sovereignty of the West was gradually surrendered to the Egyptian Pharaohs. When, therefore, we find, as we do in the Tel-el-Amarna tablets, *i.e.* about 1400 B.C., the Babylonian script and language in general use as the medium of official communications throughout Palestine and Syria, and that they were also employed in diplomatic correspondence between Babylonia (*i.e.* Palestine) and Egypt, we know that this is merely an after effect of the political hegemony so long enjoyed by Babylon in the countries of the West. Apart from such knowledge, the fact would be simply unintelligible. But, as we shall see later on, this knowledge throws a new light on a whole host of other facts, and especially on the religious history of the Old Testament. For the present, we must be content to insist on the fact, that, even at the commencement of the second millennium before Christ, Palestine and Phœnicia had fallen completely under the influence of Babylonian civilization, an influence from which neither the Phœnicians nor the Canaanites, nor any other lesser nation settled between the Mediterranean and the Euphrates, can have possibly escaped.

How these forces of civilization, which originally emanated from Babylon, came to make their way into Egypt after the close of the Hyksôs period (during the so-called Later Empire) is a matter of history: the old Egyptian civilization, which had by this time sunk into a mummified condition, derived new impulses and a totally fresh colouring from it. Thanks to her growing political influence under this later empire, Egypt, in her turn, reacted on Phœnicia and Syria. We must not forget, however, that a large part of this territory had previously been for a considerable period an Egyptian province under the eighteenth and nineteenth dynasties. It will be necessary, therefore, to extend our inquiries to a still earlier epoch. In the first place, we must endeavour to ascertain whether, since the Babylonian records have yielded so rich a harvest, the *Egyptian inscriptions* cannot be made to afford us some information in regard to the state of Palestine during the period prior to Abraham. And though the total amount of information concerning this remote epoch, which we can gather on the banks of the Nile, may not be very large, it nevertheless includes some facts of considerable importance.[1]

[1] Cf. W. MAX MÜLLER'S epoch-making work, *Asien und Europa*

Even during the Old Empire, or what is known as the Pyramid Period, it had been the ambition of the Egyptians to secure a firm foothold both in the Sinaitic peninsula and in Palestine as well. They succeeded in the first of these objects under an early Pharaoh Snofruî and his successors; the inhabitants of the Sinaitic region, which had become important in the eyes of the Egyptians on account of its copper mines and malachite quarries, were designated either by the general title of *inti* (Troglodytes, or Cave-dwellers), or by the special name of *Mentu* (*Menzu*). This name came later on to be pronounced *Menti* or *Meti*, and even at an early date the cognate form *Metthi* (pronounced *Mizzi*) seems to have come into use.

Of still greater importance for our purpose is the earliest mention of a campaign against the Asiatic (*'Amu*) "Lords of the Sands" (*heru sha*) in the time of the sixth Dynasty. The objective of this expedition was nothing short of the Philistine coast. As the inhabitants of this region are described as "rebels," it would seem as though, even at that date, a part of Southern Palestine was regarded as an Egyptian possession. That the population was not wholly a nomadic one is evident from a reference to the fig-trees and vines which the Egyptians boast of having laid waste there. The term 'Amu, which was applied in the earliest times to the whole of the Bedûin and semi-Bedûin races of the adjacent Semitic countries, is probably, as W. Max Müller suggests, derivable

nach altäg. Denkmälern, Leipzig, 1893, for the evidence of the inscriptions in support of the following statements.

from the javelin or boomerang, which was their favourite weapon: the Egyptians afterwards extended the term to all Asiatics (including the Hittites). Dr. Glaser[1] puts forward the plausible conjecture, that the biblical name "Ham" in the ethnological list of Genesis x. was originally the same word. Be this as it may, the name 'Amu has nothing to do with the Hebrew word 'am = "people," nor with the divine appellation 'Amm, which we find frequently introduced into Arab, and also ancient Hebrew, personal names. We shall have occasion to deal with this word at greater length hereafter. Thus, according to Glaser, the Katabani, a nation of Southern Arabia, call themselves "Children of 'Amm" (*walad 'Amm*), a name which has undoubtedly some connection with the title "*Benî 'Ammon*" (sons of Ammon), as frequently applied to the Ammonites of the country east of Jordan.

It is a pity that there are no personal names to be found among these early Egyptian references to Arabia and Southern Palestine; they would have been a most valuable index to the character and language of the inhabitants of these countries. Luckily, however, there have been handed down to us from the twelfth dynasty (*i.e.* the beginning of what is known as the "Middle Empire"), and therefore, most fortunately, a period prior to the time of Abraham, two detailed narratives—one of an Arabian embassy, and the other of a journey to Edom (Southern Palestine) —from which we can obtain most valuable details in regard to the formation of personal names.

[1] *Ausland*, 1891, p. 49.

I shall first take the narrative of the adventures of an Egyptian worthy named Sinûhit among the Syrian Bedûins.[1] Sinûhit was obliged to fly from Egypt, and was lucky enough to make his way under cover of night past the line of forts near the Bitter Lakes in the vicinity of the Suez Canal, which protected the frontier against the Bedûin. A nomadic chieftain took pity on the half-famished wanderer, and bringing him to his tribe invited him to remain with them. Sinûhit, however, for greater safety, preferred to retreat to some place farther away from Egypt; he was, therefore, passed on " from one tribe to another " till he at length arrived in Qedem [Kadûma], the country of the Bni Qedem [Kadmonites] or " Sons of the East " (Gen. xv. 19; Job i. 3, etc.), *i.e.* among the Bedûin of the country east of the Jordan. Here he remained for a year and a half under the protection of a king named *Ammianshi*, who is described as Prince of Upper Tenu (afterwards simply Prince of Tenu); he here fell in with other Egyptian refugees, and finally Ammianshi gave him his own daughter in marriage, and bestowed on him the government of Ia'a [Aia] (Jericho?), a district on the frontier. " There are figs there and vines; it yields wine in plenty and is rich in honey; its olives are many and fruit of all kinds is found on its trees; corn and barley are there and flocks without number." We are told that Sinûhit spent many years there, that his children " became

---

[1] Cf. AD. ERMAN, *Aegypten und ägyptisches Leben im Altherthum*, Tübingen, 1885, pp. 494—7, and quite recently G. MASPERO, *The Dawn of Civilization*, 2nd edition, London, 1896, pp. 471—3.

as heroes, each a defender of his tribe,"[1] and that he himself "subdued every nation that he came near, and drove them from their pastures and their wells, laid hands on their flocks, carried off their children, despoiled them of their sustenance and slew their people with his sword and with his bow." He also came off victor in a duel with a valiant man of Tenu who had grown envious of the multitude of his flocks. At last this nomadic existence began to pall upon Sinûhit, and, having presented a petition to Pharaoh, he obtained permission to return to the Egyptian court and spend the rest of his days there. Thereupon he left to the Bedûin "the lice of the desert, and coarse garments, the sand to those who dwelt thereon, and the oil of the trees to those who anointed themselves therewith," and was able once again to enjoy in their stead all those delights which the more refined Egyptian civilization had to offer him.

The Asiatic Bedûin who, in addition to their pastoral pursuits, also occasionally dealt in corn and wine, are here for the first time called *Seti* (or, according to the popular Egyptian etymology, "archers"), which is identical with the Babylonian term *Suti*, the name given in the Tel-el-Amarna tablets to the nomadic tribes who roved to and fro between Mesopotamia and Palestine. The land of *Tenu*, which closely resembles in sound the Biblical "Dedan"[2] and the Babylonian name for the "coun-

---

[1] This statement throws an important light on the history of the constitution of Semitic tribes and tribal allies in primitive times (cf., for instance, the sons of Jacob, and the Twelve Tribes of Israel).

[2] Tana is mentioned in the Tel-el-Amarna tablets as being hostile to

tries of the West," "Tidanu," is manifestly the land of *Tana*.

Of even greater importance than these are the two following identifications. First, the name of the king of Tana *Amîanshi*, or, to be more exact, Am-muï-en-shi, *i.e.* Ammî-anisha. This name, which means "my uncle (*i.e.* God as my paternal friend) is propitious," is found in South Arabian inscriptions under the form Ammî-anisa: the Arabs in the time of Mohammed made a deity whom they called 'Amm-anas, out of a certain famous 'Ammi-anisa of the land of Khaulân. From this it is clear that these names compounded with *'Ammi*, in which God is described as "my uncle" (in the sense of "my paternal friend"), are to be found among the Semites of Western Asia as early as the time of the twelfth Egyptian dynasty. The second important feature in the story of Sinûhît is the homely and simple, but none the less life-like picture which it gives us of the lives and pursuits of these Semitic nomads. We have here a near approach to the state of things described in the traditions of the Hebrew Patriarchal period, and this too in an epoch prior to that of Abraham.

But the Egyptian monuments are still more helpful. The narrative of events in the time of the Pharaohs Amenemhâît I. and Ûsirtasen I., referred to on a previous page, is concluded by a most inter-

---

Gebal; we come upon the following passage in a letter from Rib-Adda of Gebal to Pharaoh (Winckler, No. 69, ll. 51—55):—

"Moreover the king of the land of Tana had gone out against Zumur (Simyra), and desired to draw near to Gebal, but had no water to drink, and returned to his own land."

esting pictorial illustration dating from the time of Ûsirtasen II. We have here the picture of a long procession of Asiatic ('Amu) merchants, executed in colours. These are the well-known thirty-seven Asiatics on the tomb of Khnûmhotpû, who are represented in the act of offering to the said Khnûmhoptû (a viceroy under the Middle Empire) a quantity of eye-paint (mesdemet [1]), one of the staple articles of commerce produced by distant Arabia. The history of this word is an interesting one. But even more interesting are the figures themselves, men, women, and children, in their splendid garments of many colours. One man leads with him a goat as a present, another a gazelle, while a third bears an eight-stringed lyre, a fourth a javelin with bow and arrows, and a fifth and sixth each bear a lance. Beasts of burden are represented by two donkeys, on one of which two children are seated. Most of the figures wear sandals, the women apparently being shod with regular buskins. The features of these already more than half-civilized nomads are of a strongly marked Jewish type. One of the most interesting points about them, however, is, unquestionably, the name of their chief who, as the accompanying inscription informs us, was a certain *Ebsha'a*. This is a name which, like many others, can only be rightly explained by means of the South

---

[1] *Mesdemet* really means "a box for the preservation of Stibium," *i.e.* of antimony powder, a substance in general use among the women of the East for painting the border of the eyelids with; the word has come down to us with but slight modification in the Arabic *ithmid* (pronounced *ismid*).

Arabian inscriptions. There it is given in the complete form *Abî-yathu'a* (pronounced approximately *Abî-yasu'a* or *Abî-yashu'a*). Among the Hebrews, and this too in pre-Mosaic times, it appears as Abishû'a (1 Chron. viii. 4; v. 30). Like 'Ammî-anisa, this name also possesses a religious significance, being equivalent to "My Father (*i.e.* God) helps." From its formation it evidently belongs to an important group of personal names which, unlike the Babylonian, is only met with among the Western Semites, *i.e.* the Hebrews, Arabs and Aramaeans, but chiefly among the two former, and for the most part in the earliest periods, that is, at a time when the Hebrews were still more than half Arabs. The deep significance which this name possesses for the student of religious history will be treated more fully in a special chapter. For the present it is sufficient to have established the fact that two such names occur even at this very early period, and have come down to us from a source of such unimpeachable trustworthiness as the Early Egyptian monuments. Moreover, we shall presently come upon the name *Abî-yashu'a* in the cuneiform inscriptions, a few decades after Abraham, where it appears as "Abishua" and "Ibishu," and is likewise borne by a Western Semite.

Before proceeding to deal with monuments belonging to a period nearer to the time of Abraham, it will be well in connection with the term "Western Semites" employed above, to correct an error which, though of old standing, is nevertheless to be found in most modern works. I refer to the division of the Semitic race into Northern and Southern

Semites, a division which, though still common enough, is altogether incorrect, and likely to lead to theories which are both linguistically and historically erroneous. According to this view, the other Semites would stand in relation to the Arabs (for that is what the Southern Semites really were) as a distinct philological grouping, with much the same bearings as the other Indo-European speaking peoples have to the Aryan, restricting the latter term to the Indian and Iranian branches. In confutation of this assertion I pointed out as far back as 1881 and 1884, that in designating the date-palm, olive, fig-tree, vine, and other cultivated trees, Babylonian-Assyrian either employs terms totally different from those used in the other Semitic tongues, or shows that some of these trees (such as the fig-tree, and apparently the olive and vine as well) were originally unknown, and only in course of time came to be indicated by Western-Semitic loan-words.[1] It is evident, therefore, that in many of their more important and specially characteristic features, the Canaanitish (*i.e.* Hebrew), Arabic and Aramaic tongues form a group by themselves, and are quite distinct from Babylonian-Assyrian. This is supported by the fact that in addition to the botanical terms mentioned above, there are a large number of other words both concrete and abstract in which a similar relation is to be observed; the different

---

[1] *Semitische Völker und Sprachen*, p. 63 (and 442); *Die Sprachgeschichtliche Stellung des Babylonischen* in the *Études archéol., etc., dédiées à C. Leemans*, Leide, 1885, pp. 127—9; all the views here expressed are reiterated and amplified in my *Aufsätze und Abhandlungen* (1892), pp. 92—123.

characters of the perfect tense, and other important grammatical considerations affording further confirmation of this. Finally (and it is on this point that I here desire to lay the greatest stress) the peculiar method of name-giving adopted by the Western-Semites constitutes a marked distinction between them and the Babylonians and Assyrians. From this it will be seen that my authority for the introduction of this new term, "Western Semites," is based on grounds of a most varied character, both linguistic and material. It should, moreover, be noted that within the Western Semitic group, there is, at any rate from a linguistic standpoint, a closer bond of union between the Arabs and Aramaeans than exists either between the Arabs and Hebrews or between the Aramaeans and Hebrews,[1] a fact which the history of the Aramaeans amply confirms. I shall enter more fully into this last point when I come to the chapter on Isaac and Jacob. On the other hand, the theory recently put forward by some scholars who maintain that Aramaic is more closely connected with the Assyro-Babylonian than with its Western-Semitic sister tongues, is entirely erroneous. In this case, it is clear, the influence exercised for so many centuries by Assyro-Babylonian on Aramaic, notably on the East-Aramaic dialects (both in vocabulary and in various points of grammar) — an influence which can be readily explained by geographical propinquity — has been mistaken for an intimate organic relationship between the two languages.

[1] Cf. my *Aufsätze und Abhandlungen*, pp. 110—114.

CHAPTER III

THE ARABS IN BABYLONIA BEFORE AND IN THE TIME OF ABRAHAM

WE have already seen that about one hundred years prior to the events related in Gen. xiv., a dynasty of Arabian origin had made itself master of Northern Babylonia. The establishment of these Western-Semitic nomads in Babylon was probably the result of an invasion on their part, or perhaps the consequence of a peaceful and gradual infusion into the country of Arab elements, an infusion which may have taken place during the rule of the so-called "later" kings of Ur. Even at that early period, the countries of the West, including a part of Arabia, were very closely connected with Ur, a fact which is attested by numerous passages in the *Nûr Bel* referred to above. As far back as 1881, Professor Delitzsch in his book, *Wo-lag das Paradies?* p. 133, drew attention to the fact that these astrological notes " dwell with marked insistence on the countries of the West (*i.e.* Phœnicia or Palestine) and frequently contain phrases such as: ' when such and such a thing comes to pass (in the heavens), then shall a mighty king arise in the West, then shall righteousness and justice, peace and joy reign in all lands, and all nations shall be happy,' with many other similar predictions." He further points out that the New Testament story of the Magi, who no doubt had access to these early Babylonian astrological tablets is closely connected herewith; for they must have read in those records about the new-born King of the West whose star they followed as far as Bethlehem.

In regard to the close relation which existed between Martu (the land of the Amorites, the West) and Ur, we find the following passage in the *Nûr Bel:* "(when such and such a thing occurs in the heavens) then shall he (the god in question) give to the King of Kishar (*i.e.* of Akkad or Northern Babylonia) Ur and Martu for a possession"; and again: "then shall an oracle be given to the King of Kishar: 'Ur is to be destroyed and its walls are to be cast down'"; and yet again: "Disaster for Akkad, good fortune for Elam and Martu" (cf. Kudur-Lagamar, at one time Lord of the West (Gen. xiv.) and Kudur-Mabug, whose son Eri-Aku was master of Ur and King of Martu as well); and yet again: "then a west wind gets up, the King of the West (lives) long days, his reign grows old (*i.e.* lasts until he is a very old man)." There is undoubtedly some connection between these predictions and the fact that 12 stars of the land of Akkad and 12 stars of the land of Martu are mentioned immediately after in the same astrological work. Further light is thrown on them if we note that in the time of Abraham a district near Sippara bore the name "Field of Martu" (var. Amurrî, spelt *A-mur-ur-ri-i*), apparently because a colony of Amorites had settled there. The Babylonians derived their ordinary word for the West-wind moreover, from the territorial name of Martu, and at this very period the name "God (of) Martu" is frequently used for the Babylonian god of the air (Bel-Rammân), (cf. Hebrew Rimmôn), at first on seals, and afterwards in sale-contracts of the time of Abraham. Later on it seems to have disappeared altogether from every-day use.

The fact that with what is known as the First Dynasty of Northern Babylonia, the Arabs came into power there, is conclusively proved from the *personal names* which have come down to us, including not only the names of the eleven kings of that dynasty, but those of a large number of their subjects. A host of such names, belonging to persons of all sorts of callings, have been preserved in the numerous contract-tablets of this period, and especially in the lists of witnesses which occur in nearly all of them.

There are two methods by which we may distinguish these Arabic, or, to use once for all the more general term, Western Semitic, names from those of genuine Babylonian origin. In the first place, the inscriptions have already familiarized us with such an enormous number of Babylonian personal names of almost every historical epoch, that we can generally tell on *a priori* grounds, whether a name has the true Babylonian ring or not, and this the more readily from the fact that the names, as far as their composition and formation are concerned, are fairly uniform in character from the earliest period to the time of Cyrus. To this class belong especially all personal names containing either the title of a distinctively Babylonian deity, or some verb or noun which is specially peculiar to the Assyro-Babylonian language. All words, therefore, which present any obvious variation from this standard may, *primâ facie*, be suspected to be of foreign origin. The easiest names to distinguish are the non-Semitic, and especially the Elamitic, such as Kudur-Nakhunti, Simtishilkhak, Kudur-Lagamar, or the Kassite, such as Burna-buriash, Kadashman-Khardas, etc. To the Semitic scholar the foreign origin of such vocables is apparent at a glance. To single out Western-Semitic, and especially Arabic names, is a good deal more difficult, for the Western-Semitic tongues have many roots and stems in common with Assyro-Babylonian, and when a personal name contains some noun or verb which has, so far, never been represented in the portion of Babylonian literature with which we are acquainted, but is occasionally met with in some other Semitic language, it by no means follows that this verb or noun must necessarily have been absent from Assyro-Babylonian. This difficulty is increased by the fact that we often find in personal names words which are either obsolete or very rarely used in ordinary speech.

The case is somewhat different, however, when a personal name contains verb-inflections or other grammatical elements which are not to be found in the literary Semitic language of Babylon as known to us from about 3000 B.C. onwards. Thus in Babylonian the imperfect of *malak* is *imlik*, of *shakan*, *ishkun*, etc. etc., while in Hebrew it is, respectively, *yimloch, yishkon*, in Arabic *yamlik, yaskun*, *i.e.* in both Hebrew and Arabic an initial Jod [y] is prefixed, while Babylonian-Assyrian has merely "i." If, therefore, we come upon names like *Yamlik-ilu, Ya'kub-ilu, Yarbi-ilu*, in the time of the First Dynasty of Northern Babylonia, the verb-inflections show that there is every chance in favour of the owner having been a Western-Semite (or, to be more precise, an Arab) rather than a Babylonian. Or, again, let us take, for an instance, a royal name like *Samsu-iluna*, in which the form *Samsu* (in true Babylonian we should expect Shamshu) at once strikes us as foreign, while it is scarcely possible to translate this name otherwise than "the sun is our god." Now the Babylonian word for "our" is *ni* (thus, iluni = "our god"), in Hebrew it is *-nu*, and in Arabic (and, indeed, in Aramaic also, though this fact is of no importance in connection with the period in question) it is *-na*.

Finally—and now we come to the most conclusive evidence of all—we find in the South-Arabian inscriptions, and to some extent also in Hebrew tradition (and that too in the tradition of the earliest times) an entirely original method of name-formation, which must be placed in a class by itself, owing to its peculiarly religious character. To this class belong a great many names which, though of undoubted Semitic origin, yet cannot for some one of the reasons mentioned above be regarded as pure Babylonian, or at any rate as necessarily Babylonian, proper names.

The obvious course to follow in our investigations will be first of all to consider carefully the composition and religious import of the genuine Babylonian personal names, and then endeavour to obtain by a stricter scrutiny of the South-Arabian personal names, some definite criterion by which to test the remaining names of supposed Western-Semitic origin. The Hebrew names I purposely leave entirely on one side for the present.

Now, first of all, in regard to *personal names of undoubted Babylonian origin*, we are already acquainted with a fairly large number of Semitic names belonging to a period prior to the first Northern Babylonian dynasty.[1] I use the word "Semitic" merely for the sake of clearness, though it cannot be denied that there were, especially in these earlier epochs, many Sumerian names as well, even if we have to admit that many apparently Sumerian names are merely ideographic forms of genuine Semitic words. The great majority of the Semitic-Babylonian names contain the name of some god as an element, nearly all the personages in the Babylonian Pantheon, known to us from the religious texts, being found among them.

Thus we find at a very early date such names as *Narâm-Sin* ("Beloved of Sin or of the moon-god"), *Amîl-Bel* ("Man of Bel"), *Ini-Ma-lik* ("Apple of the Eye of the god Malik"; Malik meaning, however, originally "king"), *Ishbi-Nirgal* ("The god of war is satiated"), *Ishmi-Dagan* ("Dagon hearkened,"—

[1] For the sake of brevity, I intend henceforward to describe this dynasty by the name of its most famous and prominent member, Hammurabi (or rather Khammurabi), the sixth of the eleven kings belonging to it.

Dagon being another name for Bel), *Nur-Rammân* ("Light of the Storm-god"), *Sin-banî* ("Sin creates"), *Gimil-Ea* ("Gift of Ea"), *Gimil-Samas* ("Gift of Samas, or of the sun-god"). Names compounded with the general word *ilu* = "god," such as *Ilu-bani* ("God creates"), are rare at this period, though it is true that we find a name like *Ibni-ilu* ("god created it") in one of the very earliest inscriptions extant.[1]

For the benefit of those who are not familiar with the names of the Babylonian gods, I may mention that the god of the sky (really of the Celestial Ocean) *Nun* or *Anum* (shortened into *Nu* or *Anu*,) stood at the head of the Babylonian Pantheon; he had a son, *In-lilla*, the god of the air (the Semitic *Bel* or "Lord") and *In-lilla* had a son *Ea* (Sumerian *En-ki*, "Lord of the Earth"), the god of earth and sea. These three, Anu, Bel, and Ea form the earliest triad of divinities; yet they do not occupy a prominent place in personal names. In order to bring such names into a form more easily apprehended it became the practice at an early date to replace Bel, the god of the air, by Rammân (ideogram Im), god of the storm and wind; Ea, god of the earth and sea, by Sin the moon-god (in South Babylonia Sin receiving the special name of *Uru-ki* or *Siski* = "Protector of the Earth"). For the atmosphere in motion is to the atmosphere at rest, as the concrete is to the abstract, and the moon which transmits the

---

[1] This is a Sacrifice-list written in semi-hieroglyphic characters; it should, however, be noted that even in this case there is a possible alternative reading, viz. *Anu-bani*, or *Ibni-Anu* ("The god of the sky creates or created"), the symbol in question being used for both *Anu* (sky, or god of the sky), and *ilu* (god = Hebr. *el*).

reflected light of the sun by night was recognized even by the Babylonians as the satellite of the earth. We therefore find that Rammân and Sin occur with relatively great frequency in personal names, as does Samas (properly *Shamash* or *Shamshu*), the sun-god; this latter, in the genealogical system of Babylonian deities, corresponds to *Mirri-Dugga* or *Amar-uduk* (Marduk, the Biblical Merodach) the morning sun rising out of the ocean. The sister and consort of the sun-god is Ishtar, his hostile brother is Nirgal (Sumerian *Girra*), who again is mated with Ghanna[1] or Gula; another name for Nirgal was Nin-Girsu (Lord of Girsu). Nirgal is also a solar deity, but like his "double" Nin-dar (or Ninip) he represents the evening sun after it has sunk beneath the horizon, or the winter sun which appears at no great height above it. Nindar is, therefore, more particularly the war-god, and Nirgal the god of the plague and of husbandry; regarded as planets, Nindar is Mars, Nirgal Saturn, Marduk Jupiter, Ishtar Venus, and a god not mentioned above, *Nabu* or Nusku (the biblical Nebo, in Sumerian, *Nin-gish-zidda*, *Dun-pa-uddu*, *Pa-sagga*, *Pa-bil-sag*, or simply, *Pa;* in Semitic, *Ishu* = Fire) is Mercury. Whereas Nindar (spelt Ninip) has no place in the genealogical system, but is replaced by Nirgal—a deity who appears comparatively seldom in personal names—Nebo, on the other hand, is joined

[1] Symbol *ab* (=house) with inserted symbol *kha* (=fish). The reading *Nind*, which is frequently given in modern Assyriological works, is undoubtedly wrong; the reading Ghanna, suggested by me in 1885, is practically certain; *Gula* (properly *Gulla*) is only a later form of *Ghanna*.

either with Marduk or with his brother Nirgal as their son, his wife being the harvest-goddess, Nisaba, who, however, also bears the special Semitic name of *Tashmit* (*i.e.* hearkening).

These are the more important among the deities of Ancient Babylonia, especially those of whom a knowledge is essential to a right understanding of personal names. There is nothing furthermore so conducive to the correct apprehension of the latter as a proper appreciation of the relationship between the various gods. The Babylonians themselves were not very clear on this point, though now and then we get a more definite glimpse of these relations. When, for instance, in the journey of Ishtar to Hades we read—

> Then went forth Samas, before Sin his father wept he,
> Before Ea, the king, came his tears,

the so-called *parallelismus membrorum*, which is the guiding principle of all early Semitic poetry at once suggests that Sin, the moon-god, and Ea, the earth-god, are interchangeable terms; just as "wept" is equivalent to "came his tears," so Sin is equivalent to Ea. According to the genealogical system, Merodach (Marduk), the Morning Sun, was the son of Ea; here Samas, the Sun, is the Son of Sin. Ishtar, as sister and wife of Merodach, is thus daughter of Ea, while in the Epos, on the contrary, she is represented as daughter of Sin, who is thus assumed as the equivalent of Ea. Ea's wife is called Dam-gal-nunna (Great Wife of the Celestial Ocean), while Sin's consort receives the designation Nin-gal ("Great Mistress"). to which I may add that the signs for

"Nin" and "Dam" are almost identical in meaning. Ea is called *Gushgin-banda*, that is "Small Gold," by which silver is meant, and Sin is also distinguished by the appellation *Lugal-banda*, "The Little King," Silver being the symbol of the Moon, as Gold is of the Sun. As Ea, according to the genealogical system is the son of Bel, Sin, on the other hand, as well as his equivalent, Lugal-banda, is represented in the religious texts as the first-born of Bel, who furthermore appears in the genealogical system as Son of Anu, and in the religious texts—through his representative Rammân—also as Son of Anu, the Celestial Deity. Wherever the Fire-God (Gibil)—who is on other occasions identified with Nabu or Nusku —is also called Son of Anu, Bel or Rammân, the God of Lightning, is meant. As for the female divinities, the wife of Bel is designated *Ninlilla*, "Mistress of the Air," or *Ba'u ;* wife of the Ea, as has been already said, is called *Dam-gal-Nunna ;* while the wife of Merodach (or Samas), is named *Ishtar* (sometimes *Ninni*, or even *Aï*), and the consort of Nergal (or Nin-ib), Gula. They are collectively feminine personifications of the Celestial Ocean, and it is only as a Planet-God that Ishtar has the distinctive designation of the Morning and Evening Star. The readiness with which these female deities are made to represent each other tends to produce the impression that there was but one Babylonian goddess, that is to say Ishtar, the Astarte of the Phœnicians. But here again, the various positions assigned to her in the genealogical tree enable us to give her her proper place. Ishtar, the daughter of Anu, is the wife of Bel; "Ishtar, the first-born daughter of Bel" is the wife of Ea; "Ishtar, the daughter of Sin" (which means the same thing as "the daughter of Ea") is the real Ishtar (who, as wife of the sun-god, also bears the distinctive title *Anunit* or *Aï*), or the name may also refer to Ea's other daughter, Gula.

An exceptionally large number of personal names belonging to the closing centuries of Khammurabi's dynasty have come down to us from the epoch of the so-called "later" kings of Ur (*vide supra*, pp. 36 *et seq.*).[1] Thousands of contract-tablets and trading-accounts of this period have been acquired during the last few years by the museums in Constantinople, Philadelphia, Paris, Berlin, and apparently in London also: unfortunately very few of these have as yet been published. Quite recently, however, an American scholar has printed a number of these tablets *in extenso*, so that we are now in a position to pronounce judgment on the personal names which occur in them. The twenty records[2] edited by Dr. Arnold contain nearly a hundred personal names, and of these hundred names, about a dozen contain the word *Gimil* = gift, and about twenty the word *Amil* = man, both of them in conjunction with the name of a god. Here *gimil* is represented by the symbol *shu* = hand, and *amil*, in some cases, by the symbol *gullu* = human being, in others by the

---
[1] The majority of the names quoted above, on pp. 61—62, are taken from inscriptions of a still earlier period.

[2] *Ancient Babylonian Temple Records in the Columbia University Library*, edited with transcriptions into Neo-Assyrian characters by W. R. Arnold, New York, 1896.

symbol *ur* = man. As to the names of deities, Samas, Sin (both in the form *En-zu* and in the usual South-Babylonian form *Uru-ki*), Nirgal and Aï are the most frequent: though we also find the names of Rammân, Ishtar, Ba'u, Gula, Nin-girshu, Ea, Marduk (in the form *Gal-alimma*), Anu, Tammuz (a manifestation-form of Marduk), and a god called *Shalim* (in the name *Amil-Shalim*), as well as another god, *Damku* ("the gracious one," apparently a sobriquet of Sin). Similarly, there are also a number of names compounded with *ilu* = God *e.g.* *Amur-ila* = "I beheld God," *Ilu-bani* (*vide supra*, p. 62), *Ilu-ni* = "our god," *Gimil-ili* = "gift of God." It is an open question whether all these names, every one of which has the true Babylonian ring, are also of genuine Semitic origin, or whether a good many of them ought not to be ascribed to Sumerian, the language of the aboriginal inhabitants of Babylon. For while it is clear that names which are represented by phonetic elements, such as those contained in *bani* = creating, *amur* = I saw, *ni* = our, *akhu* = brother, cannot be anything but Semitic; in the case of those written ideographically, we can only say that it is possible but not absolutely certain that they were pronounced in the Semitic manner. For instance, it is conceivable that all names beginning with *Ur*—the Sumerian word for "man"—may have been thus pronounced, and not perhaps as the Semitic sound *Amil.* Possibly the numerous texts which have yet to be published may enable us to clear up this point; for the purposes of our present investigation the question is of merely minor importance. So long as we are in a position to recognize the essential Babylonian character of all these names, and to ascertain the true Babylonian mental attitude which underlies their formation, it is immaterial whether an element in them is pronounced in one way or the other.

The personal names which occur in deeds of sale of the Khammurabi Dynasty, to which we shall now turn our attention, present far less difficulty in this respect. Here, names of undoubted Semitic origin are in a decided majority, even among the documents obtained from Southern Babylonia (Tel Sifr, near Larsa).[1] In order to make the matter more generally intelligible, I here append a list of the eleven kings belonging to this Dynasty with the length of the reign of each.

Shumu-abi				15 years.
Sumu-la-ilu				35 "
Zabium or Zabum	son of the preceding king,			14 "
Apil Sin	"	"	"	18 "
Sin-muballit	"	"	"	30 "
Khammurabi	"	"	"	55 "
Samsu-iluna	"	"	"	35 "
Abi-eshu'a	"	"	"	25 "
Ammi-satana	"	"	"	25 "
Ammi-zaduga	"	"	"	22 "
Samsu-satana	"	"	"	31 "

[1] It should be borne in mind that, so far as I know, all of the abovementioned documents belonging to the time of the later kings of Ur come from Telloh in Southern Babylonia, whereas the deeds of sale of the subsequent epochs belong for the larger part to Northern Babylonia, a region which had been subject to Semitic influences from the earliest times: this fact must not be lost sight of in weighing the evidence.

As nearly all the contract tablets of this epoch are dated in the reign of one or other of the above-named kings, we are justified in asserting, on *a priori* grounds, the pre-Abrahamic origin of a certain number of them, about twenty-five in all (exclusive of those not yet published), containing about four hundred personal names; for, as briefly indicated above (p. 44), Khammurabi was a contemporary of Abraham, therefore Khammurabi's five predecessors and individuals who lived in their time may be rightly described as pre-Abrahamic. If we include the time of Khammurabi also, then the total number of personal names at our disposal becomes substantially larger. For, as far back as 1882, twenty-three sale-contracts of the time of Khammurabi, and twenty-three more of the time of his rival Eri-Aku, or Rim-Sin of Larsa, were published by Strassmaier alone in the *Proceedings* of the Berlin Congress of Orientalists. To these Bruno Meissner added a dozen more (all of North Babylonian origin) in his *Beiträge zum altbabylonischen Privatrecht*, published in 1893, a work containing no less than one hundred and eleven contracts of the Khammurabi Dynasty. The names occurring in the period before, and down to, the time of Khammurabi, however, supply enough material to enable us to determine the usual system of name-formation which obtained in Babylon at that time. But lest this limitation of the field of investigation should make it seem as though the names prior to Khammurabi differ from those found during and after his time, I may as well mention here that the personal names of the whole epoch, from Shamu-abi down to Samsu-satana are all of the same type, viz. pure Babylonian-Semitic, with the exception of a few names of private individuals, which I shall deal with later on; these exceptions amount to about 5 per cent. (or perhaps more) of the whole.[1]

Let us now examine the names themselves, and the religious ideas of the Babylonians of that time to which they are an index. The first peculiarity we notice is that by far the greater number of these names contain two elements, and some of them as many as three. These latter, which had hitherto only been found among the names of Babylonian and Assyrian kings of a later period (*i.e.* about 1500 B.C. Cf. *Assur-nadin-akhi* = Assur giver of a brother), are met with here also, each of them forming a whole sentence. As instances of such names belonging to the first half of the Khammu-rabi Dynasty, I may here mention *Samas-nûr-mâte* = Samas is the light of the country, *Martû-bani-amêli* = The Storm-god is the creator of mankind, *Sin-kalama-idi* = Sin knows everything, *Mannu-shanin-Samas* = who can contend against Samas? *Shumma-ilu-la-ilia* = If god be not my god (then will such and such a thing befall me); to these may be added the following names which occur under the latter half of the dynasty: *Samas-natsir-apli* = Samas is the

---

[1] It is true that the proportion is totally different in the case of the eleven names of the kings: here there are nine names which, though of Semitic origin, are not Babylonian, but rather Arabic. It must be remembered, however, that while the reigning dynasty was of foreign origin, the great bulk of their subjects remained Babylonian as before.

guardian of the son, *Sin-nadin-shumi* = Sin is the donor of the name (*i.e.* the giver of a son), *Samas-shar-kitti* = Samas is king of justice, *Sin-akham-idin-am* = Sin give a brother, *Mannu-balu-ili* = who (can exist) without God, *Ilu-ishme-khani* = God listens to the wretched, *Zanik-pi-shu-Samas* = His mouth is closed, O Samas,[1] and finally, *Abum-kima-ili* = A Father like God.

Personal names composed of two elements nearly all contain the name of a god, sometimes at the beginning, sometimes at the end of the compound. Let us first examine those in which the *final* element consists of a divine name. Whereas, under the later kings of Ur, names beginning with *Gimil-* = gift, and *Amil-* (or *Ur*)- = man, appear, as we have seen, to be in a majority;[2] under the Khammurabi Dynasty another set of words come to the front, *e.g.* those commencing with *Ipik-* or *Ipku* = Might (?), *Nûr-* = Light, *Arad* = servant, *Tsili* = my protection, *sha* = he of (*i.e.* a retainer or servant of such and such a god), etc., etc. Of the names of deities found in conjunction with these elements, by far the most frequent is that of Sin, the moon-god, who had his most ancient fane at Harân; in his later holy temple at Ur he was worshipped under the name of Nannar (written *Uruki*). At the time, however, in which these personal names originated the cult of the

[1] *I.e.* he is silent in thy presence. Cf. Habakkuk ii. 20; Ps. xxxvii. 7, or perhaps interrogatively, "Does Samas, then, close his mouth?" for which parallels may be found in Ps. l. 3 or xxviii. 1.

[2] Unless, of course, the evidence of the many texts still unpublished should reverse this verdict, a result which for various reasons I do not regard as probable. Cf. p. 104, note 1.

moon-god had spread over the whole of Babylonia, and was undoubtedly more popular than that of any other deity. It should also be noted that Ur and Harân, the chief centres of this worship of the moon-god are, at the same time, the two places which play an early and important part in the migrations of the Patriarch Abraham; for it was from Ur that he set out for Harân, and from thence he afterwards went on to Palestine. Next to Sin the most frequent elements in names are *ili* = " of God," or *ili-shu* = " of his God,"[1] Samas and Rammân, and the lesser gods and goddesses, such as Ishtar, Aï, etc., occurring much less frequently. After what has been just said, it is, perhaps, hardly necessary to adduce specific examples: in addition to ordinary compounds, such as *Nûr-ili-shu*, *Nûr-Samas*, *Nûr-Sin* (= Light of his god, Light of Samas, Light of Sin respectively), *Arad-Râmman* = servant of Rimmon, *Arad Nirgal* = servant of Nirgal, we may also notice such names as *Irishti-Aï* = My desire is Aï (Goddess of the sky), *Imgur-Sin* = Sin was gracious, *Ana-pani-ili* = before the face of God (cf. Num. vi. 25), *Na-bi-Sin* = Harbinger or Prophet of Sin (or Harbinger is Sin (?), cf. *Bani-Sin* = The creator is Sin), *Sha-Martu* = He of the storm-god,[2] Apil-Sin = Son of Sin, *Bur-Rammân*

[1] *I.e.* of the special patron-deity of the person in question, who seems, in most cases, to have been Sin, though we meet with such names as Ilu-ka-Samas and *Samas-ilu-ka-ni* = Thy god is Samas.

[2] This name is borne by a witness to a contract concluded under Apil-Sin, who is further described as "son of Abî-râmu" (which proves that even at that time there were names similar to the Hebrew "Abraham"). MEISSNER, *Beiträge zum altbabylonischen Privat-recht* No. III. Cf. *infra* p. 94, Note 1.

= scion of Rammân, *Pir-i-Aï* = scion of Aï, *Mar-Istar* = Son of Ishtar, *Apil-ili-shu* = Son of his God (cf. a similar expression in the bi-linear religious texts " The sick man, the son of his god"), *Kish-ili* = Gift of God, and *Ishmi-Sin* = Sin gave ear.

Even more numerous are those names compounded of two elements in which the *first* element consists of the name of a deity. From an examination of instances it is clear that a much greater freedom was allowed in the choice of verbal forms which might be tacked on after the name of a god. While verbs and participles are of comparatively rare occurrence as first elements, they are quite common as second elements. This may be best shown by a series of examples. *Sin-rimêne, Rammân-rimêni* = S. or R. have shown mercy on me, *Sin-rimênishi* = S. have thou mercy on us, *Beli-ishmeanni* = my Lord hearkened unto me, *Sin-shimî* = S. hearkens, *Samas-taïru* = S. turns again, *i.e.* is gracious, *Sin-iragam* = S. makes protest (*i.e.* in favour of sinners), *Sin-putram* = S. releases or frees (viz. from guilt), *Samas-natsir* = S. protects, *Sin-magir* = S. is compliant, *Sin-liki* = S. accepts (sc. my complaint), *Aku-daïnu* = the moon-god is judge (viz. of the dead as Samas was of the living), *Ilu-damik* = God is gracious, *Sin-gamil* = S. gives (cf. *Sin-ikisham* and *Sin-iddinam*), *Samas-bani* = S. creates, *Sin-muballit* = S. awakens the dead, *Sin-pilakh* = Fear Sin!, *Sin-imûki* = S. is my wisdom, *Sin-illatsu* = S. is his strength, *Samas-mudi* = S. is omniscient, *Sin-abushu* = S. is his father, *Ilushu-abushu* = His god is his father, *Samas-abuni* = S. is our father—all these are not merely evidence of what I have said above, but also of the prevailing religious tendency in Babylon—in spite of its polytheism—shortly before Abraham and during his time. It is, moreover, worthy of note that Ishtar scarcely ever appears in such personal names as commence with the name of a god: I have been able so far to find among feminine names only *Istar-ummasha* = Ishtar is her mother, and a few names beginning with Aï, such as *Aï-rishat* = Aï is the highest. Speaking generally, the only gods represented in names of this type are Sin, Samas, *ilu* (God), and Rammân (= Bel). Notwithstanding, therefore, the countless greater and lesser deities in which Babylonian Polytheism abounded, the names in general use seem to prove that it was only the moon, the sun, and the sky which conveyed an impression of deity to the Babylonian mind; and if we substitute the simple word "God" (*ilu*) for the moon, the sun, or the sky, these names express no sentiment which is inconsistent with the highest and purest monotheism. The exalted conception of the deity possessed by the Semites of Northern Babylon will be dealt with later on, when we come to speak of the primitive history of Babylon and Israel.

Our present object, however, in introducing all these names, is not so much to show the relatively high religious feeling which they evince, as to put before our readers some of the general principles which underlie the formation of Babylonian appellations, and to point out a few of their most characteristic elements. Compared with them, other names which occur, it is true, in the same documents, but which I have provisionally described as Arabian, seem obscure and unintelligible—I refer to such names as *Ammi-zaduga, Abi-eshu'a* (or *Abîshu'a*), *Sumu-abi, Mûdadi, Zimrî-rabi, Yashup-ilu, Natunu, Yadikhu,* etc. For the individual constituents or general meaning of such appellations we may search the Babylonian-Assyrian vocabulary in vain. The key of the enigma can only be supplied by a study of the system of name-formation which obtained in Southern Arabia. This system we must now briefly examine before concluding the present chapter.

In Southern Arabia we come upon traces of a high state of civilization at a very early period. Evidence of this is supplied by the ruins of ancient temples, towns, and aqueducts, and, above all, by the numerous inscriptions which still survive. These latter are written in an alphabet which belongs, at the very lowest estimate, to the same period as the so-called Phœnician alphabet, and must therefore be referred, together with the Phœnician, and the Greek alphabet, which is derived from it, to one and the same source, viz., the Western Semitic alphabet, the structural source of which has not yet been made out. This circumstance alone is an argument in favour of ascribing these inscriptions to the middle or perhaps even the beginning of the second millennium before Christ. The question as to whether they take their origin from the Egyptian hieratic script or, as seems far more probable, from the ancient Babylonian is quite a separate one.

The South Arabian inscriptions are to be respectively distributed among the kings of Ma'ân,[1] those of the Hadramaut and those of Katabân—whose monuments have lately been discovered by Dr. Glaser —and to the kings of Saba (Sheba). They are written in two dialects—the Hadramautic, Katabanian,[2] and Minæan[3] inscriptions being in Minæan, while the Sabæan inscriptions are in the Sabæan dialect. The earliest Sabæan inscriptions, those in which the rulers are referred to—not as kings—but as priest-kings (*mukarrib* or *makrûb*), belong to the commencement of the first millennium before Christ, being certainly not later than 800 B.C., and probably as early as 900 B.C. or 1000 B.C.; in the Hebrew tradition we find a queen of Saba mentioned as early as the time of Solomon. Next in order come those Sabæan inscriptions in which the rulers are named simply "Kings of Saba" (700—200 B.C.), and lastly the neo-Sabæan inscriptions (in which the title appears as "King of Saba and Dhu-Raidân"), the last of these being as late as 600 A.D. (from about 300

[1] Usually pronounced *Ma'în*; the history of the pronunciation of similar names in Southern Palestine and the region east of Jordan seems to indicate that the original pronunciation must have been *Ma'ân*, the Hebrew word in both these cases being *Ma'ôn* (from *Ma'ân*). At the present day, however, we have *Tel Ma'în* (south of Hebron), and *Ma'în* (from whence we get the river *Zerka Ma'în*). The Babylonians probably transcribed it by *Magan*.

[2] Cf ED. GLASER, *Die Abessinier in Arabien und in Afrika*, Munich, 1895, p. 72.

[3] The Greeks (in the Septuagint and the writings of Strabo) transliterate the Hebr. *Ma'ôn* and Arab. *Ma'ân* into Μιναῖοι. Hence the terms Minæans and Minæic have passed into common use, and, for the sake of convenience, I adopt them in the present work.

A.D. onwards it is "King of S. and Dh.R. and Hadramaut and Yemnat"). Of the Hadramautic inscriptions, unfortunately only two or three have as yet been discovered, and of these only one has any claim to high antiquity, though it is quite certain that there were kings of the Hadramaut in the time of the priest-kings of Saba, and probably long before it: of the Katabanian inscriptions, none of which, I regret to say, have yet been published, a part at any rate are, according to Glaser, contemporary with the earliest Sabæan records. Finally, the Minæan inscriptions, several of which have also been found at el-Oela in N.W. Arabia, ought, in the opinion of several scholars who have made a special study of the subject, to be assigned to the period between 900 and 200 B.C. One of them, which is specially important, owing to the fact that it contains a reference to Egypt and to Minæan colonies in Edom has been attributed to the time of Cambyses (525 B.C.), although an ingenious theory put forward by Dr. Glaser and supported by him with extraordinary ability, assigns the kingdom of Ma'ân to a pre-Sabæan era, a conjecture that seems to become every day more probable. While Glaser (and at one time I was prepared to agree with him) refers the earliest of these inscriptions to the end of the Hyksos period, I now confidently believe that the South Arabian kingdom of the Minæan dynasty, must, at the very latest, have flourished in the period between Solomon and Moses: at any rate, it seems to me that the inscription mentioned above (which other authorities wish to assign to the reign of Cambyses) belongs to this epoch, and Glaser has already adduced evidence from monuments lately discovered by him, to prove that the kingdom of Ma'ân was totally [1] destroyed by Kariba-ilu Watar, one of the priest-kings of Saba.

The personal names which occur in all these inscriptions—and especially in the earliest of them, such as the Minæan and early Sabæan, are of a fairly uniform type, their main characteristics being briefly as follows.

We are struck first of all by the fact that though the South Arabian religion was of a polytheistic character—as the *ex voto* offerings to the various gods conclusively show [2]—yet the names of the various gods are, in almost every instance, excluded from personal names in favour of the generic term *ilu* = "God."

The usual sequence in which the gods are mentioned in the Minæan inscriptions is as follows: *Athtar* (pronounced Astar) of *Kabâdh*, *Wadd*, *an-Karih* (another rendering is *Nakrah*), *Athtar* of *Yahrak*, and the Lady of *Nashk*. To these some inscriptions add an "Athtar the Ascendant" (*i.e.* apparently, the Morning Star), and an Athtar of Yahir. Athtar and Wadd occupy the highest place. The first of these, though originally borrowed from Babylon, and identical with the goddess Ishtar (the

---

[1] Those who hold that the kingdoms of Ma'ân and Saba were contemporary, must necessarily assume in this case that the Minæan kingdom came into existence again after its overthrow by Saba, a view which is, for various reasons, exceedingly improbable.

[2] The majority of the inscriptions are *ex voto* offerings to the gods; even the few purely historical monuments partake of this character.

Phœnician Astarte) is nevertheless always represented as a male deity. He was also worshipped in the Hadramaut, though there his son Sin (also a Babylonian importation, but in Babylon the relationship was reversed, Sin being regarded as the father of Ishtar) took a more prominent place. As to Wadd, he is the personification of Love, just as an-Karih[1] is the personification of Hate: we have here an Arabian counterpart of the hostile brothers Marduk and Nirgal (cf. Osiris and Set). Yet in spite of all this we scarcely ever find anything but *ilu* = God, in Minæan personal names. Wadd occurs but seldom (as in *Sa'ada-Wadd* = Wadd hath blessed it, or—a better reading—*Sa'du-Wadd* = The prosperity of Wadd), *an-Karih* is not found at all; the word "goddess" only once, viz. in *Sa'du-ilat* = Prosperity of the Goddess, = Sabæan, *Sa'd-Lât ;* and *Athtar* but rarely, and generally in an abbreviated form *Atht*, *e.g. Hama-Atht* = Athtar protected it, *Haupi-Atht* = give health, O Athtar, *Bi-Athtar* = By Athtar, and in a few other instances: far more frequent are names like *Yahmi-ilu* = may God protect, and *Haupi-ilu* = God give health.

We find a very similar state of things in early Sabæan inscriptions. In the Sabæan Pantheon Athtar was also worshipped in various places and temples, but Wadd no longer accompanies him, but

---

[1] This reading (in which the "n" is assumed to be equivalent to the old North-Arabian article) is based on the fact that in certain South-Arabian inscriptions the North-Arabian-Phœnician god Ba'al appears as an-Ba'al (according to another rendering Nab'al); it is, therefore, probable that an-Karih is originally of North-Arabian origin.

Almâku-hû = his (*i.e.* the Heaven's) Lights; and in place of the generic "goddess" we have the Sun (Shamsum) represented as female, accompanied by a whole host of other lesser gods, who must originally have been nothing more than local deities, such as *Ta'lab*, *Aum*, etc., etc. Now, it is interesting to observe that it is not till we come to neo-Sabæan inscriptions that Shamsum, Aum, Athtar, and other names of deities (never, it is significant to note, that of Almâku-hu) appear as the second element in personal names, and even then they do not occur nearly so often as *ilu* = God, which moreover appears frequently as a first element.

The first deduction—and a very important deduction it is, even when taken by itself—we can draw from the above facts is, that South Arabian personal nomenclature of the earliest times contains practically no appellations save those compounded with *ilu* = God, in spite of the fact that the religion of those who bore these names was admittedly polytheistic. If we consider how frequently primitive ideas continue to persist in the personal names of any race, this would seem to indicate that there must have been a time in the history of Arabia when these gods—a number of whom, such as Athtar, Sin, and the Hadramautic deity Anbay (= Nebo), recently discovered by Glaser, were certainly imported from outside—did not receive worship, and when some higher form of devotion of a type, which involuntarily reminds one of what we are told about Melchisedek in the Old Testament, must have prevailed.

Nor is this by any means the sole deduction to be drawn from the facts. It is of special interest for us to learn all that is said of God in South Arabian personal names, and particularly the special periphrases for the simple word *ilu* which were adopted in these names.

In the first place it is characteristic that whenever the word "God" appears as the first element of a name, it is nearly always accompanied by a suffix denoting the first person singular of the possessive pronoun, thus *ilî* = my God. In the following examples I have purposely chosen appellations containing such predicates as occur most frequently in the second elements. For instance:

Ilî-awwas   my God has presented [1]
"-*wahaba*   "   "   "   given
"-*dhara'a*   "   "   "   created
    (or   "   "   "   sown the seed)
"-*dharaha*   "   "   is resplendent
"-*za'ada*   "   "   commands awe (?)
"-*yada'a*   "   "   is (all) knowing
"-*yapi'a*   "   "   shines (or is resplendent)
"-*kariba*   "   "   has (or is) blessed
"-*ma-nabata*   "   stepped into the light, shone
"-*'azza*   "   "   is mighty
"-*'amida*   "   "   came forth (to help)
"-*padaya*   "   "   has set free
"-*rabbi*   "   "   increase! (probably imperative)
"-*rapa'a*   "   "   has healed
"-*radsawa*   "   "   is well pleased

[1] As the vowel points are not given in the South Arabian script, it is possible that in many of these names we ought to read an imperative instead of a third person of the perfect (*e.g. Ilî-awwis* = Give, O my God).

Ili-sharraha my God causes to thrive
"*-shara'a* " " has ordained, ordered
"*-sami'a* " " " hearkened
"*-sa'ada* " " " blessed

A large number of these predicates also occur in reverse order, and in these cases the verb preceding the word *ilu* (God) is generally in the so-called imperfect tense (with a present or probably even an optative significance), *e.g. Yasma'-ilu* = May God listen to it! *Yu'awwis-ilu* = May God grant it! and many others of a similar kind, including names in which occur verbs not mentioned in the above list, such as,— *Yadh-kur-ilu* = May God remember it! *Yahmi-ilu* = God protect it! *Yahram-ilu* = God averts it! etc., etc. Names consisting of a verb in the imperfect by itself, such as, *Yashûpu* = he regards, are abbreviated forms of a longer name as, in this case, *Yashûpu-ilu*. Moreover, the perfect tense also appears as a first element, *e.g. Kariba-ilu* = God blessed it, *Warawa-ilu* = God cast it (sc. the lot), *'Adhara-ilu* = God defended it, though in the case of words like these, it is sometimes difficult, in the absence of vowel points, to be quite certain whether the first element is a noun or a verb; *Wahbu-ili, Zaidu-ili, Widâdu-ili* (= Present from God, Gift of God, Love of God) are, for instance, more probable readings than *Wahaba-ilu* (= God gave it) *Zayyada-ilu* and *Waddada-ilu*. We also find semi-verbal adjectives (often from the same verbs that are elsewhere combined with the name of a deity) used as personal names, *e.g. Natanum* (= Giver meaning originally God and not the bearer of the name), *Tsaduku*, *Yathu'u* and *Yathi'um*, *Yapi'u*, *Akibu* (with a strong *k*-sound) and other names of one element, to which we shall again refer later on.

We find moreover—and here we come to the most characteristic feature of this method of name-formation—instead of the names originally beginning with the word *ili* = my God, a number of synonymous terms, (to some extent periphrases of the divine name), taking its place. The more frequent and important of these terms are *Abi* = my Father, *ammi* = my Uncle,[1] (in the sense of "guardian" or "protector") or, in place of it, *khâli* = my Uncle; we also occasionally find *dâdi* = my Cousin and *akhi* = my Brother, and lastly *sum-hu* = His Name. But even more general expressions such as, *dhimri* = my Protection,[2] *yith'i* = my Help (or Salvation), *nabti* = my Splendour, *tsidki* = my Justice, *wir'i* = my Fear, with a few others of still vaguer significance, such as, *ma'di*, *tubba'i* (perhaps = *malki* = my king?) and *nash'i* are used quite indifferently with *ili* = my God. We thus obtain at one and the same time a confirmation of the phrases contained in the above list and a whole series of additional predicates of the deity, as the following names—se-

---

[1] Probably = Paternal Uncle as opposed to Khâ'i = brother of my mother. In these personal names *ammi* never occurs in the sense of "my people."

[2] The vocalization has been arrived at through names that occur in the cuneiform inscriptions such as *Zimri-rabi* and *Zimrida* (from *Dhimri-yada'a*), and also by comparison with Hebrew names such as *Zimri*, *Yish'i* [*Ishi*] *Tsidki-yâhu* [*Zidkyah*] and *Yir'i-yah*.

lected either for their frequent occurrence, or special significance—will readily prove:

Abi-amara, Sumhu-amara, Khâli-amara, Ammi-amara, Yith'i-amara, Wir'i-amara = My father etc. has commanded.

'Ammi-anisa = My uncle is well affected (cf. supra, p. 51).

Sumhu-apika = His name is powerful (or excellent)—with a strong *k*-sound.

Abi-wakula, Khâli-wakula = My father etc. rules.

Sumhu-watara = His name is above all others.

Abi-dhamara = My father was protecting.

**'Ammi-dhara'a* = My uncle created (or sowed seed).

**Abi-za'ada* = My father inspires fear (or awe).

**Abî-yada'a, Ammi-yada'a, Khâli-yada'a, Dhimri-yada'a* = My father etc. is omniscient; cf. also the inverted forms *Yada'a-abu, Yada'a-ilu, Yada'a-sumhu*. This last name taken in connection with that of *Sumaida* which occurs in the later South Arabian tradition, seems to point to *Sumhu-yada'a* as a name which must have originally existed somewhere among the inscriptions. Cf. p. 110.

Sumhu-yapi'a, Ammi-yapia, Yith'i-yapia, Nabti-yapia = His name etc. shines.

Abi-yathu'a (cf. supra, p. 53), *Ammi-yathua* = My father etc. helps.

**Abi-kariba, Ammi-kariba, Khâli-kariba, Dâdi-kariba, Akhi-kariba, Sumhu-kariba, Dhimri-kariba, Yith'i-kariba, Nabti-kariba, Ma'di-kariba,*[1] *Tubbaï-kariba, Nash'i-kariba, Dhar'i-kariba* = My father etc. has (or is) blest.

Rabbi-nadiba = My Lord is generous.

Abi-'ali, Sumhu-ali, Dhimri-ali, Nabti-ali = My father etc. is sublime.

Ammi-tsaduka = My uncle is just—with strong *k*-sound.

Sumhu-riyâmu = His name is sublimity.

Abi-shapaka, Ammi-shapaka = My father etc. gives rich gifts —with strong *k*-sound.

**Abi-sami'a, Ammi-samia* = My father etc. hearkened.

---

[1] This is one of the most common names, and continued to be in actual use up to late times, that is, to the time of Mahomed.

An asterisk is prefixed to those names of which the second element has already appeared in the earlier list on pp. 81—82, in conjunction with *ili* = my God.

By far the greater number of all these names, including both those on p. 81, and those just enumerated, belong to the Minaean and early Sabaean inscriptions. Careful calculations—some results of which are given elsewhere—tend to show that many of these names, and especially those beginning with *Ammi-*, *Kháli-*, and *Sumhu-* appear less and less frequently as time goes on, and that the vogue of this whole system of name-formation practically began and ended in the earliest epochs of South Arabian history.

In regard to the *religious significance* of this name-system, it may, I think, be confidently asserted that no parallel can be found for it in the nomenclature of any ancient people. It is true, that in so far as the attributes ascribed to the Deity are concerned, genuine Babylonian names, which we have already considered at some length, offer points of resemblance with those of South Arabia. In the Babylonian, no less than in the South Arabian, we find evidence of a belief that the Deity gives men all things that are good, that He blesses, protects, rescues, assists, and delivers, that He is mighty, and shines with a pure radiance; that He creates and preserves all things, is omniscient, just, sublime, and kingly, increases, and commands; that He is nevertheless gracious and merciful to all who approach Him as suppliants, even as a father is to his children, and hearkens to the prayers of them that call upon Him and serve Him in holy fear. If we add to this the fact that in Babylonian names, references to "judgment," "raising from the dead," and "forgiveness" occur with comparative frequency, it would almost seem as though the Babylonians had possessed a deeper sense of religion than the Arabs. Apart, however, from the fact that with few exceptions—as, for instance, in the case of expressions like "hearken," "know," and one or two others—Babylonian and Arabic rarely employ the same or even etymologically identical verbs, but generally use totally distinct words even when they wish to express the same or a similar meaning, there is another radical distinction between them, which places the Arabic nomenclature on a far higher and purer level than the Babylonian. I refer to its almost invariable use of the word "God" (*ilu*) as contrasted with the polytheism observable in Babylonian names (Sin, Samas, Rammân, Nirgal, etc.). Even the synonymous alternatives for the word "God" which are found in South Arabian inscriptions, such as "Father," "Uncle," "Protection," "Help" (cf. the analogous use of *Tsur* = "rock" in the O. T.), and especially the substitute "His name" which occurs so frequently, are merely so many witnesses to the lofty conception of the Deity entertained by the earliest Arabs. Compared with that held by the Babylonians, it can only be described as a very advanced type of monotheism not unworthy to rank with the religion of the patriarch Abraham as presented in the Biblical narrative. If we look at the part played by the sublime and holy

" name of Yahveh " in the Old Testament scriptures dealing with Mosaic times, we find that a growing reluctance to pronounce this sacred name led to its being replaced by the designation $Shem$ = " Name (κατ' ἐξοχήν)." The fact, moreover, that the worship of a number of deities is prominently mentioned, even in the earliest South Arabian inscriptions, merely serves to throw into still stronger relief the persistent monotheism of the personal names, which even the lapse of a thousand years or so had been powerless to efface. How deeply this monotheistic principle must have rooted itself in the hearts of this people from the earliest ages is proved by its having been able, in face of the growing encroachments of polytheism, to retain for so long an undisputed position in their appellations.

Having now sufficiently described the system of name-formation peculiar to South Arabia, both as regards its form (viz. the verbs and nouns which are employed in it) and as regards its meaning, it will be a comparatively easy task to separate the Arabic names referred to above (pp. 59—62) as occurring under the Khammurabi Dynasty, and especially the names of the kings themselves (see list p. 68) from those of purely Babylonian origin. And first of all it is only fair to credit with their due meed of praise, and in their proper order, the various scholars who have directly or indirectly helped to elucidate this most important point, and to show how modern investigators were gradually led to determine the Western Semitic (or, to be more precise, Arabic), origin of the Dynasty in question.

As far back as December 1880, the English Assyriologist, Mr. T. G. Pinches, in dealing with the list of eleven kings and the periods for which they reigned, then first published, called attention to the fact that another list showed a long series of names of Babylonian rulers, the greater part of them of Sumerian and also Kassite origin with their explanation in Semitic. Among these translations into the Semitic dialect of Babylonia were found also the two names *Kha-am-mu-ra-bi* (pronounced *Khammurabi*) and *Am-mi-di-ka-ga* (for which read *Ammi-sadugga* or *Ammi-didugga*, since the symbol *ka* when it appears in conjunction with *ga* is equivalent to *dug*); the Babylonian scribe explains them by *Kimta-rapashtu* (*i.e.* "a widely extended family") and *Kimtu-kittu* ("just family"). According to the view of the Babylonian interpreter, in these names (which he evidently regards as foreign or, at any rate, as not of genuine Babylonian origin) the first element *Khammu*, or *Ammi* = Family, the second element *rabi* (ostensibly good Babylonian for "great," from *rabû* = to be great) = "widely diffused" or "extended," while the other second element *sadugga* = "just." That the pronunciation intended was really *sadugga* and not *didugga* is proved by certain ancient Babylonian contract tablets of Tel Ibraham (Kutha), the dates of which were given in a translation by Mr. Pinches in 1886;[1] in these contracts the name of the king in question is spelt *Ammi-zaduga* by his contemporaries.

In December 1887, that able Assyriologist, M. H.

[1] *Guide to the Nimroud Central Saloon*, (London 1886) p. 82.

Pognon, French Consul at Bagdad, carried the matter a step further. In a note contributed to the *Journal Asiatique* (Series VIII., vol. xi., 1888, pp. 543—547)—which seems unfortunately to have been buried in that publication, and has, in any case, received no further attention from Assyriologists—he identified *zaduga* with the Hebrew and Arabic verb *Tsadak* = "to be just": explained *Khammu* and *Ammi* as equivalent to the Hebrew '*am* = "people," basing this latter conclusion on the Babylonian paraphrase *kimtu* = family, and correctly translated *Samsu-iluna* as "Samas is our god." From these data he argued that the dynasty in question must have been of "Arabic or Aramaic origin." The last sentence of his paper (in which, by the way, he does not even touch on the most important point of all, viz. the existence of South Arabian and Hebrew names beginning with *Ammî*) runs as follows: "I am, however, quite prepared to admit that my opinion (sc. as to the foreign, but incontestably Semitic origin of the dynasty) is purely hypothetical, and I have no intention of presenting it to my readers as a certainty."

It was not till the year 1890 that this hypothesis, which Pognon had done little more than suggest, at length took tangible shape. In that year the gifted English Assyriologist, A. H. Sayce, pointed out that a name almost identical with Ammi-zaduga occurs in a well-known South Arabian inscription (Hal. 535) in the form '*Ammi-tsaduka*, thus furnishing obvious confirmation of the existence of the Western Semitic verb, meaning "to be just," postulated by Pognon's theory. Meanwhile Eduard Glaser had (in 1889) drawn fresh attention to this document, hitherto invariably misinterpreted, in which the writer, '*Ammî-tsaduka*, returns thanks to the gods for his safe escape out of Egypt, Glaser making reference to it in connexion with his hypothesis as to the higher antiquity of the Minæans.[1] This, together with certain contributions towards the elucidation of this important inscription which I gave in my *Aufsätze und Abhandlungen*,[2] and a further discussion of the same text by Glaser in the second volume of his book[3] (which appeared in May 1890) led Sayce to suggest the Minæan name *Ammî-tsaduk*.[4] This identification of Ammi-zaduga, the name of a Babylonian king with the South Arabian name 'Ammî-tsaduka (for this was, of course, the complete pronunciation)—an identification of the utmost importance to all who seek to elucidate the earliest history of the Western Semites—occurs in Sayce's Preface to the third volume of the New Series of *Records of the Past* edited by him, and dated September 1890. Sayce here supports his case by a reference to the Hebrew names Ammiel, Amminadab (I had already adduced these in *Aufsätzen und Abhandlungen*, p. 6, note 1),

---

[1] *Skizye der Geschichte Arabiens*, Pt. I. (which is unfortunately not yet obtainable through the booksellers), Munich, 1889, pp. 57 *et seq.*

[2] Pt. I., Munich, 1892; pp. 1 — 66 were, however, sent to various scholars and libraries as early as March 1890.

[3] *Skizze der Geschichte und Geographie Arabiens*, vol. II. (*Geographie*), Berlin, 1890.

[4] This had already been correctly transcribed by me in my *Aufsätzen und Abhandlungen*, p. 26, note 1, though on p. 6 I gave it as 'Ammî-tsadik.

Balaam and Jeroboam, to the Arabian names Ammu-ladin (under Assurbanipal in the seventh century B.C.) and to the name borne by the Shuhite god Emu (for 'Ammu), and in conclusion expresses his conviction that certain kings of the first North Babylonian dynasty, not all of them, but from Khammurabi, the sixth member of the dynasty, onwards, belonged to "tribes of Arabian origin from the western and eastern frontiers of Babylon." On this last point he is, however, mistaken, since Samsu-iluna, the son of Khammurabi, calls Sumu-la-ilu "his mighty ancestor, his fifth predecessor" (cf. the third (1887) Part of my *History of Babylonia and Assyria*, pp. 353 and 415); Sayce ought, therefore, to have described the whole dynasty as Arabian, but appears to have been misled by the seemingly pure Babylonian names of the first five kings. In addition he drew attention to the fact that the name of the eighth of these kings is Ibishu according to the list, and *Abi-esukh* in the contracts (the correct and more accurate form is, however, Abîshu'a), and that it contains the element *Abi* = "father"; he also regards as a later interpolation the assertion in the list to the effect that Samu-la-ilu, the second king, who was probably brother to the first, was the progenitor of the whole dynasty.

But now a fresh difficulty arises which did not occur to Professor Sayce when he claimed an Arabian origin for the second half of the Khammurabi Dynasty. Since names beginning with *Ammi* are found among the Hebrews, the absence of such a name as *Ammi-zadok* from the Old Testament may be purely accidental. There is, moreover, the possibility that the names of the second half of the Khammurabi Dynasty may have been Canaanitish instead of Arabian. In that case Samsu-iluna instead of being equivalent to "Samsu is our God" (Hebr. *Shemesh-elênu*, or in Babylonian script *Shamash-ilênu*) would have to be explained as "Samsu is God" (*Shemesh-elon*), as indeed I myself had at one time proposed to do.[1]

Meanwhile, we learn from texts recently discovered that both Khammurabi and his great-grandson, Ammi-satana, were not only kings of Babylonia proper, but also kings of the land of Martu, (which included Palestine);[2] the obvious explanation seemed, therefore, in my opinion, to be that both Khammurabi and his successors must have assumed Canaanitish names either for political reasons with a view to conciliating their Canaanite subjects, or possibly because they had married Canaanite wives and thus condescended to show their love for them.[3] I was encouraged in this view by the following remark of H. Winckler's (*Altorient. Forschungen*, Leipzig, 1894, p. 183): "The name Ammi-saduga is generally admitted to be merely another form of Ammi-tsaduk;

---

[1] *Geschichte Babyloniens und Assyriens*, p. 415, note 1.

[2] Cf. H. WINCKLER, *Altorientalische Forschungen*, Leipzig, 1894, pp. 144—146 and 198, also p. 45 of the present volume.

[3] Cf. my *Geschichte des alten Morgenlandes* (p. 59) which was written early in 1894 and published in the spring of 1895, in the *Sammlung Goeschen*. There also I characterized Abishu'a as "a Minæo-Canaanitish name" (Hebr. *Abîshû'a*, Min. *Abîyathu'a*; cf. also *supra* pp. 57 and 59, and also *infra* p. 94, note 1).

according to Sayce and Hommel;[1] Khammurabi, Ammi-sadugga, and Ammi-satana are West-country names, cf. *supra* p. 146 (Khammurabi, King of the countries of the West)." Indeed, in 1895, Winckler went still further, for in his *Geschichte Israels* (pp. 130 *et seq.*) he declared the names Sumu-abi and Sumu-ilu to be Canaanitish (giving as a reason their analogy with Shemu-el and with a hypothetical Sam-'al-el) and that hence the whole Dynasty must have been Western Semitic or rather Canaanitish conquerors; "as a matter of fact," he writes, " of the whole eleven names of the Dynasty, eight bear the true Canaanite stamp, two-Apil-Sin and Sin-muballit —are Babylonian, for the victors could not entirely escape the influence of Babylonian culture—and one (Zabu) is uncertain, but can hardly be Babylonian." But even should this theory prove to be really correct, Sayce's identification of Ammi-zaduga with Ammi-zadok (or Ammi-tzaduka), on which the whole superstructure depends, would still be of immense importance to the student of ancient oriental history, and more especially of the early history of the Hebrews. For Abraham's migration from Chaldæa would thus assume a totally different complexion if it were true that the Dynasty to which Amraphel,[2] (*i.e.* Khammurabi), belonged were of the same nationality and spoke the same language as Abraham

---

[1] Here Winckler evidently has in his mind a passage in my *Südarabischen Chrestomatie*, p. 12, "The names Ammi-zaduga and Ammi-satana, as Sayce has already pointed out, are pure Western Semitic formations."

[2] Gen. xiv. 1.

and his followers; in other words, if they were of Canaanite origin. This result would be inevitable if we were to accept Winckler's tacit assumption that Hebrew and Canaanite, in the time of Abraham, were practically convertible terms—an assumption, however, which, as recent investigations convince me, is untenable.

Towards the close of 1895 appeared two further contributions towards the solution of this question, one from the pen of Professor Sayce and one published by myself. In the latter, I succeeded, I believe, in proving conclusively by a comprehensive review of the whole body of available material, (including not merely the names of the kings, but more particularly the other personal names of the period) that Sayce was perfectly right in his first contention as to the *Arabian* (not Canaanitish) origin of Khammurabi's dynasty, but that it was the whole dynasty that was Arabian, and not, as he supposed, the half only. But before I deal with this, and recapitulate here the reasons which led me to this conclusion, it will be well to consider the preface to Sayce's *Patriarchal Palestine*, a small volume which appeared in November 1895, in which he again returns to the subject.

Sayce first points out that not only is the personal name Ab-ramu (more properly *Abi-ramu*) to be found in Babylonian contract-tablets of the Khammurabi epoch,[1] but that Mr. Pinches has also discovered the

[1] Cf. my *Assyriological Notes*, § 5 (*Proceedings* of the Bibl. Archæol. Soc., May 1894), where I drew attention to the first evidence of this that was forthcoming, viz.: the mention of a certain Sha-Martu, son of

names *Ya'qub-ilu* (Jacob-el) and *Yasup-ilu* (or rather *Yashup-ilu* or *Yashub-ilu*) in these tablets, and " other distinctively Hebrew names, like Abdiel." From this he proceeds to make the following deductions to which I attach so much importance that I quote the passage in full :

" There were therefore Hebrews—or at least a Hebrew-speaking population—living in Babylonia at the period to which the Old Testament assigns the life-time of Abraham. But this is not all. As I pointed out five years ago, the name of Khammurabi himself, like those of the rest of the dynasty of which he was a member, is not Babylonian but South Arabian. The words, with which they are compounded and the divine names which they contain, do not belong to the Assyrian and Babylonian language, and there is a cuneiform tablet in which they are given with their Assyrian translations. The dynasty must have had close relations with South Arabia. This, however, is not the most interesting part of the matter. The names (Khammurabi, Ammizaduga, etc.) are not South Arabian only, they are Hebrew as well.[1] . . . When Abraham therefore was born in Ur of the Chaldees, a dynasty was ruling there which was not of Babylonian origin, but

Abî-ramu in a contract-tablet of the time of King Apil Sin (grandfather of Khammurabi). I there went on to say that this was not surprising since both Khammurabi and the third king in succession after him, Ammi-satana, style themselves " Kings of the countries of the West." Also cf. *supra*, p. 72, note 1.

[1] Sayce here refers to Hebrew names such as Amminadab, and verbs like *tsadak* [*Zaduqa* or Zadoq] = to be just, which though foreign to Assyro-Babylonian, are common enough in Hebrew and Arabic.

belonged to a race which was at once Hebrew and South Arabian. The contract tablets prove that a population with similar characteristics was living under them in the country. Could there be a more remarkable confirmation of the statements which we find in the tenth chapter of Genesis? There we read that 'unto Eber were born two sons; the name of the one was Peleg,' the ancestor of the Hebrews, while the name of the other was Joktan, the ancestor of the tribes of South Arabia. The parallelism between the Biblical account and the latest discovery of archæology is thus complete, and makes it impossible to believe that the Biblical narrative could have been compiled in Palestine at the late date to which our modern 'critics' would assign it. All recollection of the facts embodied in it would then have long passed away."

This modification of Sayce's former view is clearly due to observations made by Winckler and myself, but Sayce rightly avoids the expression "Canaanite," and uses the term "Hebrew" in its place.

And now I come to the real object of this whole chapter, which is to prove the Arabian origin of the kings of the Khammurabi Dynasty collectively. The reader is now sufficiently familiar with the general characteristics of genuine Babylonian nomenclature, and has, on the other hand, obtained such an insight into the principles of South Arabian name-formation as to be able to form an opinion for himself, even without a knowledge of Arabic Hebrew, or the cuneiform texts; much more will the majority of theologians, or at any rate all those who understand Hebrew—and it is to this class that I specially address the present volume—be in a position to follow my arguments unaided.

In November 1895, and therefore simultaneously with the appearance of Sayce's *Patriarchal Palestine*, and also—a fact to which I attach importance—with the publication of H. Winckler's *Geschichte Israels*,[1] my review of Meissner's *Babylonian Common Law*— comprising a collection of over a hundred contract tablets of the Khammurabi Dynasty, most of which had never been previously published—appeared in a German periodical.[2] Shortly before this an article of mine, entitled "Discoveries and Researches in Arabia," was published in the Philadelphia *Sunday School Times* of October 12, 1895, and was afterwards reprinted in Professor Hilprechts' *Recent Research in Bible Lands* (pp. 131—158). This article (the MS. of which is dated April 30, 1895) also dealt with the Arabian origin of the Khammurabi Dynasty.

In the following pages I will give a brief general summary of these two articles, adding at the same time a number of additional facts which have since come to hand.

We must notice in the first place that the names of the first two kings of the Dynasty, *Shumu-abî* and *Sumu-la-ilu* contain an element which plays an important part in South Arabian names, viz. *sum-hu* =

---

[1] Winckler's book did not appear until after my MS. had been sent to the printer, in the summer of 1895.

[2] The *Zeitschr. der Deutschen Morgenl. Gesellsch.* vol. xlix., pp. 522— 528, (*on* MEISSNER'S *Beiträge zum altbabylonischen Privatrechte*).

his name (*i.e.* God's name; cf. *supra*, p. 85); these two appellations mean respectively "Sum-hu is my Father," and "Is not Sum-hu God?" The Babylonians also occasionally employed in personal names the word *shumu* (which originally meaning "a name," came afterwards to indicate "a son"), *e.g. Shum-irtsiti* = son of the earth; (cf. the alternative name *Mar-irtsiti* which means the same thing).[1] It is evident from the meaning attached to the latter that it was not used in the same way as the term *Sumu* in the two names mentioned above. It is much more probable that the first element in Sumu-la-ilu[2] is simply a divine appellation—just as Sumu-abi is a parallel of Samas-abi, Ilu-abi, etc. (= Samas is my Father, God is my father, etc.). This name cannot therefore mean "The Son is my father," but simply and solely "Sumu is my father." Now we nowhere find *sumu-hu* (abbreviated to *sumhu* and contracted to *Sumû*, cf. Hebr. Shemû-el, Samuel), still extant as a periphrasis for "God," except in South Arabian personal names, to which, therefore, we must look in the first instance for information. The Hebrew name *Shemu-el* (the pure Hebraic form of which would be Shemô-el), which occurs first in Num. xxxiv. 20 (the Simeonite "Shemuel, the son of 'Ammî-hud) and then in 1 Chron. vii. 2 (the name

---

[1] In the contract tablets the expression *Mârat-irtsiti* = Earth-daughter (or according to Meissner = a daughter of one's own blood) is used for "adopted daughter" (Meissner, Beitr., p. 154).

[2] Cf. the analogous name *Pa-la-Samas* = Is it not then Samas? (where the particle *pa* = "then," "thus," is Arabic) and *Ea-ma-la-ilu* = Is not Ea God?

AS ILLUSTRATED BY THE MONUMENTS 99

of a grandson of Issachar) and elsewhere only in Samuel the name of the great judge and prophet, and in Shemîda (a son of Gilead mentioned in Num. xxvi. 32) also contains the element Sum-hu, and this appellation also can only be explained by a reference to ancient Arabic; the name *Sum-hu-yada'a* appears, so Glaser informs me, in the Katabanian Inscriptions, as Sumîda'a, a contraction very similar to the Hebrew *Shemîda*, while a name of analogous formation such as Sumu-hu-yapi'a is generally given in full in the South Arabian inscriptions.

In regard to the two names of witnesses *Shumu-litsi* and *Shumu-libshi* (otherwise Shumu-ma-libshi and Shumi-libshi),[1] it cannot be denied that both *litsi* (= may he come out or proceed!) and *libshi* (= may he be!) are perfectly regular Babylonian forms, and that a possible translation of these two personal names would be "May a son come forth!" and "A son may it be!" Considering, however, that a similar name, Shuma-lib-shi, occurs in the bilingual list (mentioned on p. 89, *supra*), in which Khammurabi and Ammi-sadugga are explained, and is there paraphrased into Sumerian as *Mu-na-tilla* = His Name lives, I prefer to regard the names in question as being Babylonian in form but Arabian in meaning. We come upon names like *Ikun-ka-ilu* = God existed for thee (stood thee in good stead?) and *Ibshi-na-ilu* = God came into existence for us (shewed himself as existing for us),[2] which not only offer a

---
[1] We also find *Shumi-abia* and *Shumi-abu* in the Ancient Babylonian contract tablets as names of private individuals.
[2] MEISSNER, *Beiträge zum altbabylonischen Privatrechte*, No. 78

close analogy with the name *Shuma-libshi* (which I take to mean "His (viz. God's) Name comes into existence"), but also furnish a remarkable parallel to the Hebrew divine appellation Yahveh (= the Existing One). I ought, moreover to point out that when we find expressions like "may his name be, or exist," and "his name lives," as variants of the same Babylonian name, the chances are that they are translations of a Western Semitic original *Sum-hu-yahvi*; for the only distinction between *yahvi* = "he is" and *yahvi* = "he lives," is that the latter is pronounced with a somewhat stronger guttural aspirate, a sound which in the Hebrew script is represented by a *kh* (Hebr. *yikhych* = "he lives" as opposed to *yihych* = "he is") though it is really more of an *h* than a *kh*, as any one who is familiar with colloquial Arabic will readily admit. I may here mention that Yahveh[1] does not mean "He who strikes down" (*i.e.* the God of battle or of lightning)—as the higher critics fondly imagine—but is an Arabic rather than a Hebrew (Canaanitish) form of the ancient verb *hawaya* = Hebr. hayah = "to be, to come into existence," and belongs to the very earliest language of the Hebrews, as spoken in the time of Abraham and Moses, prior to the epoch of Canaanitish influence. In the later Hebrew idiom, which was employed from the time of the Judges

(Khammurabi Period). The variant *Ib-shi-na-ilu*, side by side with *Ib-shi-i-na-ilu* and especially the analogy of *Ikun-ka-ilu* prove that Meissner's reading, Ibshi-ina-ili = he was with or near God, is erroneous. Note the Arabic -na = us (genuine Babylonian -ni).

[1] Jehovah is a wrongly formed word and never really existed.

onwards, the name Yahveh came to be pronounced more like *Yihyeh*, and is actually written as *Ehyeh* = I will be, cf. Ex. iii. 14.[1] In so far as form is concerned *Yahveh* stands in precisely the same relation to *yihyeh*, as Yamlech (1 Chron. iv. 34) does to the ordinary Hebrew verb-form *yimloch*, (*vide supra*, p. 60). The names of the witnesses in the Ancient Babylonian contract tablets of the time of Abraham bear witness, therefore, to the correctness of the traditional Biblical explanation of the All-holy name of Yahveh.

There is another name, compounded with *sum-hu* which seems to afford a clue to the origin of the Babylonian personal name Samsu-riâmi (found in a contract tablet of the time of king Zabium). As the Babylonians generally omit the *h*, they would naturally write the Arabic *sumu-hu* = "his Name" either *sumu* or *shumu*, as in the name discussed above, or perhaps transliterate it *sumsu* (properly—*shumu-shu*), which in genuine Babylonian means "his Name." In this latter case, the probabilities are that they would have intentionally altered *sumsu* = his name = God, into *Samsu*, the name of the Babylonian sun-god, which closely resembles *Sumsu* in sound, and would at the same time be more in harmony with the Babylonian polytheistic system. In the South Arabian inscriptions we find the name Sumhu-riyâm, *riyâm* (allied to *râmu* = "high" in *Abî-râmu*) being a word peculiar to South Arabia; we are not likely to be far wrong, there-

[1] Cf. Hosea i. 9, *ehyeh lachem* = "I will be for you," an expression in many respects analogous to the Babylonian names mentioned above.

fore, in identifying the name Samsu-riâmi with Sumhu-riyâm. Nor ought we to lose sight of the fact that in the Minaean dialect, *sumu-su* = "his name" was used in place of *sumu-hu*, a fact which was obviously due to Babylonian influence, while only in personal names the old Western Semitic *sumu-hu* maintained its existence with few exceptions (*e.g. Sumu-su-amina* = "His Name is true").

If this explanation of Samsu-riâm be correct, then there is every reason for believing that a similar transformation may have occurred in the names Samsu-iluna and Samsu-satana, especially as here the final element in each case is Arabian.[1] The original form of these two names would, therefore, be *Sumu-hu-ilu-na* = "His Name is our God" and *Sumu-hu-Sata-na* = "His Name is our Mountain."

Taking the names of the kings in their order (*vide supra*, pp. 68 *et seq.*) we pass from Sumu-la-ilu to Zabum, or (as it is entered in a whole series of contract tablets) *Zabium*. This name means "a warrior," and, since nearly all of these names possess a religious significance, it is probably an abbreviation of Ilu-zabi = "God fights (for me)."[2] This name is also found in the South Arabian inscriptions, but does not appear in any of the Assyro-Babylonian records, although it is clear that there was also a Babylonian word tsâbu = "warrior"; moreover, the uncontracted form Zabium (instead of tsab'u or

---

[1] Cf. what is said in regard to *ilu-na* on p. 60, *supra*, and as to *satana* a few pages later on.

[2] The name *Damku* = "gracious" otherwise *Ilu damik* = "God is gracious" offers a close analogy.

tsâbu) points rather to an Arabian origin, just as *Nabium* = herald, is probably a Western Semitic loan-word imported into Babylonian. Indeed the Semitic root which lies at the base of Zabium must be familiar to every student of the Bible; it contains the same root as *tsaba'a* which is involved in the Biblical attribute of God, *Yahveh Tsebaoth* = "Lord of Hosts."

Apil-Sin and Sin-muballit, who come next in order in the list of kings, are the only members of the whole dynasty who bear genuine Babylonian names. This circumstance has quite recently induced an Assyriologist, who has so far shown himself to be a mere amateur in questions of historical and archaeological research, to throw ridicule on the theory of the Arabian origin of Khammurabi's Dynasty. Because, forsooth, Khammurabi's father "bore the stately Babylonian name of Sin-muballit, and his grandfather the no less irreproachably Babylonian name, Apil-Sin" and because other persons who possess names which I have claimed as Arabic have either sons or fathers with pure Babylonian names, it follows, so we are told, that the assumed Arabian origin of the Khammurabi dynasty, supported as it is by so much indisputable and irrefragable evidence, is none the less a baseless and untenable conjecture. We have, however, in the succeeding Kassite Period a case which presents the closest analogy with that of the Khammurabi Dynasty. There we find that the son of King Ramman-shuma-utsur bore the Kassite name, Mili-Shipak, while his son, who was every bit as good a Kassite as his forefathers, reverts to the pure Babylonian name Marduk-apli-idinna. And, moreover, among the names of witnesses occurring in contracts of the Kassite period, as my friend Professor Hilprecht of Philadelphia informs me, there are numberless instances in which a son is called by a Semitic name and the father by a Kassite name and *vice versa;* and as the Kassites—or, in the present instance, the Arabs—fell more and more under the influence of Babylonian culture, so much the oftener do we come across this practice of adopting Babylonian personal names. We need not therefore allow objections of this nature, which are founded on nothing but crass ignorance of the Minaeo-Sabaean language and antiquities, to detain us further, but will merely lay stress on the fact that both of the appellations referred to above, Apil-Sin and Sin-muballit, involve the name of a Babylonian deity who had, even in the earliest ages, been honoured as far as South Arabia, viz.: the name of the moon-god Sin (*vide supra*, p. 79).

As we have already discussed the elements *Khammu* and *ammi* (pp. 89 *et seq.*) not much more remains to be said about the next name on the list, that of Khammurabi. One point only is worthy of note. In a series of contracts and letters of very early date published by Mr. Pinches[1], we find the variants

---

[1] *Cuneiform texts from Babylonian Tablets in the British Museum*, Pt. II. (50 plates), London, 1896. I take this opportunity of mentioning that Pt. I. (also with 50 plates) merely contains lists of the time of the later kings of Ur written in the manner described above on pp. 67 *et seq.*; these new texts amply confirm all that I have said in regard to the personal names of that period on p. 67 (also on 70, Note 1).

Ammu-rabi and *Khammi-rabi*. This serves to remind us of the fact that in a contract of the time of King Zabiu (Zabum) the Western Semitic name ʿAbdel (Abdallah), which also begins with the guttural letter ʿ*Ayin*, appears in one place as *Abd-ili*, in another as *Khabdi-ili*. The original form of the king's name must therefore have been ʿAmmi-rabi. The variants Ammu-rabi, Khammurabi and Khammum-rabi are merely the result of attempts to give a Babylonian aspect to the name of a man who was, as far as his deeds were concerned, the most truly national of all the Babylonian kings. Indeed these attempts went a step farther. There is in existence a seal which bears the name *E-ki-rapal-tu*,[1] king of Gish-galla (*i.e.* Babylon); this is none other than our old friend Khammurabi, who is mentioned in the bilingual list as Kimtu-rapaltu and in the Bible (Gen. xiv. 1) as Amraphel (LXX: Amarpal). In the text moreover edited by Mr. Pinches, which is a triumphal ode celebrating the overthrow of Kudurlagamar by Khammurabi, the former is referred to as *Girra* (= Nergal-) *la-gamil* (according to Pinches a play on the name Kudur-lagamal) and the latter—a fact which has hitherto passed unnoticed—as En-nun-dagal-la = E-nun (or *Kummu*) *rapaltu*. Both *E-ki* and *E-nun* are mythological terms which indicate the southern region of the zodiac, in which the Babylonians placed the constellations of Ea (Fish-Goat, etc.) and the entrance to the under-world. Now, seeing that there is a Babylonian word *Khum-*

[1] Cf. my note in the *Proceedings* of the Soc. of Bibl. Arch., January 1893, p. 110.

mu (synonymous with lummû) for Aries (the sign of the God Ea), and that on the other hand we find *kummu* (syn. lummû), a word closely resembling *kimtu* in sound, used to indicate that Watery-region in the heavens in the same manner as *kimmatu* is used for the ideogram for Fish-Goat, we can readily understand how it was the Babylonians came to paraphrase the, to them, outlandish name Ammi-rabi (Khammirabi etc.) in this manner. Moreover, the element *-rabi* which is found in a number of seemingly genuine Babylonian names of the same period, such as Samas-rabi, Ramman-rabi, Ilu-rabi, must have sounded strange in Babylonian ears, for they replaced it by *rapashtu* or *rapaltu* (feminine of *rapshu* = broad); probably the name *Yarbi-ilu* (p. 60), which from its formation is manifestly Arabic, is closely related to this word *rabi*. Among the South Arabian inscriptions we find a parallel in the name Ili-rabbi (My God, increase, cf. *supra* p. 81), which might, it is true, be also read Ilu-rabbi = "God is my Lord."

Although I have headed this chapter, "*The Arabs in Babylonia before and in the time of Abraham,*" it is manifest that here, where we have to deal with the evidence in favour of the Arabian origin of the Khammurabi Dynasty as a whole, it is impossible to disregard the names of Khammurabi's successors, and we must consequently include the generations immediately subsequent to Abraham within the scope of our inquiry. In addition, I propose to discuss (pp. 110 *et seq.*) one or two other personal names that occur in the contract tablets of this dynasty, which, in the light of the knowledge gained in the preceding pages, the reader will readily recognize as Arabian.

In regard to the name of the next king on the list, Samsu-iluna, enough has already been said. Other names containing the suffix *-na* (= our) in place of *-ni*, are *Ipik-ili-na* and *Ilu-na* (in contract-tablets of the time of Ammi-zaduga). We have already dealt with all the more important facts in connection with the name of *Abîshu'a* (pp. 53, 84, and 93 *et seq.*) and of his grandson *Ammi-zaduga* (pp. 84 and 88 *et seq.*)[1] the latter being further noteworthy from the fact that it furnished Sayce with the clue to his theory in regard to the Arabian origin of the Khammurabi Dynasty—a theory which has been so strikingly confirmed by the results of further investigations. There now only remain the names of the kings *Ammi-satana* and *Samsu-satana* to deal with. As there is no verb *Satana* or *Sadana* to be found in the Western Semitic nomenclature, the most likely hypothesis as to its origin seems to involve the assumption that the last syllable *-na* is the same Arabic pronominal suffix which we had already found in Samsu-iluna. What sort of noun, we may ask, is the remaining word *Sata?* In the inscriptions of Khammurabi we come for the first time on a very

[1] When we find in the list of kings the form *Ibishu* in place of *A-bi-i-shu-'u-a* or *A-bi-i-shu-'a* (cf. the name of a private individual *A-bi ia-shu-kha* in Meissner No. 97), it is evidently with the aim of giving the name a Babylonian form. It is possible, however, that even in Abishûa's time the name was pronounced Ebishu (which may easily have changed into Ibishu); cf. Hebrew Ebiasaph (or Abîasaph) and Ebyatar, as well as the variants Emi-zaduga for Ammi-zaduga and the divine name Emu cited on p. 91.

peculiar-looking word for "mountain," viz. *satu*, which is treated as a Sumerian ideogram, and for this reason its genitive is written *SA-TU-im* instead of *sa-ti-im;* in a bilingual text, apparently of the same period, this word appears as *sati* and finally, under Nebuchadnezzar, when the tendency was to imitate the language of Khammurabi's time, the word appears in an indeclinable form, *sa-tu-um* (pronounced *satu*). From all this it follows that the word was really Semitic but not Babylonian in form: had it been Babylonian it would have been written *shadû*. Now in Arabic *saddu* or *suddu* means "barrier," "dam," "mountain," nearly related to which are the words *tsaddu* and *tsuddu* = mountain. It is, therefore, clear that the Babylonians endeavoured to reproduce the Arabic double *d* (or accentuation of the syllable) by means of their *t*.

But this Arabic word for "mountain" must have had a religious significance as well. This is manifest from its employment in the name Ammi-satana = "my uncle (*i.e.* as we have already learned, "God") is our mountain." And here Babylonian comes in to enlighten us. Just as the Babylonians called the goddess of the air or clouds "the Mistress of the Mountain," so, too, their distinctive name for Bel was "the great mountain" (*Shadû rabû*), a term probably due to Western Semitic influences. Among the Assyrian personal names of the eighth century B.C. we find Marduk-shadûa = "Marduk (*i.e.* Bel-Merodach) is my mountain," and Bel-shadûa, and in the next century Bel-Harran-shadûa = "the Lord of Harran (*i.e.* Sin) is my mountain," with which may be coupled the names Sin-shaduni = "Sin is our mountain" and Shadûnu or Shadûni = "our mountain (sc. is God)" obtained from other texts (cf. DELITZSCH, *Prolegomena*, pp. 205 and 208). For this reason the word *shadû* in Assyro-Babylonian has come now and then to mean "Lord" or "commander." It is, therefore, something more than a mere coincidence that in Ancient Hebrew, and that too as early as the time of Moses, if we may accept the testimony of tradition, a name '*Ammi-Shaddai* occurs, which not only contains the subsequently obsolete divine name Shaddai, but also exhibits almost exactly the same elements as Ammi-sata-na. Now it matters not whether we adopt the later or earlier system of vocalization of the Hebrew word Shaddai (LXX. Σάδδαι)—it is, for instance, quite within the range of possibility that the original reading was *El Shaddî* = "God my Mountain"— the fact remains that this divine name by which Yahveh revealed himself to Abraham and Jacob (Gen. xvii. 1 and xxxv. 11) must, as has been abundantly proved by the facts stated above, be of the very highest antiquity.[1] At the time at which Abraham migrated from Ur, both the Arabic *saddu* (spelt *satu* by the Babylonians) and the Babylonian rendering *shadû* possessed the same religious mean-

[1] Moreover, the fact that in Babylonian the word is written Ammi-*sata*-na (and not Ammi-*satu*-na), probably points to the existence of a previous form Ammî-saddai-na. Such a word as Saddai = "He who dwells on the mountain," when followed by a pronominal suffix, may quite possibly have been abbreviated to Saddâ (Babylonian transcription *sata*). In this case the O. T. vocalization Shaddai would possess an antiquity no less high than that of the root letters Sh-d-y.

ing in Babylonian, viz. mountain = God; the Hebrew root Sh-d-y in *El Shaddai* (as it was pronounced in post-exilic times) is identical with one or other of these.

In regard to the name of the last of the kings, *Samsu-satana*, this must (as indicated above on p. 102), have originally been Sumu-hu-sata-na = "his name is our mountain," and it was only later that it was transformed into the Babylonian Samsu-satana = "the sun-god is our mountain."

This completes the chain of evidence which goes to prove that every one of the eleven kings of the Khammurabi Dynasty was from first to last of Arabian origin, and, as might have been expected—and it is a fact which affords ample confirmation of the above theory—a large number of names of private individuals are mentioned in the contract tablets of this epoch, of which many bear the unmistakable impress of an Arabian origin. We have already cited (p. 60) several names beginning with the Arabic sign of the imperfect (ya . . .) *e.g.* Ya'qub-ilu (cf. also p. 95 and the South Arabian 'Akibu on p. 83), Yarbi-ilu (cf. p. 106) Yamlik-ilu, and on pp. 75 and 95 Yashup-ilu, with which latter name we may compare the South Arabian Yashûpu on p. 83.[1]

[1] Were it possible, however, to read Yashub-ilu, we should have a parallel to our hand in the Hebrew Yashûb (Num. xxvi. 24). The abbreviated form stands in the same relation to the complete one as the Hebrew Ya'kob [Jacob] to the name Ya'kub-ilu mentioned above. The reading Yashup-ilu is supported by the fact that in the fifteenth century B.C. in the lists of Thûtmosis III., two places named Ya'kob-el and Yashap-el are mentioned with a number of other towns and villages of northern Palestine, though it is, of course, quite possible that here, as

AS ILLUSTRATED BY THE MONUMENTS 111

To these may be added Yakbar-ilu = "God is great" (Meissner, No. 77; cf. *Kubburu*, Meissner, No. 74 and *Akbar*, Strassmaier, No. 57), *Ya'zar-ilu* (Peek, No. 13), *Yarkhamu* (Strassmaier) and Yakhziru (cf. Samas-khazir, Nabium-Khazir and Marduk-khazir, Meissner, No. 101), which last name undoubtedly finds a parallel in the Arabic 'Adhara-ilu on p. 82 (Hebr. Eli-'ezer, El-'azar, etc.). To the names terminating with the Arabic suffix *-na* = "us," which are also mentioned above on p. 60 (Samsu-iluna, Samsu-satana) are to be added names of private individuals, such as Ipik-ili-na, Ilu-na (p. 107). Other pure Arabic forms are the names *Makhnûbi-ilu* (Meissner, No. 36) and *Makhnûzu* (*Ibid.*, No. 92), Abatia (cf. Arab. ya-abati = "O, my Father"; *ibid.*, No. 97), Pa-la-Samas (properly *Pa-lâ-sumhu; supra*, p. 98), and Samas-riâmi (Sumuhu-riâmi; *supra*, p. 102), Zimri-rabi (*supra*, pp. 75 and 83, note 2; Scheil, *Recueil*, xvi., p. 189, where the erroneous reading Zimrî-ram is given), and Abdili (*supra*, p. 105). Among names containing but a single element *Natunum*, *Mudadi* (cf. the South Arabian race El-modad, Gen. x. 26, LXX) and Yadikhum (for *Yadi'um*, an abbreviated form of Ili-yada'a) have been instanced on p. 75 *supra;* other examples are *Mazanum, Gadanum, Azanum, Gamunu* (cf. Arab. Gumânatu), *Zakunum* and many names of similar form.

A very interesting name found in a document of

occasionally elsewhere, the Egyptians have replaced the foreign *b* by a *p* (*e.g. hurp*, loan-word from Canaanite *khereb* = sword). In any case the Hebrew name Joseph (Ps. lxxxi 6, Yehoseph, cf. Egyptian Osir-sip) has no connection here.

the time of Sinmuballit, and to which I wish to draw special attention before concluding this chapter, is Aï-kalabu, W. A. I.,[1] 750 (Peiser, K.-B.,[2] IV. p. 14). In so far as its first element is concerned this name is apparently pure Babylonian, the "Aï" being written in precisely the same manner as the name of the Babylonian goddess of the sky mentioned on pp. 65 and 66. But Mr. Pinches has drawn attention to the fact that we also find in various Assyrian names, a *male* deity, Aï or Ya [Ja] (the latter reading being a perfectly possible one); now, this deity is in no way identical with the Babylonian god Ea, whose name is written with different signs. There can be no doubt, therefore, that in the name Aï-kalabu or Ya-kalabu, the first element represents a male god, who is not of Assyro-Babylonian, but of Arabian origin. *Aï-rammu*, the name of an Edomite king in the time of Sennacherib (Taylor Cylinder, 2, 54)—an appellation, as Mr. Pinches rightly assumes, to be interpreted only as equivalent to *Joram*[3]—and more especially the Arabian name Aï-kamaru borne by a Masæan in the time of Assurbanipal (700 B.C.), help us to this conclusion. It need not surprise us to find a name like Aï-rammu or Ya-rammu among a people so nearly related to the Hebrews as the Edomites were. On the other hand, it is very singular that Aï-kalabu or Ya-kalabu should occur as

---

[1] West. Asiat. Ins.   [2] Keilinschr. Bibliothek.
[3] The reading "Malik-rammu" proposed by Schrader is incorrect. There is no more ground for transcribing the divine name Aï by Malik, than for the transcription Nin-ib or Nin-dar by Adar. Both of these readings must now be finally abandoned.

the name of an Arabian subject of the Babylonian king Sin-muballit, in the time of Abraham, *i.e.* at least one thousand years before the time of Sennacherib and Assurbanipal. For this name has the same meaning as Aï-kamaru, viz: "Ya is Priest." Evidently in these early times the words *kalabu* and *kamaru* had not yet acquired the disreputable sense afterwards associated with them. In the Old Testament the maidens consecrated to the service of the heathen temples are called "Kedeshah" (Babyl. *kadishtu;* A. V., harlot), the men who occupied analogous positions "Kadesh" (literally "sanctified"); in Deut. xxiii. 17, the Israelites of both sexes are forbidden to devote themselves to such offices, a passage paralleled in the next verse: "Thou shalt not bring the hire (*ethnan*) of a whore or the wages (properly purchase-price, *mekhîr*) of a *keleb* (or "dog," Babyl. and Arab. *kalbu*) into the house of the Lord Thy God for any vow." The other word, *komer*, is never used in the Old Testament except of idolatrous priests. But in a Phoenician inscription in Cyprus it seems to cover the builders, the sacrificers, the servants of the temple, the barbers (*i.e.* surgeons), the proselytes, the door-keepers, and lastly the priestesses and kelabîm. This last word, the singular of which was originally *kalibu* or *kalabu*, cannot, of course, be identical with *kalbu* (dog), for though the Israelites may later on have applied the term dog to the slaves of heathen temples, it is inconceivable that the Phoenicians should have thus designated their own *Hierodules. Kalibu* is rather allied to the verb *kariba* (cf. South Arabian *makrûbu*

= "Priest-king"; and *mikrâbu* = "Temple"). Moreover, the fact that *Keleb-clim* occurs as a Phoenician personal name is opposed to any original identity with *kalbu*, "dog." The most important point, however, is that the name of a Western Semitic god Aï or Ya is found in two Arabian names—*Aï-* (or *Ya-*) *kalabu* (in the time of Abraham) and *Aï-* (or *Ya-*) *kamaru*. Now seeing that the Hebrew word *Yahveh* appears in personal names only as *Yô*, *Yah*, or *Yahu*,[1] and that Moses expressly states that *Yahveh* was a new name (Exod. vi. 3), (the ancient Hebrew name for God being El Shaddai), we are evidently warranted in making the following deductions: firstly, that *Yahu* or *Yah* was the earlier form, and not a later abbreviation from *Yahveh*; and secondly, that there were then thrown into a concrete shape ideas that had been current from the time of Abraham onwards, and a new significance imparted to this ancient name, by compounding it with the Ancient Hebrew verb *hawaya* = "to exist" (imperfect, or rather present, *yahvi*), thus transforming it into Yahveh = "He exists, comes into existence, reveals Himself."

As to the original etymology of the primitive Western Semitic name for God, *Ya* or *Aï*, this is a point which is never likely to be cleared up.[2] One thing, however, is worthy of note, and that is, that

[1] *E.g.* in the names Joseph (*vide supra*, p. 110, note 1) and Jochebed (the mother of Moses).

[2] Its resemblance to Aï, the name of the Babylonian Queen of Heaven (from the Sumerian *anna*, softened into *anya*, *anyï*, *aï* = "Heaven") is perhaps merely accidental.

both in Hebrew and Phoenician personal names we find a variant, I, (written with a long *i*, indicated by the letters Aleph and Jod, and probably pronounced originally "Ai"). A parallel to the well-known Phoenician woman's name *I-zebel* (Isabella) has recently been discovered in *Shemzebel* (*Academy*, Jan. 25, 1896), which shows that the first element of I-zebel is a divine name[1]; from this it follows that the Hebrew I-chabod (1 Sam iv. 21) must be from the same source as Jochebed, and that in the names I-tamar (Ex. vi. 23, R. V. Ithamar) and I'ezer (Num. xxvi. 30), and probably also in I-shai or Yi-shai (cf. Abî-shai), we are also confronted by this ancient collateral form of Yah, the true meaning of which had ceased to be intelligible to later generations.

Passing mention should be made of two other deities, Khusha and Ilâli (written E-la-li), who are also possibly of Arabian origin. The latter, at any rate (in the personal names Elâli, Arad-Elâli and Elâli-bani), at once reminds us of the Arabic *hilâl* = "new moon"; the Hebrew *Helal*, "Son of the morning" (*Is.* xiv. 12), is also probably connected with it. It is possible that this word "Ilâli" is merely the result of an attempt on the part of the Arabs of the Khammurabi Dynasty to translate the name of a Babylonian god (Sin or Uru-ki). As to Khusha (Meissner, No. 43), it is quite possible that

---

[1] The Phoenician Astarte possessed a sobriquet (Shem Ba'al name of Baal), just as the Carthaginian Tanit bore the sobriquet Penê Ba'al (countenance of Baal). Probably, however, the Shem in Shem zebel stands for I or Aï (= Yahveh), just as, later on, the Jews were in the habit of using Shem (= name) for Yahveh.

this may be an incorrect rendering of the name of the Arabian goddess 'Uzzâ; for as in these contract tablets we find the Babylonian verb *bashu* = "to be," sometimes written "*bazû*," so on the other hand *Khusha* may be an erroneous transcription of '*Uzzâ*. In that case '*Uzzâ* (properly "the mighty") would be an Arabian translation of the Babylonian name Ningal (= great mistress), the wife of the moon-god; the passage runs as follows: "in the gate of Marduk, of Shussha (lit. "her name," meaning Ishtar or Zarpanit, wife of Marduk), of Uruki, of Khusha and of Nin-Mar (mistress of Mar), the daughter of Marduk (did they pronounce judgment)." These are the only Arabic names of deities that occur. We are therefore fully warranted in assuming that what has been said of South Arabian names applies with equal force to the Arabian personal names of the Khammurabi epoch: these names indicate that their owners possessed a far purer religion than that of the Babylonians, a religion, in short, of an essentially monotheistic character.

It was from out of such surroundings as these that Abraham, the friend of God, had gone forth. By his migration from Chaldaea Abraham's higher and purer creed was preserved from absorption into the Babylonian polytheism, a fate which must otherwise have inevitably befallen it. For from that time onward we find Babylonian manners and Babylonian idol-worship steadily penetrating into the Arabian religion as they had previously done into that of the Canaanites. This is proved by the presence of the names Athtar (Astar) and Sin, Anbay (Nebo) and

Almâku-hu[1] among the South Arabians, by the Babylonianisms found in the grammatical forms of the Minaean dialect (*e.g.* the suffix *-sû* instead of *-hû*, the causative form *sakbala* instead of *hakbala*), by Babylonian loan-words, such as *satara* = " to write " (instead of *kataba*), and by many other indications of a like nature. It can be readily imagined that this influence must have operated with still greater force on those Arabs who lived in Babylonia itself. Even the Arab kings of Babylonia, from Sumu-abi onwards became almost entirely Babylonian — at first, no doubt, from policy, but ere long from habit as well, and finally from innate conviction.

[1] Lamga is a Babylonian sobriquet of Sin ; from this the Sabæans, deceived by its apparent identity with their verb *lamaka* (= glitter ?) constructed a plural Almâku.

CHAPTER IV

CHRONOLOGY OF THE TIME OF ABRAHAM

THERE are three circumstances which make the Arabian personal names of the Khammurabi Dynasty of incalculable importance to the student of religious history. First, the fact that Biblical tradition connects the history of the patriarch Abraham with Khammurabi (Gen. xiv.); a point which will be fully dealt with later on in a chapter by itself. Second, the proof, from an examination of Hebrew personal names—especially those of the time of Moses and the Judges,[1]—that even the very earliest Hebrew nomenclature is absolutely similar to that of the Arabs of the Khammurabi Dynasty and to that of the South Arabian inscriptions—nay, more, that the Hebrews, before they took possession of the territory west of the Jordan under Joshua (*i.e.* the Hebrews of the patriarchal period), were still half

---

[1] Attention has already been drawn in the preceding chapters to many of these points of similarity. The period between Moses and David naturally yields the largest amount of material; but allowing for their relatively much smaller number the names of the patriarchal period lead to the same results, as is sufficiently proved by such names as Abram (*vide supra.* p. 94, note 1), Eli'ezer, Ishmael, Ya'kob (from Ya'kob-el, *vide supra*, p. 110), and Abida'.

Arabs, and that it was not until they had permanently settled down in the Promised Land that they adopted the Canaanitish tongue in place of their original language. Third, and last of all, the fact that we have arrived at results in the preceding chapters which place us in a position of advantage in regard to our adversaries, a position from which no future attack of sceptical criticism can hope to dislodge us. We have been able, for instance, to prove that the system of name-formation which we find in the South Arabian inscriptions was already in existence at the beginning of the second millennium before Christ, and that the numerous personal names ascribed to patriarchal and Mosaic times were in general use at this very period, and could not have been invented in or after the time of the kings—when a totally different system of nomenclature obtained—and thrown back into antiquity retrospectively.

It now only remains to discover the date to which in the balance of probability we ought to assign King Khammurabi, and to account also for the fact that while some Assyriologists are inclined to place him in the nineteenth or eighteenth century, B.C., others prefer to go back as far as the twenty-third or twenty-second century, B.C. For when the general reader finds that the following dates are assigned for the fifty-five years of Khammurabi's reign, it is only natural that, in the absence of any further explanation, grave doubts should arise as to the trustworthiness of the Ancient Babylonian chronology;

according to Oppert   from 2394 to 2339 B.C.
" Winckler (1894) " 2314 " 2258 "[1]
" Maspero (1896) " 2304 " 2249 "
" Winckler (1889) " 2292 " 2237 "
" Delitzsch (1891) " 2287 " 2232 "
" Hilprecht (1893) " 2277 " 2222 "
" Peiser (1891) " 2139 " 2084 "
" Carl Niebuhr
 (1896) " 2081 " 2026 "
" Hommel (1895) " 1947 " 1892 "
and " " (1886) " 1923 " 1868 "[2]

Once, however, that the general reader has learned the true state of affairs, he will fully comprehend why up to the present it has been impossible to arrive at any sort of unanimity in regard to the date of the Khammurabi Dynasty. In the following pages I will endeavour to show as briefly as possible how the matter really stands.

Since the year 1880 scholars have been in possession of a small tablet which bears on its obverse a list of the eleven kings of the Khammurabi dynasty, together with the number of regnal years of each (*vide supra*, pp. 68). The subscription reads: "305 years (being the total of the eleven separate

---

[1] The figures given on p. 35 of Winckler's *Untersuchungen* are based on a miscalculation on his part; he makes the 1st Dynasty begin in 2403 and end in 2098, which gives 2292—2237 as the date of Khammurabi (these figures being practically the same as those placed in brackets after the date 1923—1868 on p. 169 of my *History of Babylonia*).

[2] My earlier conjecture 2168—2113 *Semitische Völker und Sprachen*, vol. i. p. 422, 1883, was based (prior to the discovery of the list of Babylonian kings) on Berosus and the dates assigned to his first two dynasties by the data of the tablet containing lists of dynasties A and B.

items 15 + 35 + 14 + 18 + 30 + 55 + 35 + 25 + 25 + 22 + 31 years), eleven kings of the dynasty of Babylon." On the reverse of the same tablet is a list of eleven other kings, but unaccompanied by any statement as to the length of their reigns, the superscription merely containing the name of a town or country thus: "Uru-ku-ki."[1] The names are as follows: Ilû-ma-ilu, Itti-nibi, Damki-ili-shu, Sapin-mât-nukurti (written Ish-ki-bal), Shusshi, Mu'abbit-kissati (written Gul-ki-shar), Mamlu-Ea,[2] Apil-Ea-shar-mati (written A-ea-kalamma), Apil-Bel-usum-shamê (written A-kur-ul-anna), Milam-mâtati (written Me-lam-kur-kurra), and Ea-gamil, after which comes the subscription: "Ten (a clerical error for "eleven") kings of the dynasty of Uru-ku-ki." This superscription, which obviously means that: "[on the other hand the kings of] Uruku [are as follows]" clearly points—as the French Assyriologist Halévy rightly surmised some years ago—to the assumption that the two dynasties were contemporaneous.

When, however, the great list of Babylonian kings was discovered and published by Mr. Pinches in

[1] Written with the symbol *Uru* (or *Sis*) and *ku* (or *azag*), and a local suffix (symbol *ki*), so that it is quite possible to read Uru-azag, Sis-ku or Sis-azag in place of Uru-ku. The name of the well-known town Uruk (Erech) is written quite differently but is none the less probably the place here referred to.

[2] Followed by the note, "son of the foregoing"; a similar note is attached to the name of his successor. It would, therefore, appear that of these eleven kings, Mu'abbit-kissati, Mamlu-Ea and Apil-Ea form a genealogical sequence (Father, Son, and Grandson). For further details as to the names of the second dynasty, cf. my review of Hilprecht's *Assyriaca* in the *Berl. Phil. Wochenschrift*, xv. 1895, cols. 1586—1590.

1884, it seemed as though this theory of the co-existence of the two first dynasties would have to be abandoned — for the list in question placed the Khammurabi dynasty first and the Uru-ku dynasty second. The close of the third or Kassite dynasty, however, being once fixed—a matter of no great difficulty (according to the subscription: 576 years, nine months, thirty-six kings), it would now seem to be possible to arrange the two first dynasties in correct chronological order. For, (and this seemed at first to be a most important point,) the list gives figures for the kings of the second dynasty also (viz.: 60+55+36+15+27+55+50+28+26+7+9, the subscription making out the total to be: " 368 years, eleven kings of the dynasty of Uru-ku"). From this it would seem as though one had only to determine approximately the end of dynasty C and then calculate backwards, in order to ascertain the desired date for every king of the Khammurabi dynasty. In regard to the close of dynasty C, which, provided there were no gaps in the list, appears at first sight to be easily ascertainable within a year or so, the authorities are fairly unanimous:

Hommel (1886)	1154 B.C.
Winckler (1889)	1155 "
Delitzsch (1891)	1150 "
Hilprecht (1893)	1140 "
Winckler (1894)	1177 "
Hommel[1] (1895)	1178 "
Carl Niebuhr (1896)	1169 "

[1] In my short *History of the Ancient East* (Stuttgart, Goeschen) the MS. of which had been sent to the publishers before the second volume

By this it will be seen that Hilprecht's date for Khammurabi is 2277—2222 B.C., whereas the dates suggested by Winckler and myself in 1894—95, are 2315—2259 (or 2314—2258), the difference between these two last dates being in the case of so remote a period practically immaterial. Moreover, the statement in later Babylonian records (of the sixth century B.C.) to the effect that the interval between Khammurabi and Burnaburiash (either Burnaburiash I., ca. 1450, or Burnaburiash II., ca. 1400 B.C.) was, in round numbers, 700 years (800 would be more nearly what we should expect) seems to be far more in favour of the successive rather than of the simultaneous existence of the two first dynasties. In any case the Babylonian chronographers of the time of King Nabonidus (sixth century B.C.) add the two dynasties together, although this does not, of course, preclude us from eliminating the period covered by the second dynasty from our calculations. Their principal source of information must have been the list of the Babylonian kings, and in all probability a version of this list, which either fixed the duration of the second dynasty at 248 years (in place of 368) or made out the third dynasty to be 120 years (*i.e.* 2 × 60) shorter than in the existing text.

of Winckler's *Altorientalische Forschungen* appeared : we had both therefore arrived quite independently at our conclusions (1177 and 1178), and mainly in consequence of our mutual objections to Hilprecht's absurdly late date 1140. So far as our knowledge extends at present the dates suggested by Winckler and myself are the most probable.

How comes it then, one might ask, that in spite of this, the estimate for Khammurabi given by me (on p. 120) is not 2315—2259, but only 1947—1892 (or in round numbers 1900 B.C.)? And, again, why does Peiser adopt the period 2139—2084 half-way between these two extremes?

The lower of my two estimates is simply due to the fact that I still persist in placing the third (or Kassite) dynasty immediately after that of Khammurabi. This had been my view even when I was engaged on my *History of Babylonia and Assyria*, only that at that time I believed the first two dynasties should have been made to change places, whereas I have now come round to Halévy's view and regard them as contemporary with one another. Taking the year 1178 B.C. as the likeliest date for the close of Dynasty C, I thus obtain 1753—1178 as the period covered by it; and consequently for the Khammurabi dynasty the 304 years which immediately preceded it, *i.e.* 2058—1754 B.C., the reign of Khammurabi himself (the Amraphel of Gen. xiv. 1) occupying 1947—1892 B.C.

This theory (of the co-existence of Dynasties A and B) which receives strong confirmation from the small tablet previously mentioned (and especially from the absence of figures in the case of the second dynasty), is further supported by two considerations or facts which no one has, so far, been able to invalidate. First, we have the circumstance—and it is one which now, in the light of recent research, possesses even greater weight than formerly—that Biblical tradition also refers the time of Abraham to the twentieth century B.C.; and second, the fact that, from a purely Assyriological standpoint, there is good reason for doubting whether the so-called "second dynasty" ever really existed in that capacity. It is becoming clear to the historian that the "Dynasty of Uru-ku" is entirely apocryphal and the less that one has to do with its chronology the better.

In regard to the chronology of the Bible, it cannot be denied that from the time of David and the Judges backward it is deficient in that high degree of definiteness which the scientific historical investigator is inclined to demand. There are, however, certain important events the dates of which can be determined with approximate accuracy. Such, for instance, is the Exodus of the Israelites from the land of Egypt, which must have taken place either in the closing years of Ramses the Great (1348—1281) or, which is more likely, in the fifth year of his successor Minephtah[1] (1277 B.C.). If we add to this last figure the traditional sojourn of 430 years in the land of Goshen we get a total of 1707. The patriarch Jacob is said to have migrated into Egypt with his people at the age of 130; this gives the year of his birth as 1707 + 130 = 1837 B.C. At that time his grandfather Abraham was, according to the tradition, 160 years old, therefore, 1837 + 160 = 1997 = birth of Abraham. This patriarch migrated from Haran to Canaan in his seventy-fifth year, i.e. about

---

[1] In any case the Israelites were not settled in Palestine at the date of the Tel-el-Amarna tablets (ca. 1400 B.C.). The Biblical tradition also clearly indicates Ramses II. as the Pharaoh of the Oppression.

1922, and the battle in the valley of Siddim described in Gen. xiv. must have taken place very soon after, that is at a time when Khammurabi had been at least fourteen years on the throne. This, as nearly as possible, coincides with the period postulated above for the reign of Khammurabi, viz. 1947—1892 B.C.

But now let us return to Dynasty B (*i.e.* the eleven kings of Uru-ku mentioned on p. 121) which seems to stand in open contradiction with this later date. In the first place, the figures added to the list of kings are open to grave suspicion. Compared with those given in the case of Dynasty A, these figures, and indeed the whole constitution of this Uru-ku dynasty, give the impression of an artificial scheme. As in the case of Dynasty A (the existence of which is amply attested by the evidence of contracts and royal inscriptions), we here find exactly eleven kings. Again as in Dynasty A, in which the sixth king, Khammurabi, reigned fifty-five years, so here too, the sixth king Gul-ki-shar or Mu'abbit-kissati (= destroyer of the world) also reigned exactly fifty-five years. Such a long reign in a dynasty of eleven kings is for once in a way conceivable enough; it is singular, however, that this high figure recurs at precisely the same place in Dynasty B as it occupies in its twin-brother, Dynasty A, and —more remarkable still—in Dynasty B the figures 60 and 55 also appear in the first and second place, and 50 in the seventh place, just as in Dynasty A.[1]

[1] It is true that the sacred number 60 at the beginning of the list is written as the figure 1; that this, however, was read as 60 (viz. 1 Sos)

Add to this that the sixth, seventh, and eighth kings (with reigns of 55 + 50 + 28 = 133 years) form a genealogical series of three (*vide supra*, p. 121, Note 2). Reigns of 55 + 35 + 25 years (Dynasty A, Nos. 6—8) are intelligible enough in the case of a father, son and grandson, but successive reigns of fifty-five, fifty, and twenty-eight years can only be explained on the assumption that the first king of the three ascended the throne at a very tender age, a thing which is extremely improbable in the case of Gul-ki-shar, since he is not described as the son of his predecessor. Moreover, the fact that the period from the central date (the death of Gul-ki-shar) to the end of the dynasty is exactly 120 years, or two Sos, (viz. 50 + 28 + 26 + 7 + 9) is highly suspicious. All this goes to prove that the figures, at any rate, are apocryphal, since the numbers appear in the List of Kings only and are not to be found on the Tablet in connection with Dynasty B (see p. 120 *et seq.*), a fact which I again desire to emphasize.

A similar remark may be applied to the individuals of the dynasty. There are only two of the whole eleven kings of Uru-ku in regard to whom we possess any information, although if they succeeded to those of the Khammurabi dynasty, they must presumably like them, and like the dynasties who followed them (*e.g.* Dynasty C, etc.), have ruled in Babylon. These two kings are the first, Ilû-ma-ilu (abbreviated to Ilû-ma in the List of

at any rate by the copyist of the list of kings is evident from the total of 368 years. Otherwise the total would be only 309.

Kings), and the sixth, Gulkishar (Mu'abbit-kissati). But what title do they bear in those inscriptions that mention them? That of Kings of Babylon? By no means! One of them (in a short contemporary inscription) is described as "King of the hosts of Erech," and the other (in an inscription of the time of Dynasty D) as "King of the country of the sea," *i.e.* of the southernmost part of Babylon on the Persian Gulf. The first of these inscriptions (which is of interest in other respects as well) runs as follows:[1]

>Ilû-ma (written in the Sumerian form DINGIR-A-AN)
>Sheikh (written ab-ba, *i.e.* shîbu) of the hosts of Uruk (Erech)
>Son of Bel-shimîa,
>has the walls of Erech
>the ancient building
>of Gibil-gamis (*i.e.* of Gishdubar or Nimrod)
>again repaired.

With this inscription, as Hilprecht afterward pointed out, must be classed another of the time of the kings of Erech (and therefore probably contemporary with the predecessors of King Eriaku of Larsa who conquered Erech), published by Peiser and Winckler (*Keilinschr. Bibl.* III. p. 84:) "To Nirgal, the king of the lower world, his king, has Ilûma-Gishdubba, son of Bel-Shimêa, built his temple for the preservation of the life of Sin-gamil, king of Erech." From this we learn the full name of this

---

[1] HILPRECHT, *Old Babylonian Inscriptions*, No. 26, first translated by me in the *Proceedings* of the Bibl. Arch. Soc., Nov. 1893.

king Ilû-ma-ilu (= God is God), viz. Ilû-ma-Gish-dubba (*i.e.* "God is Gishdubba," the deified Gishdubar, whose ancient wall Ilû-ma had restored and whose name he had taken). Ilû-ma was, therefore, the vassal of one of the contemporaneous and still independent kings of Erech, and, as it would seem, the chief of some tribe of Semitic nomads; Gishdubar, his patron deity, was also, as we have seen above (p. 39), intimately associated with Arabia. This is in no way incompatible with my assumption that he was a contemporary of the Arab monarch Shumu-abi, the founder of the Khammurabi Dynasty, and very possibly one of his allies. For, that there were several Arab princes ruling in Babylon at that time is proved by the date-formula of a contract discovered by Mr. Pinches, in which the "kings" Shumu-abi and Pungunu-ilu[1] are mentioned.

Gulkishar is described as king of "the country of the sea"[2] on a boundary stone published and translated by Hilprecht and dated in the fourth year of king Bel-nadin-apli (ca. 1122—1118 B.C.) the immediate successor of king Nebuchadnezzar I. (ca. 1145—1122). From this monument we learn that from the time of Gulkishar, king of the countries of the sea (*i.e.* from his death), to Nebuchadnezzar a period of one Ner (= 600 years) one Sos (= sixty years) and thirty-six years, or 696 in all had elapsed; that is to

---

[1] As to this latter, cf. the personal names Piknanum, Paknu and Pikinnu, which are also probably Arabic.

[2] Probably a part of Arabia, viz. the region bordering on the Babylonian frontier; cf. the expression "Ass of the Sea," used of the camel.

say, that we have only to add to this the four years of Bel-nadin-apli's reign in order to obtain a total of 700 years. It is needless to remark, that these are merely round numbers similar to the period of 700 years fixed by the chronographers of Nabonidus as the interval between Khammurabi and Burnaburiash (*vide supra*, p. 123 and note).[1] Let us now go back to the year 1820 B.C., a date which, according to my calculations given above would fall somewhere in the reign of the Babylonian king Ammi-satana. At the first glance it will be evident that Gulkishar ("Destroyer of the World") is not the sort of name which a Babylonian prince would be likely to receive from his father at his birth, but rather a sobriquet like Ish-ki-bal (Sapin-mat-nakurti = Overthrower of hostile countries) bestowed by posterity on a mighty conqueror, and there is nothing more probable than that, after the fall of the Arabian dynasty of Khammurabi, one of its kings should have been handed down in the Babylonian tradition, under the awe-inspiring name of "destroyer of the world." That the records of the genuine Babylonian dynasty D to which Nebuchadnezzar I. and Bel-nadin-apli belonged, should describe him as king of the country of the sea (N.E. Arabia), and not as king of Babylonia is perfectly intelligible.

[1] In the List of Kings the duration of Dynasty C is given as 9 Sos ($9 \times 60 = 540$ years) and 36 years; probably the figures of the boundary stone would agree with these but for the fact that a period of sixty years has been added at the beginning and at the end, in order to arrive at the full total of $696 + 4 = 700$ years in round numbers. Extreme accuracy was evidently not the object in view.

Moreover the name of the region referred to in Bel-nadin-apli's boundary mark, viz. Bit-Sin-magir, is a reminiscence of the Khammurabi dynasty. Indeed the personal name Sin-magir frequently occurs in the contract tablets, especially in those of the time of kings Sin-muballit, Eri-aku, Khammu-rabi and Samsu-iluna. Revillout in his well-known work *Les obligations en droit Egyptien comparé aux autres droits de l'antiquité* makes special mention of a certain Sin-magir as the head of a widely-distributed family; in a contract tablet of the time of Khammu-rabi express reference is made to the house (*bîtu*) and garden of this Sin-magir.

All this goes to show that until the matter is definitely decided by some future discovery, our safest course will be to regard the Uru-ku dynasty as apocryphal. The ultimate decision may be in favour of my theory, or on the other hand it may confirm the later Babylonian view, according to which the 304 years of the Khammu-rabi dynasty, and the (as we have seen, extremely uncertain period of) 368 years of dynasty B ought to be added together in our chronological calculations. I look forward to future discoveries of this kind with an untroubled mind, for I am firmly convinced beforehand, that they will merely tend to confirm the evidence of the ancient records and monuments so far known to us. Among ancient monuments, however, I can only include those parts of the List of Kings which can be checked by contemporary records and thus proved to have come down to us intact. This verification has actually been made in the case of all the other dynasties, that of Uru-ku being the sole exception.

The whole question is one of decisive importance for the Biblical chronology of the earliest period, and, therefore, has been specially dealt with in the present chapter (p. 118 *et seq*). For if we admit that Khammurabi reigned, not from 1947 to 1892, but from 2314 to 2258, then the period between Abraham and Moses would be not 650 but 1,000 years, and between Abraham and Joseph not 200 but 550 years: we should in that case be obliged to assume one of three things. Either that a later generation, looking back on the vistas of the past, was deceived by some optical illusion similar to that which makes two hilltops that are really separated by spacious valleys seem to stand quite close to one another; or else that there may possibly have been two patriarchs named Jacob who lived at periods centuries apart from one another, one of them the grandson of Abraham, the other the father of Joseph, and that a later tradition merged these two individuals into one; or lastly, that Abraham did indeed flourish about the year 1900 B.C., but that his association with Khammu-rabi, Kudur-laghamar and Eri-aku is apocryphal. I need hardly say that the acceptance of any one of these hypotheses would be merely bringing grist to the mill of the modern critics of the Pentateuch.

A very acute and ingenious attempt to solve this difficulty was made by Felix Peiser in the year 1891 (*Zeitschrift für Assyriologie*, VI. pp. 264—271 ; *Zur Babylonischen Chronologie*), and as I have already promised my readers an explanation of the differences between Peiser's results and my own in regard to the date of Khammu-rabi 2139—2084 (*vide supra*, p. 120), I cannot do better than give a brief summary of the solution proposed by him. He starts from the hypothesis that the much-debated dynasty lists of the Babylonian priest Berosus, ends, not as has hitherto been assumed, with Nabonassar (in 747 B.C.), but rather with the accession of Alexander the Great (in 331 B.C.) Now the total duration of the historical dynasties of Berosus as carefully estimated by A. von Gutschmidt is 36000—34080 = 1920 years. If we add 331 to this total we get 2251 B.C. as the beginning of the Khammu-rabi dynasty. Peiser thus obtained for Dynasty A (lasting 304 years) the period 2251—1947 (*i.e.* 2139—2084 as the reign of Khammu-rabi), for Dynasty B (368 years) 1947—1579, and for the (Kassite) Dynasty C (the final close of which Peiser agrees with Winckler and myself in fixing at 1180 B.C.) 1579—1180, that is a duration of 399 years instead of the 576 years given in the List of Kings. He explains this result by assuming that some later copyist instead of reproducing the 6 Sos and 39 years (*i.e.* 360 + 39 = 399) of his original, wrote 9 Sos and 36 years (*i.e.* 540 + 36 = 576) in error. Peiser was the more firmly convinced of this, because it agrees with the estimate which fixes the interval between Khammurabi († according to Peiser 2084 B.C.) and Burnaburiash (ca. 1400 B.C.) at 700 years: for 2084—1400 = 684 years, which is as near the round number of 700 as we can ever hope to get in matters of this kind. Now

Peiser might very well have asked himself whether the mistake in the List of Babylonian Kings, instead of occurring in the total of Dynasty C, ought not rather to be looked for in Dynasty B, the individual figures of which lie open to such grave suspicion. It is true enough that the total of 576 years, as Peiser rightly points out, is somewhat questionable. Dynasty C includes 36 kings; and if it had lasted for 576 years this would give each king an average reign of 16 years, ($16 \times 36 = 576$). Now the names of the last 15 kings of this dynasty and the periods for which they reigned are known to us: the total comes out at 186 years, and the average reign at $12\frac{1}{2}$ years. Assuming, therefore, that 576 is the correct total, the first 21 kings must have reigned for a period of 390 years, or an average of $18\frac{1}{2}$ years each, a result which Peiser regards as improbable. Or, since we can fix the date of the reign of Burnaburiash II. (the 18th king of the dynasty), approximately at ca. 1410—1380 B.C. the total reign of Nos. 18—36 (19 kings in all) would then be 222 years, or an average of barely 12 years each: the first 17 on the other hand would, according to the list, have reigned 343 years, or an average of over 20 years each.

But even allowing, for the sake of argument, the improbability of the average of the second half having been only 12 years as against 20 years for the first half, Peiser's reduction of the total from 576 to 399 years (*i.e.* from 9 to 6 Sos omitting odd years) goes too far. Even assuming that the average length of reign was the same in both halves (viz. 12 years) this would give us a total of about 420 years [432]: or if we assume that the average reigns in the first half was 14 years and in the second only 12 years, this would give a total of about 460 [456] years (*i.e.* 7 Sos, 36 years, instead of the 9 Sos, 36 years recorded in the list). Peiser has, moreover, entirely overlooked the fact that an average of 12, far from being a normal one, is exceptionally low and that therefore the balance of probability would be in favour of a higher average for the first half, and, consequently, for the dynasty as a whole. I will try to make this clearer by one or two parallel instances. Eighteen kings ruled over Assyria during a period of 322 years (*i.e.* from ca. 930 to 608 B.C.); in other words for an average of nearly 18 years each; the first nine of these reigned for a total period of 176 years (an average of over 19 years each); the remaining 9 reigned for a total period of 146 years (an average of $16\frac{1}{4}$ years). The first Babylonian dynasty (in which from the time of the second king onwards the throne descended from father to son) included 11 kings with a total duration of 304 years; an average of over 27 years each. The Neo-Babylonian Empire consisted of 6 kings who ruled for 88 years, an average of nearly 15 years, while for the 16 kings who preceded them, the average was barely 7 years each: this however is sufficiently explained by the dependent state of Assyria during this time, and the frequent change of rulers necessitated by this: such an epoch cannot be fairly used as a basis of comparison. The first half of the Kassite dynasty was, in the main, a time of peaceful development, while in the second half the rise of Assyrian power and its intervention in Babylonian affairs, together with the growing national Babylonian reaction against the Kassites, rendered the political situation much less stable. We know that the first three monarchs of this dynasty reigned for 60 years altogether (16 + 22 + 22), while the reign of the seventh Agukakrimi was very probably a rather long one (30—40 years); and, besides, the Babylonian kings who exercised a supremacy co-equal with that of the Pharaohs of the XVIIIth dynasty (notably Kurigalzu I. and Burnaburiash II.) also belong to the first half of the Kassite dynasty. All the evidence, therefore, goes to prove that the average reign of the kings in the first half of the Kassite Dynasty was much longer than in the second half.

And yet Peiser's attempt deserves most careful attention; only we must seek to effect the principal reduction somewhere else and not in the Kassite dynasty. For example, we should arrive at precisely the same result if we assumed the duration of the Kassite dynasty to have been 516 years in the document from which Berosus obtained his information (*i.e.* only 60 years less than in the List of Kings), but that the second dynasty which he and the later Babylonian chronographers add on to it, lasted for 2 Sos (or 120 years) less than the 368 years given in the list, *i.e.* 248 years. We thus obtain the following result:

End of the Dynasties of Berosus   331 B.C.
Beginning: 331 + 1920   =2251 "
Khammu-rabi Dynasty   2251—1947 "
Khammu-rabi   2139—2084 "
Uru-ku Dynasty   1946—1699 "
Kassite Dynasty   1698—1183 "

The close of Dynasty C would in this case fall in the year 1183 instead of 1180 as assumed by Peiser, or instead of 1178 as I estimate it, an absolutely trivial disparity.

That Berosus was probably in error when he estimated the duration of the Kassite Dynasty at 8 Sos and 36 years (instead of 9 Sos and 36 years), and thus reduced the period for the Babylonian dynasties, up to the time of Alexander, from 1980 to 1920 years, is evident if we add this one Sos to all the dates mentioned above, thus:

Dynasty A   2311—2007 B.C.
Khammu-rabi   2199—2144 "
Dynasty B   2006—1759 "
Dynasty C   1758—1183 "

This estimate harmonizes much more closely with the period of 700 years between Burnaburiash (ca. 1440 B.C.) and Khammu-rabi (*i.e.* the death of this latter in ca. 2140 B.C.) than does Peiser's (Khammu-rabi 2139—2084). For, since in the estimate in question there is nothing to show which Burnaburiash is intended, it is best to assume that it was Burnaburiash I. (ca. 1440 B.C.) rather than Burnaburiash II. (ca. 1410—1380). As I have already pointed out, however, the whole estimate depends on the mistaken addition of Dynasty A to Dynasty

B. The key to the whole problem lies in the fact that this addition is inadmissible. In so far as the proposed emendation of Berosus is concerned, it matters not whether we decide in favour of 2251 as proposed by Peiser, or 2311 as suggested by me, for our point of departure; it will be necessary, in either case—if we wish to get at the original record, and consequently, the real date of the first dynasty —to subtract the number 248 (which I have shown above to be the most probable estimate of the total duration of Dynasty B). We shall thus finally obtain the following dates:

    Dynasty A   either 2003—1699 or 2063—1759
    Khammu-rabi   " 1891—1836 " 1951—1896
    Dynasty C   " 1698—1183 " 1758—1183

The second alternative approaches very nearly the estimate given by me quite independently of Peiser on p. 120, viz: Dynasty A, 2058—1754 (Khammu-rabi 1947—1892) and Dynasty C, 1753—1178. The first alternative is based on the assumption that the 576 years assigned to Dynasty C in the List of Kings, ought to be reduced by at least 1 Sos ($=60$ years), and harmonizes pretty closely with the Bible figures in so far as Khammu-rabi and the date of Abraham are concerned. Even were Peiser right in reducing the duration of Dynasty C by 180 years and accepting the 368 years of Dynasty B unaltered (though I repeat that this latter total must at all costs be excluded from our calculations!) which in the face of what I have said above is extremely improbable, we should have the following *minimum dates:*

Dynasty A   1893—1579 B.C.
Khammu-rabi 1771—1716 "
Dynasty C   1578—1180 "

These minimum dates, however, could only be made to harmonize with the Biblical chronology if we were to assume that Abraham, Isaac and Jacob (the last-named, it will be remembered, migrated with his people into Egypt at a very advanced age) never attained the extreme longevity ascribed to them in the Bible, and that the episode narrated in Genesis xiv. did not take place until thirty years after the birth of Isaac.

We have, therefore, every reason to believe that the year 1900 B.C. was, in round numbers, the approximately correct date of Abraham's migration from Haran and of his participation in the campaign conducted against the king of Sodom by Chedorla'omer, Arioch and Amraphel, a subject which I propose to examine more closely in my next chapter.

In addition to the identity of its founder Ilûma with a vassal of the kings of Erech (*vide supra*, pp. 128 *et seq.*) we possess further direct evidence of the simultaneous existence of the problematic Uru-ku Dynasty and that of Khammu-rabi. It comes to us from a quarter in which no one had hitherto dreamt of looking for it.

It is a well-known fact that the beginnings of the Assyrian empire can be traced back to somewhere about the year 1850 B.C. We are told by Tiglath-pileser I. (ca. 1120) that some sixty years before his time, his great-grandfather Assur-dan, a contemporary of the last king but one of the Kassite Dynasty wished to restore a temple, which had been built 641 years earlier by the priest-king (patesi) of Assyria, Samsî-Rammân, son of the priest-king Ishmi-Dagan of Assyria; Assur-dan pulled the old temple down, but was prevented by some cause or other, most probably by his death, from rebuilding it, and thus it remained until Tiglathpileser took the task in hand. This brings us to the year 1820, or so, for the date of the Samsî-Rammân (⌐ my Sun is Rammân,) in question. He had, however, been preceded on the throne by another *patesi*, also named Samsî-Rammân, son of Bel-kap-kapu (written Igur-kap-kapu), who is mentioned in the original monuments, and probably in several others as well. It has always been rightly assumed that, as the Assyrian civilization was merely a copy of the Babylonian,[1] this priest-king of the 19th century B.C. must have been intimately connected with Babylon either as a vassal or as a voluntary ally.

Now, if the Khammu-rabi dynasty was in power from 2050 to 1750 B.C. it must have been with this dynasty that the earliest Assyrian princes were connected either as dependents or as allies. That it really was this dynasty and no other can be proved beyond dispute by evidence of a two-fold nature as I shall now proceed to briefly explain.

In the first place, the early Assyrian contract

---

[1] Cf. Gen. x. ii. : " out of that land [Babylonia] he [Nimrod] went forth into Assyria and builded Nineveh, and Rehoboth-'Ir, and Calah and Resen " (= Nisin? This must, therefore, have been a colony of the Babylonian Nisin, cf. Ishmi-Dagan, which occurs both as the name of a king of Nisin and of a *patesi* of Assyria).

tablets discovered in Cappadocia (not far from the modern Caesarea) shew both by the various characteristic personal names that occur in them and also by their script and style such striking resemblance to the contract-tablets of the Khammu-rabi dynasty that it is impossible to assign them to any other epoch.[1]

It is true that Delitzsch had already noticed one or two of these coincidences, but had not drawn from them the only possible conclusion in regard to the date of the tablets in which they occur; here and there indeed he seems to have some inkling of the true state of the case (cf. for example pp. 66 and 270, note 1 of his treatise), but he nevertheless ends by declaring that for the present the period to which they belong seems to be an enigma to which no answer is, as yet, forthcoming.

[1] We have only to compare such names as Amur-Ashir, Amur-Samas, Ashir-Emûki, Ashur-ishtakal, Ashur-rabi, Ashir-tayar, Ashur-bani, Ilubani, Ishtar-lamazi, Ashur-imîti, Ennam-Ashir, Ennam-Aï, Pilakh-Ashur, Zili-Ishtar, Manum-bali-Ashir (= who would be without Ashir?), Manum-ki-Ashur (= who is like unto Ashur?) taken from the 22 tablets recently annotated by Delitzsch, and which had previously been edited by Golenischeff,* with names of precisely similar formation found in the tablets of the Khammu-rabi Dynasty, such as Ilîma-amur, Ilî-emûki, Ili-ishtikal, Samas-rabi etc., Marduk-taiar, Samas-bani, Lamazi, Sin-imîti, Ennam-Sin, Sin-pilakh, Tsilî-Ishtar, Manum-balu-ili, Manum-balu-Ishtar, Manu-shanin-Samas (see p. 70 and earlier, the last-mentioned name = "who can withstand Samas?").

* W. GOLFNISCHEFF, *Vingt quatre tablettes Cappodociennes de la collection W. Golenischeff*, St. Petersburg, 1891 : F. DELITZSCH, *Beiträge zur Entzifferung und Erklärung der Kappadokischen Keilschrifttafeln*, Leipzig, 1893 (*Abh. der Sachs. Gesellschaft, d. Wiss.*, Vol. xiv. No. 4).

Peiser[1] goes back as far as the time of the Assyrian king Shalmaneser I. (ca. 1300 B.C.), but he too is misled into identifying such unimpeachable Babylonian names as Sugalîa, Garîa and the like (where the termination *ia* denotes a hypocoristic contraction of a longer name), with the divine appellation Yahu, and therefore concludes that the contracts must have been indited at the time of a Phoenicio-Canaanite colonization of Cappadocia. All this, however, in the face of the coincidences mentioned above, is to no purpose; the time of the Khammurabi dynasty is, here, the only one worth consideration.

In the second place, we also find in these Cappadocian contract tablets unmistakeable traces of that Arabian element which had previously impressed us as the characteristic feature of the contracts of the Khammu-rabi dynasty — itself an Arabian *régime*, viz.: names like Ikib-ilu (cf. *supra* Ya'kub-ilu), Ashupi-ilu (cf. *supra* Yashup-ilu, p. 95), Elali (written E-la-ni, cf. p. 115), Mashkhûru (for Mash'uru? cf. Makhnûzu on p. 111), Nabatî (with an emphatic dental sound, cf. the Arabic names beginning with Nabti on pp. 83 *et seq.*), Gamaru etc. And, what is of still greater importance, these names continue to be a feature of Assyrian nomenclature up to the close of the Assyrian Empire, a fact which is proved by the occurrence of such names as Ilu-milki (Eponym 886, B.C.), Tsidki-ilu (Ep. 764 B.C.), Abu-râma (Ep. 677), Milki-ramu (Ep. 654 B.C.), Atar-

---

[1] *Keilinschrift Bibliothek*, Vol. IV. Introduction, p. viii.

ilu (Ep. 673, cf. the South Arabian Watar-il), Makhdi (for Ma'di cf. p. 83—Ep. 725 B.C.), Ilu-amar (in the time of Sennacherib, cf. Arab. Abî-amara, p. 84), and particularly of the numerous names compounded with Aï in the sense of a male deity (pp. 112 et seq.). Mr. Pinches has recently proved that the element Aï (which is always represented by the symbol of deity) must not be read as "Malik" in personal names, but as equivalent to the Hebraic Yah [1] (originally a word in general use among the Western Semites, but especially among the Arabs); thus we find Abu-Aï (Ep. 887 B.C.), Nindar-Aï (Ep. 864), Ashur-Aï (Ep. 862 and 651), Nirgal-Aï (Ep. 831), Samas-Aï (Ep. 819), Marduk-Aï (Ep. 818), Bel-Aï (Ep. 769), in addition to the names Sharru-Aï (Aï is king) and Shadû-Aï (*vide supra* pp. 108 *et seq.*), with which latter may be compared the peculiarly Assyrian names ending in Shadûa (= "my mountain") mentioned on p. 108. In a word, the Assyrians, (like the numerous Arabs of the Khammu-rabi dynasty who in time developed into Babylonians) were similarly of Arab blood, and like their kinsmen they quickly assimilated the Babylonian traditions, and finally developed into the warlike Assyrian race with which history has made us familiar, though they maintained their blood much freer from admixture than the Babylonian Arabs. For it is a well-

---

[1] *Journal of the Transactions of the Victoria Institute*, vol. xxviii. (1896), pp. 11 *et seq.* in his essay on *The Religious ideas of the Babylonians* (pp. 1—21 cf. 34—46) (cf. also my "remarks" on pp. 34—36): Pinches also draws attention to the highly interesting variants Ya and Yau for Aï.

known ethnological fact, which, though occasionally noticed before,[1] has till now never been satisfactorily explained, that the Assyrian type which we find on the royal monuments presents far purer Semitic features than are to be discovered on Babylonian monuments of any epoch whatsoever, with the sole exception of that of the Khammu-rabi dynasty.[2]

The names cited on the previous page, meaning respectively " Father is Aï (or Ya)," " Nindar is Aï," etc., belong to the eponymous rulers, that is, the highest dignitaries of the Assyrian Empire, and examples of these extend from the beginning of the 9th century B.C. (a time when there had been as yet no contact with the kingdom of Israel) down to Assurbanipal. They reflect, without doubt, the earlier Arabian monotheism of the Assyrians, for nearly all of the deities borrowed from the Babylonian Pantheon, first of all Ashur, then Bel, Samas, Marduk, Nindar, and Nirgal, are here identified with the ancient Aï or Ya. From this it is at once apparent that Jonah's mission to preach Jehovah to the Ninevites, is by no means so absurd as the modern "critics" would have us think: he would here have found ready to his hand a text for his sermon not a whit less apposite than that Athenian altar to " the unknown God," which later on supplied a theme to S. Paul.

It is to the Assyrians, therefore, whose existence as a nation began in the time of the Khammu-rabi

---

[1] See my *History of Babylonia and Assyria*, pp. 483 *et seq.*

Cf. the representation of Khammu-rabi himself in Winckler's *Altorient. Forschungen*, p. 197.

Dynasty, that we must look for the sole possible date of this last piece of evidence. The sole and only period, therefore, in which we can place the memorable association of the history of Abraham with that of Khammurabi is not the 23rd century B.C., but the close of the 20th or beginning of the 19th, in other words about 1900 B.C. That this association is a real one, I hope to prove more fully in the following pages.

CHAPTER V

ABRAHAM AND KHAMMURABI

The fourteenth chapter of Genesis is, in many respects, one of the most remarkable in the whole of the Old Testament, containing as it does the account of that Elamite campaign against Sodom and consequent liberation of Lot, which form an episode in the history of Abraham. It is true that we can draw no particular doctrinal lesson from this chapter; it conveys no special message from Moses, and even the magnificent figure of Melchizedek as he comes forth bearing bread and wine to Abraham, is but a faint symbol of future spiritual gifts, the true significance of which it is impossible to understand save in the light of New Testament teaching (cf. Heb. v. 10). There are of course episodes in the history of the children of Israel of far higher importance than that here narrated; for even had Lot, Abraham's nephew, been left a prisoner in the hands of the enemy, the sacred story, grouped as it is round the person of Abraham and not round that of Lot, would have proceeded without a break, and no one could have blamed Abraham had he hesitated to set off with his three hundred and eighteen slaves to rescue Lot and his possessions out of the hands of a superior hostile force. Nor can we pretend that this chapter bears any special message of consolation to afflicted souls, or that it is more edifying than other passages in the writings of the Old Covenant. No; its real interest lies in the fact that in this chapter we obtain a glimpse of the general history of the world in the 20th century B.C., such as is nowhere else vouchsafed us in the Bible. In it we catch sight of a political background instinct with life and movement, and full of the deepest human interest, the more important details of which are now being confirmed and amplified in a most surprising manner by modern research and excavations in the territory of Ancient Babylonia.

A mighty despot, Chedor-la-'omer,[1] king of Elam, a country lying to the south of Babylon, on the shores of the Persian Gulf, afterwards known as Persia, appears on the scene. His allies are Tid'al,[2] king of the Goi [Goiim], Amraphel, king of Shin'ar,[3] and Arioch, king of Ellasar (verse 9). In the first verse, which enables us to fix the date of the episode, we learn that Amraphel was king over the region in which Haran, Abraham's second adopted home, was situated; next comes Arioch, who at that time was still in possession of Ur, Abraham's native place, holding in addition the supremacy over Sumer and

[1] LXX Chodollogomor, the Hebrews must have pronounced it Chedorlaghomer.
[2] LXX Thargal; originally, however, as has only been recently discovered, it was Tudkhul.
[3] *i e.*, according to Gen. x. 10 and xi. 2 *et seq.*, the country of which Babylon was the capital.

Akkad (*i.e.* the whole of Babylonia), and lastly Chedor-la-'omer and Tid'al, whose names stand out prominently in the narrative of the campaign itself (verses 5—9). That Chedor-la-'omer was the prime mover in the matter, and the others merely his allies, is clearly stated in verse 5 (cf. also verse 4). For twelve years had the kings of the Five Cities of the Dead Sea paid tribute to Chedor-la-'omer, in the thirteenth they rebelled, and in the fourteenth there followed the expedition against the " Countries of the West," undertaken in order to bring the rebellious vassal kings to their senses. Chedor-la-'omer invaded Bashan (the Rephaïm in Ashteroth-Karnaim), Ammon (Zuzim), Moab (Emim), and Edom (the Horites in mount Se'ir), one after the other as far as the Ælanitic gulf (El-Parân); he then retraced his steps to En-Mishpat ("The Spring of Judgment," known as Kadesh Barne'a in the exodus of the Israelites from Egypt to Moab), and smote the Amalekites and the Amorites who dwelt in Hazezon-Tamar (Engedi on the western shore of the Dead Sea). At last the kings of the Five Cities, whose domain evidently included Edom and the whole region east of Jordan, seem to have rallied, and to have determined to give battle to Chedor-la-'omer in the open field. The fight took place in the valley of Siddim (a region rich in asphalt, and afterwards, owing to a convulsion of nature, invaded by the waters of the Dead Sea), and resulted in the defeat of the allied princes of the Five Cities. Moreover, Lot, Abraham's nephew, who was living in Sodom, fell into the hands of the victors. As soon as Abraham was informed of this, **he set** out, with 318 of his men, in pursuit of the enemy, now on their homeward march towards Babylonia, and came up with them near Dan on the northern frontier of Palestine. Falling on them by night as they lay intoxicated with victory and manifestly never dreaming of pursuit, he drove them in disorderly flight as far as the neighbourhood of Damascus. The booty left behind by the enemy, together with the prisoners—among whom, of course, was Lot—fell into the hands of the pursuers; these latter included not only Abraham's own followers, but also the people of Mamre' (Hebron), 'Aner, and Eshcol, his allies, whose suzerain was apparently Melchizedek, King of Salem, who is mentioned a little lower down.

If we carefully examine the concluding verse of the chapter, we shall find what would seem to be traces of two different recensions; according to one of these, it would appear that it was the King of Sodom who came out to meet Abraham as he returned home victorious and laden with the spoil; according to the other, it was Melchizedek of Salem, as the following parallel passages shew:

16. And he [Abram] brought back all the goods and also brought again his brother Lot, and his goods, and the women also and the people [the other prisoners].

| 17. And the King of Sodom went out to meet him after his return from the slaughter of Chedorla'omer and the kings | 18. And [there came out] Melchizedek, King of Salem [to meet him] . . . . |

that were with him at the *Emek sharre:* (gloss) *i.e.* the King's vale.[1]

21. And the King of Sodom said unto Abram; give me the persons and take the goods to thyself.

22a. And Abram said to the King of Sodom:
. . . .
. . . .

23. I will not take (*i.e.* keep) a thread nor a shoe-latchet nor aught that is thine, lest thou shouldest say, I have made Abram rich: 24. save only that which the young men have eaten and the portion of the men which went with me; Aner, Eshcol and Mamre, let them take their portion.

[and] brought forth bread and wine; and he was priest of El 'Elyôn (= God most High). 19. and he blessed him and said, Blessed be Abram of El 'Elyôn, possessor of heaven and earth: 20. and blessed be El 'Elyôn which hath delivered thine enemies into thy hand. And he gave him (= offered him) a tenth of all (*i.e.* of the spoil).

[Then said Melchizedek to Abram: . . . .
. . . .
but Abram said to him]
22b. I have lifted up my hand unto El 'Elyôn,[2] possessor of heaven and earth.
. . . .
. . . .

---

[1] *Emek Shaveh* in the Hebr. text, cf. *shaveh Kiryathaim* in verse 5 (the LXX reading is Σαυη in verse 5, Σαβυ in verse 17; the emendation of *shaveh* into *sharre* is an obvious one (*r* and *v* being represented by somewhat similar characters in the Ancient Hebrew script)—cf. Babyl. *sharru* = king.

[2] Here a later editor has inserted " Yahveh " for El 'Elyôn.

In verse 10 we are told that "the vale of Siddim was full of slime pits [*i.e.* the ground was honeycombed with asphalt quarries], and the kings of Sodom and Gomorrah fled, and they fell there, and they that remained flew to the mountain;" now since the King of Sodom had fallen in the rout, it was impossible that he should have come out to meet Abraham. Moreover, the opening words of Abraham's reply (verse 22) possessed a special significance for Melchizedek, since he alone employs the title Elyôn (= Highest), the word used by Abraham being rather Shaddai (cf. p. 109). In all probability therefore the recension which represents Melchizedek as coming out to meet Abraham is the earlier of the two. As matters stand with the two recensions intermingled as they are, the Melchizedek episode rather destroys the coherence of the other; we have no right, however, to conclude from this that verses 18—20 are a later interpolation, since verse 22*b*. unmistakably shows that here the person originally referred to was Melchizedek and not the King of Sodom. On the other hand, if we were to omit verses 18—20, verse 21 would follow on somewhat abruptly after verse 17; in order to make it read properly we should have to supply some such clause as: "then in order to express his good will to him, Abram offered him a share in the booty." For the rest, the very fact that the text has fallen into confusion[1] from verse 17 onwards—taken in con-

---

[1] In view of the facts disclosed above, the question naturally arises whether in the original it was really a tenth (and not rather the whole of

junction with the presence of so many obscure and archaic expressions, which it was necessary to explain to later generations by means of glosses—is the best possible proof of the very high antiquity of this whole chapter. Probably the original, which seems to have been written in Babylonian, was rescued from the archives of the pre-Israelitish kings of Salem, and preserved in the archives of the temple at Jerusalem.

It is also important to note that the author of the Epistle to the Hebrews must have been familiar with a version in which verse 18 contained a supplementary clause, somewhat to this effect: "who had not received the kingdom from his father and mother," a clause intended to give prominence to the fact that the office of Priest-King was elective and not hereditary. The kings of Edom mentioned in Gen. xxxvi. 31 *et seq.*—no one of whom was the son of his predecessor—furnish a somewhat parallel instance, especially the second on the list, Bela' son of Beor, who is doubtless identical with the well-known prophet Balaam son of Beor, in Num. xxii. 5 *et seq.*, and xxxi. 8. It is evident, therefore, from the apostle's metaphorical comment on Melchizedek (Hebr. vii. 1), that the phrase "without father, without mother," in Hebr. vii. 3, was not suggested by Ps. cx. 4, "thou art a priest for ever after the order of Melchizedek" (Heb. vi. 20), nor by the phrase "Priest of God Most High" (Heb. vii. 1), but must

the booty) that was offered, also whether the original wording has been preserved in verse 21*b* and in verse 24. But see my explanation offered below on p. 157.

have appeared in the version from which he was quoting. We need only compare—

Quotation from Gen. xiv.	Metaphor:
a) Melchizedek	= King of righteousness (Hebr. vii. 2)
b) King of Salem	= King of Peace (Hebr. vii. 2)
c) without father, without mother, (cf. v. 1 " Priest of God most High.")	= without genealogy, having neither beginning of days nor end of life, but made like unto the Son of God, abideth a priest continually (Heb. vii. 3).

—especially as the words are preceded by the following introduction (Heb. vii. 1): "This Melchizedek, king of Salem, priest of God most High, who met Abraham returning from the slaughter of the kings and blessed him, to whom also Abraham divided a tenth part of all" (cf. v. 4, where it is still more clearly stated that it was "a tenth out of the chief spoils"). We are forced to conclude, therefore, either that there existed in the time of S. Paul a version of the Bible which contained in Gen. xiv. 18 the supplementary clause, "without father and mother," or that independent of the Biblical text there was an ancient oral tradition current among the priesthood at Jerusalem in which the epithet, "without father and without mother," was applied to the ancient office of the Priest-King.

Indeed we find confirmatory evidence of this even in inscriptions of pre-Mosaic date, which throw an historical light of the most striking character on the expression in question, as well as on the history of the kingdom of Salem generally in primitive times.

In the letters from King 'Abd-khiba of Uru-Salim to the Pharaoh Amenothis (ca. 1400 B.C.) preserved to us in the Tel el Amarna tablets, we find an asseveration which occurs in nearly every one of these writings and which I give below in parallel columns:

Berlin No. 102, lines 9 *et seq.*	B., No. 103, lines 25 *et seq.*
Lo, in so far as I am concerned.	Lo in regard to the region of this city of Jerusalem
It was not my father who installed me in this place nor my mother,	It was not my father, not my mother who gave it me
but the arm of the mighty king has allowed me to enter into my ancestral house.[1]	but the arm of the mighty king gave it to me.

and again in a third letter B., No. 104, lines 9 *et seq.*:

" Lo, I am no prefect (*i.e.* no Egyptian viceroy), but a " Friend (*rukhi*—Hebr. *rê'eh*, cf. 2. Sam. xv. 37) of the king's, and one who brings [voluntary] offerings to the king (*ubil bilti*, Canaanite *obel belet*), am I; it was not my father, it was not my mother, but the arm of the mighty king, that placed me in my ancestral house."

The expression "mighty king" (*sharru dannu*)—a title which, though borne by Babylonian and Assyrian monarchs in the context given above, reminds us very strongly of the El 'Elyôn of Melchizedek — finds a parallel in another passage in Letter

---

[1] *bit abi-ya*, cf. the Hebrew expression *bêt ab* which has the same general meaning.

No. 104 in the Berlin edition of the Tel-el-Amarna
texts:
" So long as there is a single ship on the sea,
So long does the arm of the mighty king hold
  in possession .
The land of Naharim, [1] and the land of Kapasi,
Now, however, shall the Khabiri [2] possess themselves of the Cities of the King? [3]
It is evident from this that the "mighty king"
mentioned in the letters of 'Abd-khiba must be an
earthly potentate. But in the numerous letters addressed by Canaanite princes to the Egyptian Court
that have come down to us, although they abound
in servile protestations of subjection, we never find
Pharaoh described by this title. On the contrary,
Rib-Addi, governor of Gebal, complains to Pharaoh
that his enemies, the sons of 'Abd-Ashirti [Ashera]
in Coele Syria, have taken his territory away from
him and given it to the "mighty king," *i.e.* in this
case to the king of the Hittites (Berl. No. 76); for
in another passage Rib-Addi describes the sons of
'Abd-Ashera as "creatures of the king of Mitanni,
of the king of Kassi (Babylonia), and the king of
Khâti," and as a matter of fact the Hittite influence
was at that time daily gaining ground in Syria.

[1] Western Mesopotamia and Northern Syria, the hegemony over which was at that time an object of rivalry between the Hittite kings and the kings of Mitanni (a region between the Euphrates and Belikh). Kapa-s is probably the country on the gulf of Issos, called the Land of Kef-t in the Egyptian inscriptions.

[2] Bedûin, from whom Kirjath Arba' first received the name of Hebron ; see, as to this, a future chapter.

[3] *i.e.* of Pharoah. The environs of Jerusalem are here referred to.

Nevertheless, the asseveration of 'Abd-khiba of Jerusalem, which he thrice repeats in his letters to Pharaoh quoted above, sounds for all the world like the echo of some ancient sacred formula, or of a phrase that originally possessed a religious significance, and receives just as much light from the facts narrated of Melchizedek in Gen. xiv. 18 *et seq.*, and Heb. vii. 1 *et seq.*, as it, in its turn, throws on them. To Pharaoh, of course, the "mighty king" meant nothing more than his rival the king of the Hittites; but in Jerusalem the original significance of the words "not my father and not my mother, but the arm of the mighty king" (*i.e.* of El 'Elyôn) must still have been perfectly familiar. In Babylonian (the language employed by the kings of Jerusalem when addressing Pharaoh) El 'Elyôn (the Most High God) would appear as *bêlu asharidu;* the ideogram for *sharru* king, however, in the bilingual texts, also stands for *bêlu* = Lord, or *ilu* = God, and the ideogram for *dannu* = mighty is also used to represent *asharidu*. And, if further proof were needed, it is furnished by the fact that in the Shuhite country, the home of Bildad [*i.e.* the Shuhite] the friend of Job, the war-god, Nergal, was called not only Emu, but also "mighty king" (W. A. Inser., ii. 54, No. 5, l. 65 *et seq.*); from this it is evident that there must have been a Western Semitic deity who was known by this name.

And now to return to our investigation in regard to the original text of the closing episode narrated in Gen. xiv. The fact that the King of Sodom had, as stated in verse 10, already perished, supplies a clue to the correct emendation of the text. I believe that there are ample grounds for assuming that the passage originally ran as follows:—

17. " And *Melchizedek*, the king of *Salem*, went out to meet him, after his return from the slaughter of Chedorla'omer and the kings that were with him at the 'emek sharre,[1] (gloss) the same is the King's vale.

18. And Melchizedek king of Salem brought forth bread and wine; and he was Priest of God Most High [and had not inherited the kingdom from his father or his mother[2]].

19. And he blessed him and said, Blessed be Abram of El 'Elyôn possessor of heaven and earth: (20) and blessed be El 'Elyôn which hath delivered thine enemies into thy hands. And he (Abraham) gave him [= offered him] a tenth of all (*i.e.* of the whole booty).

21. But *Melchizedek* said unto Abram: give me the persons and take the goods to thyself. . . . I have lift up my hand to El 'Elyôn possessor of heaven and earth, (23) that I will not take a thread nor a shoe-latchet, nor aught that is thine, lest thou shouldest say thou hast enriched *me:* (24) save only that which the young men have eaten and the portion of the men which went with *thee:* 'Aner, Eshcol, and Mamre', let them take their portion."

Only the words in italics have been changed. The chief mistake, to which all the others may be traced, lies in the insertion of the words "king of Sodom"

---

[1] *Vide supra*, pp. 90 and 107, note 1, and cf. the Katabanian divine name 'Amm mentioned on p. 48.

[2] As to this restoration see what I have said on pp. 152 *et seq.*

instead of "Melchizedek" in verse 17. The only omission necessary is at the beginning of verse 22, where the words, "And Abram said to the king of Sodom," are inconsistent with the general sense. For the invocation of El'Elyôn is only rightly intelligible when placed in the mouth of Melchizedek. That Melchizedek should have desired possession of the prisoners is no more than we should expect: for after the death of the king of Sodom and Gomorrah he must naturally have regarded himself as master of the Jordan. Moreover, it is quite possible that some of his own people may have been included among the prisoners rescued by Abraham. And, finally, in regard to those who had lent Abraham a helping hand, viz. the men of 'Aner, Eshcol, and Mamre', we can readily understand Melchizedek's anxiety that they should receive their share, since they were his own subjects; Hebron is, indeed, a natural annex of Jerusalem. My emendation, which leaves the existing text practically untouched, may therefore be allowed to speak for itself. The Melchizedek incident has now, for the first time, been shown to form an integral part of the whole chapter in which it occurs; nay, more, it supplies the *raison d'être* for the introduction of the narrative of the military expedition which precedes it, and which we are now about to examine more closely; the suggestion that we owe the narrative to a desire to invest Abraham with a halo of military glory is absolutely groundless.

But are the events narrated in Gen. xiv. actual historical facts? Is it conceivable that at this early

AS ILLUSTRATED BY THE MONUMENTS 159

date, an Elamite king not only exercised supremacy over the whole of Babylon but even penetrated as far as the Sinaitic peninsular in his lust for conquest? Or ought we, as some would have us believe, to regard the whole matter as originally nothing more than the narrative of some predatory raid against Canaan by a party of Bedûin Arabs, to which legend had tacked on the names of Lot and Abraham, the whole story being afterwards elaborated by some later writer into the shape it now presents in Gen. xiv.?

As a matter of fact, a distinguished Orientalist long ago declared this chapter to be a fantastic grouping together of names, which either belonged to some remote period, or were expressly invented for the occasion, and since that time it has become the fashion among the "higher critics" of the Old Testament to echo this view. Ever since 1869, when Theodor Nöldeke attempted to prove the xivth chapter of Genesis to be the biased invention of a later—though possibly pre-exilic—date,[1] modern "critics" have unhesitatingly endorsed his verdict. Scholars began afterwards to study the cuneiform texts and shewed that king Arioch of Ellasar was identical with king Eri-Aku (G. Smith, 1871) of Larsa (H. Rawlinson); they next pointed out that there was an Elamite goddess called Lagamar or Lagamal (G. Smith), and that there were two ancient Elamite kings, one named Kudur-Mabug, father of the aforesaid Eri-Aku, and the other Kudur-nan-

---

[1] *Untersuchungen zur Kritik des alten Testamentes* (1869).

khundi (G. Smith). What did the modern critics do in the face of this evidence—since to admit the presence of such an ancient tradition in the Old Testament would be virtually equivalent to cutting the ground away from beneath their own feet? They could not, of course, deny that Kudur - Lagamar (Chedorla'omer in Gen. xiv.) is a genuine Elamite name, or that the supremacy of the Elamites in Syria (including Palestine) is proved by one of Kudur-Mabug's inscriptions—though the reading Eri-Aku, as the name of a son of Kudur-Mabug, was at one time, though wrongly, disputed.[1] They were therefore obliged—since there seemed no other way out of the difficulty—to fall back again on the theory of a post-exilic forgery, and to suggest that, like a nineteenth century novelist in search of "local colour," the Jewish writer must have gone to the Babylonian priests for his antiquarian details. "It would seem, therefore"—I quote Meyer's own words from the first volume of his *History of Antiquity* (Stuttgart, 1884)—" that the Jew who inserted the account (Gen. xiv.), *one of the latest portions of*

---

[1] By many it was regarded as nothing more than an ingenious conjecture, and was occasionally quoted as such, but its accuracy was questioned by Assyriologists (such as Fr. Delitzsch in his little book on the Cossaeans, which appeared in 1883), the result being that the identification came to be discredited by theologians and historians alike: the present writer stood alone in his disregard of the doubts cast on this theory, and thanks to a mass of fresh evidence which now no longer admits of question, he has been able to establish both the correctness of the reading Iri-Aku and the identity of the bearer of this name with Arioch. (Cf. *Semiten* vol. 1, and more fully, *History of Bab. and Ass.* pp. 357—74.)

the whole Pentateuch,[1] in its present position, must have obtained in Babylon exact information in regard to the early history of the country, and, for some reason which we are unable to fathom, mixes up Abraham with the history of Kudur-Lagamar; in other respects his version of the story accords perfectly with the *absolutely unhistorical* [1] views held by the Jews in regard to primitive ages."

By adopting this attitude, it was no longer necessary for modern critics to deny that the events related in Gen. xiv. rest on an actual basis of historic fact; they had now to admit, whether they liked it or not, that the names of the hostile kings especially were not pure inventions. But that the history of Abraham, whom they regard as not merely a legendary but rather a purely mythical being, should contain in its midst an ancient historical tradition, was something which they could not accept; for in that case the whole theory, according to which everything before the time of David is wrapped in the mist of legend, would begin to totter on its base, and the account drawn up by Moses would begin to appear in another and far more authentic light; in a word, the whole doctrine of the untrustworthiness of the earlier history of Israel—so dear to the hearts of modern critics of the Pentateuch—would suddenly find itself attacked in a vital part. In order, therefore, to save this master principle from ruin, there was nothing for it but to adopt the above opportunist expedient, the inherent absurdity of which

---

[1] The words printed in italics occur at the beginning, and the other part at the end, of paragraph 136 in Meyer's book.

must, one would think, be patent to every unprejudiced observer. This merely serves to show us once again how true it is that once the critic refuses to be convinced by the sheer force of facts because to do so would involve the sacrifice of a carefully elaborated theory, he is apt, like a drowning man, to catch at the various straws, provided they seem to promise him a way out of his difficulties. For it is absolutely inconceivable that a Jew of the post-exilic period should have been the first to derive from the sacred Babylonian records such exact information in regard to an incident in the history of the earliest kings of Babylon[1]—an incident, moreover, in which the king of Babylon played a passive and comparatively subordinate part. Besides, even assuming Gen. xiv. to be nothing more than a "very late narrative of a Midrash character" belonging to post-exilic times, how came its author (who, by the way, may be congratulated on the production of such a masterpiece as this chapter) to introduce into it a whole host of ancient phrases and names, to which he himself is obliged to add explanatory glosses in order that they may be better understood? It is merely necessary to glance at verses 2 and 8, "king of Bela [the same is Zoar];" verse 3, "the vale of Siddim, [the same is the (later) Salt Sea];" verse 7, "En-Mishpat [the same is Kadesh];" verse 14, "his trained men, *i.e.* born in his house;" and verse 17, "in the vale of Sharre (*vide supra*, p. 150, note)

---

[1] It must be remembered that the only continuous tradition we have refers to the kings of Babylon and not to those of Ur, Nisin and Larsa. Cf. for instance the List of Kings.

[that is the King's Vale]." Are we to assume that he did this intentionally in order to invest his story with an air of higher antiquity? In that case, all we can say is, that no similar example of literary finesse can be found throughout the whole of the Old Testament, and that if he was capable of such subtlety in this one instance, it is strange that he should have limited himself to dressing up this one scene from the life of Abraham in Canaan, in finery borrowed from the Ancient Babylonian archives, when there were so many other episodes, both in the story of Abraham and elsewhere in the primitive history of the Israelites, which would have readily lent themselves to similar adornment and elaboration. To take only a few instances, we have the migration of Abraham from his original home in Ur (Gen. xi. 28 and 31), the building of the tower of Babel (Gen. xi. 1—9), the account of Nimrod (Gen. x. 8—12), of which there is not a single one that would not have amply repaid him for the expenditure of a few explanatory additions and interpolations taken from Babylonian history and mythology. Besides, if Meyer's view be the correct one, we may rest assured that the editor of Gen. xiv. would not have refrained from pointing a moral, by showing that the insolence of the kings of Elam and Larsa drew down upon them a divine Judgment, in that they were soon afterwards overthrown by the hand of Amraphel. Yet he does none of these things. Such an enrichment of the stock of Ancient Hebrew history and tradition, direct from cuneiform sources, in exilic or post-exilic times, as is here predicated by Meyer, Kuenen and Wellhausen, etc., is open to the gravest suspicion from the fact of its being an isolated instance, not to speak of its being otherwise unprecedented and inconceivable. Moreover, if we accepted their theory, we should expect to find the names of the kings given in the Hebrew texts in a different form, and one more in harmony with the text of the later Babylonian tradition: the chronographers of Nabonidus' time certainly wrote nothing but "Khammu-rabi" and the form of the name "Chedor-la'omer," even in the Epos current in the time of the Achaemenides (of which we shall hear more anon), was Kudur-dugmal or Kudur-laga-mal, while the contemporary texts give Ammurabi as well as Khammu-rabi, and the name of the Elamite king as Kudur-luggamar instead of Kudur-luggamal, *i.e.* with the earlier *r* in place of the later *l*.

The reader will now understand why it is that this fourteenth chapter of Genesis has come to be a sort of shibboleth for the two leading schools of Old Testament critics. The purely literary question as to whether the so-called "Priestly Code" is the oldest or latest of the sources of the Pentateuch, is, by comparison, of merely minor importance. It is the question of the nature of history itself which divides the students of the Old Testament into two irreconcilable factions. The authenticity of a narrative such as that under consideration is, however, in itself, an unanswerable criticism upon the views which are now in fashion with regard to the credibility of the ancient Hebrew tradition. The subject matter of the present chapter will, therefore, for ever remain a stumbling-block in the path of those who refuse to recognize a single line of the Pentateuch — not even the Decalogue and the Blessing (Deut. xxx.)—to be genuine, and, try how they may to remove it, it will continue to defy their persistent efforts.

Having now sufficiently explained the true state of this question, I propose in the following pages— as a kind of supplement to what I have already said at the beginning of this chapter, and to the outlines sketched on pp. 43 *et seq.*—to institute a closer comparison between the historical scene which we find depicted in Gen. xiv. and the evidence of the monuments. The monuments in question may be divided into two classes. First, the contemporary records dating from the time of Abraham; and secondly, the later Babylonian tradition, which is not altogether free from a tinge of poetic fancy: the monuments of the first class consist of the Ancient Babylonian inscriptions of Kings discovered at Ur and Larsa, of letters, and lastly of the date-formulae of the contract tablets—documents which yield a fruitful harvest of knowledge in regard to the personal names and legal relations of the people.

I shall begin with examples of *ex voto* offerings of the kings of Larsa, and shall, first of all, allow one or two of them to speak for themselves, as I feel convinced that the reader will be interested to learn something of the actual wording of these important monuments, now fortunately rescued from the accumulated *débris* of four thousand years which had covered them in Southern Babylonia. They are written in the primitive Sumerian language, an idiom somewhat akin to modern Turkish, which was used in royal inscriptions right down to the Kassite period and even later, but had long before ceased to be employed colloquially.

An *ex voto* now preserved in the Louvre runs as follows:—"To the goddess Ishtar, the lady of the mountain. . . . . the daughter of Sin to their mistress, have Kudur-Mabug, the prince (*adda = malik*) of Yamutbal, the son of Simtishilkhak, and Ri-Aku, his son, the exalted shepherd of Nippur,[1] the guardian of Ur, king of Larsa, king of Ki-Ingi (Sumer) and of Akkad, built the temple of Mi-ur-urra, her favourite holy place, for the prolongation of their lives, and have made high its summit and raised it up like a mountain."

A second inscription discovered at Ur (W. A. I., i. 2, No. 3) runs as follows:—"To the God Uru-ki (the Moon-god of Ur) his king, has Kudur-Mabug, the prince of Martu (*i.e.* of the "countries of the West," Palestine) the son of Simtishilkhak, on the day in which the god Uru-ki hearkened unto his prayer, built the temple of Nunmagh for the preservation of his life and the life of Iri-Aku, his son, the king of Larsa."

In another similar inscription Iri Aku comes forward to speak for himself, but mentions his father Kudur-Mabug as well. On the other hand the following inscription (W. A. I., i. 3, No. 10) must evidently have been indicted after the death of

[1] Lately identified with Nuffar [Niffer] by Peters, Hilprecht and Haynes.

Kudur-Mabug, since, contrary to the usual practice elsewhere, he is not named:

"To the god Nin-Shagh..... his king, does Iri-Aku, the shepherd of the possession (or income) of Nippur, who fulfils the oracle of the sacred tree of Eridu, the guardian of Ur (and) of the temple of Uddaim-tigga, king of Larsa, king of Sumer and Akkad, consecrate this; on the day in which Anu, Bel, and Ea, the great gods, gave the ancient Uruk (Erech) into my hand, have I built to the god Nin-shagh, my king, with good and loyal intent, the Temple of A-agga-summu, the abode of his pleasure, for the preservation of my life."

This presupposes the *conquest of Erech*, which not long before had been the capital of an independent dynasty, just as the references to Nippur in this inscription, and in the one first translated on the preceding page, presupposes the occupation of Nisin, a city whose fortunes were closely bound up with those of Nippur. The taking of Nisin plays an important part in contract tablets of the time of Ri-Aku, found at Tel Sifr (near Larsa), many of which are dated from this event. One of these date-formulae is worded thus, "in the year in which he with the exalted help of Anu, Bel and Ea, conquered Nisin, the city of the kingdom," and other tablets of the time of Ri-Aku are dated from the 5th, 6th, 7th, 8th, 13th, 18th, and 28th year after the taking of Nisin. Now in the time of Sinmuballit, the predecessor of Khammu-rabi, we find the following dated example (Meissner No. 32): "in the year in which he (*i.e.* Sinmuballit) conquered Nisin." From this it would seem that the struggle for the ancient royal city of Nisin (cf. p. 36) had gone on between Sinmu-ballit and the kings of Larsa, until Ri-Aku succeeded in obtaining undisputed possession of it, and held it for at least twenty-eight years—in fact, until he was himself dethroned by Khammu-rabi. It is also obvious that Ri-Aku must have enjoyed a very long reign —probably, over thirty years. This same capture of Nisin is, moreover, mentioned in yet another dated example, which reads: "in the year in which Ri-Agum, the king, and the prince of Yamutbâlu [with] the tribes (*nin - ki - sulub - gar*, Semitic, *ummanâti*) of Ishnunna (*i.e.* Ashnunnak, on the Elamite frontier) overthrew Nisin and he. . . . ." The rest of the inscription is unfortunately illegible.

In this last example the name of the king is written quite phonetically *Ri-im-A-gam-um* which can only be read as Ri-Agu[1] (Agum or Agu is a sobriquet of the Moon-god, as is also the more strongly articulated form Aku). On the other hand, in the inscriptions previously translated, the name is written either as Irim-Aku (pronounced Iri-Aku) or Ri-

---

[1] The symbol *gam* also possesses, it is true, the phonetic value *gu*, as for instance in the word *Shangumakhu*, which must not be read as *Shangammakhu*. A certain hypercritical scholar, one of whose pet theories is that "the Biblical Arioch has not yet been identified," recently proposed that we should read *Ri-im-A-gam-um* as *Ri-im-A-gam-mis* (*Zeitschrift der Deutsch. Morg. Gesellsch.*, vol. l. p. 251, note 2), which though in itself possible enough, must, to say the very least of it, be described as absolutely unnecessary; for even supposing him to be right on this point, the proposed rendering would be nothing more than an Elamite amplification of the divine name *agu* into *agavis*, a parallel to which is found in the name Ur-Ziguruvas (for Ur-Zigur).

im-Aku (pronounced Ri-Aku). That we have in these two latter cases a parallel to the Semitic rendering Arad-Sin (or Rim-Sin) is proved both by the form Ri-Agu and also by the Hebraic transliteration Arioch; moreover, this is absolutely confirmed by certain Epic fragments which we shall have occasion to discuss hereafter, in which the name is written Iri-E-a-ku and Iri-E-ku-a. The name means "Servant of the Moon-god." Some writers have suggested that Kudur-Mabug had *two* sons, one named Arad-Sin, the other Rim-Sin. But seeing that *ardu* = servant, is merely a Semitic translation of the Sumerian word *irim*, *rim*, (or *iri*, *ri*) = servant, we need not take this conjecture seriously.

Now, what are the conclusions to be drawn from the texts quoted above? Firstly, that the king who is named in each one of them, Iri-aku or Ri-Aku, resided at Larsa, a city of Southern Babylonia, sacred to the Sun-god; secondly, that he also possessed the cities of Ur, Eridu, Nisin, Nippur and last of all Uruk also, while Akkad and Babylon (in Northern Babylonia) seem to have merely paid tribute to him. And thirdly—the most important fact of all in so far as Gen. xiv. is concerned—that his father and grandfather, as a single glance at their names will show, were *Elamites;* the fact that Kudur-Mabug[1] is described as "prince of Yamutbal" affords additional

---

[1] The name means " Servant (Elamitic *Kudur*) of the god Mabug" (or Mavuk, cf. the Elamite personal name Mauk-titi; see my *Assyriological Notes*, § 20).

proof of his Elamite origin. For Yamutbal is derived from the Kassite word *ia* = "land" and *Mutabil*, the name of a Semitic viceroy of Dûr-ili on the Elamite frontier who flourished long before the time of Eri-Aku; this Mutabil had, as he informs us in an inscription, subdued and conquered Anshan (*i.e.* Northern Elam), with the result that for a long time afterwards the Babylonian name for a part of Elam was simply "the land of Mutabil," abbreviated to "Mutbal." Moreover, in the Babylonian geographical lists Yamutbalu is explained as the "fore-part of Elam" (W. A. I., v., 16, 20), so that even should my proposed explanation of the name of Yamutbal prove to be incorrect, we should still have evidence to show that this region formed part of the Elamite territory.

But whereas in the first inscription Kudur-Mabug is described as "prince of Yamutbal," in the second he bears the title "prince of Martu," which, as later usage proves, was equivalent to "prince of the West," and which, for this reason, many Assyriologists take to be synonymous with Yamutbal (*i.e.* in the present instance Western Elam). But Martu, in all the Ancient Babylonian historical records, is simply another name for Palestine (including Coele-Syria), being an abbreviation of Amartu = the land of the Amorites; since the Babylonian term Martu was the same as "countries of the *West*," this word *martu* gradually came to be used occasionally in the general sense of "West," and finally became a fixed ideogram for *amurrû*, the ordinary Semitic-Babylonian expression for "West," a word which originally meant "Amoritish."[1] The title "prince of Martu," therefore, necessarily implies that Kudur-Mabug had extended his military operations as far as Palestine and had reduced it to submission, or rather that he regarded the supremacy previously exercised by the later kings of Ur as his inheritance, and duly annexed it. If we couple this fact with the obvious identity of Arioch of Ellasar with Eri-Aku of Larsa, we obtain another striking instance of the way in which the Bible narrative is corroborated by facts revealed in the inscriptions. In both one and other we find an Elamite hegemony over Canaan in the time of Arioch, in both one and other there is the closest possible connection between this South Babylonian potentate and Elam, and lastly we find in both the same initial element (Kudur-) of the name of an Elamite prince. The only link still wanting to complete the chain of evidence — the connection between Eri-Aku (Arioch) and Khammu-rabi (Amraphel) will be dealt with later on — is the discovery of some reference to Chedor-la'omer in the cuneiform inscriptions. Up to the present, we have only succeeded in proving the individual elements of his name to be of Elamite origin—Kudur occurring in the name Kudur-Mabug

---

[1] Cf. Hebr. *Emori*, patronymic for the obsolete Amoreth = Martu. I have proved conclusively (*Assyriological Notes* § 13; cf. also Zeitschrift D. M. G. vol. xlix. p. 524) that the correct reading is not *akharrû*, but invariably *amurrû*. Sayce's conjecture that the Canaanite word Emoreth (=Martu postulated by me) may be traced in such expressions as *elôn Moreh* (Gen. xii. 6), elônê Moreh (Deut. xi. 30) and gib'at ha-Moreh (Judges vii. 1), appears to me well worth considering.

of the inscriptions, and Lagamar as the title of an Elamite goddess.

Even this missing link has been recently supplied by the sensational discovery made by the Dominican Father, Fr.-V. Scheil, in the shape of an autograph letter from Khammu-rabi addressed to a certain Sin-idinam (probably a grandson of the celebrated king Sin-idinam of Larsa). Of scarcely less importance than this document are the lyrical fragments of a later epoch which refer to the devastation of North Babylonia by Chedor-la'omer, the discovery of which, as of so many other important documents, we owe to the industry of Mr. Pinches; it is only within the last few years that we have been made aware of their existence, Mr. Pinches having first communicated them to the Geneva Congress of Orientalists in September 1894.

Father Scheil made the first announcement of his discovery in October 1896, in the fifth volume of the *Revue Biblique* (pp. 600 *et seq.*), a periodical compiled in Jerusalem by the Dominican Father M.-J. Lagrange, and published in Paris, in a paper entitled *Chodorlahomor dans les inscriptions Chaldéennes*. At almost the same date (the middle of September 1896) Father Scheil wrote from Constantinople to my friend Hilprecht, who was staying at the time not far from Munich, and shortly afterward to me also, enclosing a revised transcription of the clay tablet which had appeared in the *Revue Biblique*. In view of its great importance I here append, not only a literal translation (which differs in some respects from that supplied by Father Scheil), but a transliteration of the Babylonian original as well:

    A-na Sin-i-din-nam
    ki-bi-ma
    um-ma Kha-am-mu-ra-bi-ma
    i-la-a-tim sha E-mu-ut-ba-lim
(5) it-li-ti-ka (in Scheil two words, id li-ti-ka)
    ûm (-um) sha Ku-dur[1])-nu-ukh[2]-ga-mar
    u-sha-al-la-ma-ak-ku[3]
    i-nu-ma iz-za ila ba-ni-ik-ku
    i-na tsab-im sha ga-ti-ka
(10) tsab-am lu-pu-ut-ma
    i-la-a-tim
    a-na shu-ub-ti-shi-na
    li-sha-al-li-mu

Before giving the translation of the above I should like to point out that the name of the Elamite king may be read either as Kudur-nuggamar or as Kudur-luggamar. At the time in question the symbol *ni*, for instance, was also equivalent to *li*. I need scarcely point out that the symbol *ukh* when followed, as in this case, by *ga*, must be pronounced *ug*; lakh = to glitter (Sumerian *lag*), for instance, is followed not by *kha* but by *ga* and must therefore be pronounced *lagga* instead of *lagha*. The Babylonians of Khammu-rabi's time would seem to have pronounced the divine appellation Lagamar (thus in the ancient in Elamite inscriptions, *e.g. Lagamarivi*

---

[1] Symbol *tur* (Ideogram for "small" or "son").

[2] Symbol *ukh* = *imtu* or *rûtu* (Ideogr. for *Upi*, Opis).

[3] Symbol *ku*, with emphatic *k* sound (cf. *passim* in the suffix of the 2nd person singular, in the Ancient Babylonian correspondence).

mishirmana sarrakh) with a surd *l* naturally followed by a modified *a*, a sound which they reproduced in writing by Luggamar (cf. LXX, Λογόμορ).

Father Scheil gives the following translation of this clay tablet, which, according to his account, came originally from Larsa: "To Sin-idinnam from Khammu-rabi: the goddesses of the land of Emutbal, I have given them to thee as a reward for thy valour on the day of the defeat of Kodor-lahomor. Because the god, thy creator, is angered thereat, therefore destroy with the troops which are in thy hand their people, and may the goddesses remain uninjured in their holy places." He also adds the following explanation of the historical incident to which it refers: "There can be no doubt that Sin-iddinam (whom Scheil identifies with the well-known king of Larsa) had been restored to power by Khammu-rabi, after he (Khammu-rabi) had vanquished and dethroned the prince of Emutbal (= Yamutbal) and Rim-Sin (= Eri-Aku)." Moreover, Scheil considers the prince of Emutbal mentioned in the contract tablets of Tel Sifr to be identical with Chedor-la'omer, and cites Gen. xiv. (Arioch of Larsa and Chedor-la'omer of Elam) in support of his view.

Before I proceed to contrast my own translation of this tablet with that just quoted from Scheil, it will perhaps help the reader to form a more correct judgment as to this important identification if I furnish the date to which Scheil alludes, and which associates Eri-Aku and the "prince of Yamutbal" with Khammu-rabi, just as Scheil's new tablet links Chedor-la'omer and Khammu-rabi together. One of the Tel Sifr contract tablets, dated in the reign of Khammu-rabi (Strassmaier, No. 37), bears the following subscription, which throws an important light on the history of Ancient Babylonia.

"In the year in which Khammu-rabi the king, with the help of Anu and Bel, in whose grace he lives, overthrew[1] the prince (*adda vide supra*, p. 166) of Yamutbalu and Ri-Aku (written Ri-im-Sin)."

With Eri-Aku's original inscriptions before us, our first impulse would be to identify the "prince of Yamutbal" mentioned above with Eri-Aku's father Kudur-Mabug, who nearly always bears this title, but Scheil prefers to take it as applying to Chedor-la'omer. It cannot be denied that if my explanation of the Erech inscription on p. 167 is the correct one (*i.e.* if Kudur-Mabug was no longer living at the time of Eri-Aku's conquest of Erech), it follows as a natural consequence that it is not Kudur Mabug who is referred to in the inscription in question, but his successor in the principality of Yamutbal. Whether or not, however, this latter was Kudur-Lagamar, who it will be remembered is explicitly described both in the Epic texts (*vide infra*) and also in Gen. xiv. as "king of Elam," is still to a great extent an open question. There is, nevertheless, a good deal to be said in favour of answering it in the affirmative. It is quite possible—indeed it is highly probable—that a Kudur-Lagamar of Yamutbal should have been known in distant Palestine

---

[1] *Shu-ni ki nin(n)-dug*, literally "stretched his hand to the earth;" elsewhere *shu-dug-ga* is used in the sense of "to destroy, annihilate" (so used of the soil, W. A. I., ii. 26, 11).

by the more general title of "king of Elam," of which latter region Yamutbal actually formed a part; even in the native Babylonian tradition of later times Kudur-Lagamar is called "king of Elammat," nor, so far as we can tell from the fragments that have come down to us, does any distinction seem to have been drawn between Elammat and Yamutbal.

And now to return to the letter from Khammurabi to Sinidinam, discovered by Father Scheil, the text of which is given above on p. 173. To my mind the only satisfactory way of translating it is as follows :—

> To Sin-idinam
> give the following order
> from Khammu-rabi:
> the goddesses of Emutbal,
> (5) thy mistresses,
> on the day in which Kudur-luggamar
> shall allow thee to return scatheless,
> when they (the goddesses) are angry
>   with the god, thy creator,
> destroy thou with the warriors
>   which are in thy hand
> (10) the warriors (of the enemy),
> and they (thy warriors) shall then
> the goddesses
> bring back to their abode
> again scatheless.

This rendering seems to me to be, at any rate more grammatically correct than Scheil's, viz.: "the goddesses of Emutbal have I on the day of Kudur-luggamar (*i.e.* on the day of his defeat) given over to thee unharmed ;" for *ushallam*, though it may, no doubt, also be taken as 1st person singular, is certainly in the present tense, and lines 6 and 7 are clearly parenthetical. The situation was manifestly as follows :—

Sin-idinam, probably a grandson of the famous king Sin-idinam (son of Nûr Ramman) of Larsa,[1] had evidently been originally master of Larsa and Yamutbal, but had been deposed by Kudur-Mabug and Eri-Aku. This deposition would seem to have taken place during the reign of Sin-muballit over Northern Babylonia. Many years afterwards Kudur-Mabug was succeeded on the throne by his kinsman Kudur-Lagamar, who, as the poetic fragments tell us, laid waste North Babylonia, but was at length defeated by Khammu-rabi. As a result of this, Kudur-Lagamar was forced to release Sin-idinam, who had been a prisoner in Elam for about thirty years, and it must have been on this occasion that Khammu-rabi dispatched the letter in question, in order that it might be handed to Sin-idinam on his return to Larsa. The goddesses of Yamutbal—now once more a Babylonian possession—were probably statues which had been carried off on a previous occasion by the Elamite king from Dur-ilu to some town in the interior; this was why they "were

---

[1] We also find the name of another Sin-idinam son of Gaish- . . . . . W. A. I., i. 3, No. IX., who is styled "guardian of Ur, king of Larsa, king of Sumer and Akkad." As the title "king of Sumer and Akkad" was not borne by Nûr-Rammân, but is first given to his son Sin-idinam, this second Sin-idinam must have come to the throne after the son of Nûr-Rammân, and it is evidently to him that reference is made above.

angry " (the regular Babylonian expression in such cases) with Sin-idinam's patron deity, the Samas of Larsa, who had been so unreasonable as to allow this to happen. Now, however, that Dur-ilu had once more passed into Babylonian hands, the first concern of the new Babylonian sovereign would naturally be to see that these divine images were brought back again. This is why Khammu-rabi impresses on Sin-idinam that the moment he is at liberty again he must, if necessary,[1] secure their return, by force; a threat to use force in the event of refusal would have been no empty one, now that Chedor-la'omer had been overthrown and that Sin-idinam was backed by his present suzerain, the mighty Khammu-rabi; we may safely conclude, therefore, that the images were speedily brought back to Dur-ilu, and re-instated in their former abode. For the power of Chedor-la'omer had now been broken once and for all. In a great many of Khammu-rabi's inscriptions, the conqueror of Eri-Aku and of Kudur-Lagamar appears as Lord over the whole of Babylonia, for not only does he boast in them of the great canals he has dug and the extensive cornfields he has laid out for the benefit of the people of Sumer and Akkad, but he also describes himself, almost in the same breath, as "Destroyer of adversaries, whirlwind of the battle, vanquisher of the people of the enemy, making strife to cease, conqueror of rebels,

---

[1] *i.e.* should they not be given up voluntarily on Sin-idinam's release. This possibility is provided against in line **8** of Khammu-rabi's letter, by the words, "when they (are still) angry with the god thy creator."

who shattereth warriors like images of clay, and opens up difficult paths " (?).

To complete the picture, we need go no further than the poems in which the memory of the heroes of that period was perpetuated among the Babylonians. Fragments of these poems, discovered by Mr. Pinches, as already mentioned, are preserved in the Spartoli Collection in the British Museum, and formed part of a Babylonian library in the time of the Achaemenides. They are probably copies of earlier originals, belonging, it may be, to a time not far removed from that of Khammu-rabi himself. The longest and most perfectly preserved of these fragments—all three of which take for their theme the inroads of Kudur-dugmal (or Kudur-lugmal, for this is the form which the name here assumes) into North Babylonia—may be freely translated as follows :—

(6) (Obverse:) . . . .
. . . . and pressed on against the august portals
the Istar-door, he unlocked, tore it from its hinges, threw it down in the holy dwelling like the pitiless war-god [1] went he into Dul-makh,[2]
(10) he installed himself in Dul-makh, as he looked on the temple,
and opened his mouth, thus speaking to his men,

---

[1] *Urra* (or *Girra*) *la gamil*, a play on the name Kudur-lagamal (*vide supra*, p. 105). Cf. the personal name *Urra-gamil* in the contract tablets (Meissner, No. 52). [2] Name of the desecrated temple.

unto all his warriors cried he hastily the injustice
"Take away the spoils of the temple, seize its possessions
tear away its bas-reliefs, unfasten its chambers."
(15) Then . . . . and pressed on . . . .
. . . .
(20) and there came in the overseer of the princes, he tore the doors from their hinges,
against En-nun-dagal-la[1] pressed on the enemy with evil intent,
before him was the god clothed in light,
like a thunder-bolt flashed he, the conquered ones trembled,
and the enemy became afraid, hid (?) himself,
and he descended to his priest, as he spoke the command to him
. . . . the god is clothed in light
. . . . . and the conquered ones tremble
. . the En-nun-dagal, take away his diadem
. . . . his house, seize his hand
(30) But [En-nun-dagalla] was not afraid, nor cared he for his life,
. . . . En-nun-dagalla, did not remove his diadem
. . . . . the Elamite proclaimed to the lands

---

[1] *i.e.* against Khammu-rabi; *vide supra*, p. 105 [the Semitic form was something like Kummu-rapaltu].

> . . . the Elamite, the evil one, proclaimed
> to the fields (?)
> . . . .
> (Reverse:) . . . . . . a dish of . . . . .
> When the lurking dæmon (his) greeting. .
> then descended his (evil) spirit who the
> temple . . . .
> the hostile Elamite, when he hastily sent
> misfortune,
> (5) and Bel against Babel evil plotted.
> When right no longer existed, and mischief
> took its place,
> from the temple, the house of the whole
> body of the gods, came down his (evil) spirit
> the hostile Elamite took away his goods
> (9) Bel, who (at other times) dwelt therein, him
> had anger taken hold of
> . . . . ordered destruction
> . . . . . . him had anger taken hold of,
> . . . . . Bel the Manda-tribes the road
> to Sumer
> Who is Kudur-luggamal, the author of evil?
> and he summoned the Manda-tribes. . of Bel
> and laid in ruins . . . . . on their side
> When from E-zidda (in Borsippa) . his .
> (25) and Nebo the guardian of the world caused
> his dæmon to descend,
> down to the country of the sea did they turn
> their face
> I-ne-Tutu[1] who in the country of the sea .

---

[1] Or I-bil-Tutu? Tutu is another name for Bel-Merodach. Hence probably (cf. *ibil* = Sem. *aplu*) Apil-Bel of dynasty B. (*supra*, p. 121)?

and he passed through the country of the sea and set up an evil dwelling-place E-zidda, the everlasting house, its chambers came into distress.

(30) The hostile Elamite, made ready his team
down towards Borsippa turned he his face
and he descended the high-road of darkness
the high-road to Mish(-ki)
the evil-doer, the Elamite, destroyed his wall (?)
the princes . . . . destroyed he with the sword

(35) All the spoil of the temple plundered he
he took their gods and carried them away to Elam
. . . . annihilated their kings,
(they) . . . and filled the land (therewith).

In regard to the form of these fragments there is one point which escaped Mr. Pinches' notice, but which is none the less of immense importance when we come to criticise them as a whole. I mean the fact, discovered by Gunkel and Zimmern, that they are cast in an epic metre, every line being divided into two half-verses, each containing two accented syllables; I have tried to imitate this here and there in the translation (*e.g.* reverse l. 5 "and Bél against Bábel—évil plótted"). The metre alone is enough to show that the fragment in question must have formed part of an *epic poem*, and the same remark applies to the two smaller fragments in which a similar metrical arrangement is also discernible.

The large fragment (Sp. 158 + Sp. II. 962) shows

us the victorious enemy just as he is on the point of looting the Temple of Bel at Babylon. Ennun-da-galla, (Kimtu-rapaltu), *i.e.* Khammu-rabi himself, had taken refuge in the Holy of Holies. But when his pursuers burst open the door, the statue of the god blazed out in dazzling radiance in order to protect him, and Kudur-luggamal, blinded by the glare, was forced to ask the priest to seize the king and tear the royal diadem from his head. Khammu-rabi seems, however, to have been preserved from falling into the hands of the victor by another miracle. Kudur-Luggamal made up for this by plundering the temple (Reverse l. 1—9), and then proceeded to play similar havoc with the temple of the god Nebo at Borsippa (Reverse l. 24—38). In this last passage the fate of Borsippa is manifestly associated with the country of the Sea (*i.e.* Arabia), a name which at that time was evidently applied to the whole region in the direction of Arabia lying to the west of the Euphrates, from Borsippa to the Persian Gulf, and even as far as Bahrein, where began the road leading to the Land of Darkness[1] (reverse l. 32), known also as the road to Mish-ki.[2] The association of Borsippa with the country of the sea is eminently suggestive of the Arabian origin of the Khammu-rabi dynasty.

The only absolutely novel point about the other two fragments lies in the fact that they both contain

[1] Cf. the date of the contract tablet quoted on p. 35 *supra*, Meissner, 77.

[2] From Mash-ki, *i.e.* Ki-mash, elsewhere simply Mash, in Central Arabia, cf. pp. 34, 35, and 38, *supra*.

a reference to a fresh personage, viz., Dur-mach-ilâni, son of Eri-Aku of Larsa, with whose name the reader must by this time be familiar; one of the fragments also mentions—in a context which is unfortunately obscure—a certain Tudkhula (written Tu-ud-khul-a) son of Gaz-za . . . . . who can of course be no other than Tid'al (properly Tidghal), king of the Goiim,[1] whose name occurs in Gen. xiv.

And now let us examine one of these two smaller fragments, Sp. III. 2, a little more closely. It is only from line 9 on the obverse side, onwards, that we can make any sense out of it.

       it did Dur-mach-ilâni, son of Iri-Aku overthrow
(10) . . . plundered, waters (came) over Babylon and Bit-Saggil
his son (?) with the sword of his hand, slew him a lamb.
. . . in order to . . . . old and young with the sword
. . . *tur-gu-di-is* (*vide supra*) Tudkhula, Son of Gazza . . . . . .
. . . . . plundered he, waters (came) over Babylon and Bit-Saggil
(15) his son with the sword of his hand struck down his skull
the . . . of his guardian office (?) before the goddess Anunit (brought he?)

On the reverse side the inscription is still more fragmentary, as may be seen from the following lines—

[1] Cf. the word Tur-*gudis* (?) which immediately precedes the name Tudkhula.

AS ILLUSTRATED BY THE MONUMENTS 185

(1) [the king] of Elam the city . . . . . on
the high-road (?) of the land Rabbâtu
plundered he
. . . . like a whirlwind made he his *zuhâti*,
the land of Akkad, all their holy places
. . . . . held back Kudur-dugmal his son,
with the iron dagger his middle
his heart transfixed (?) he,
. . . . . his enemy, Nabu-kima-ab'i-shar-
rani (?), *pirûtu* (scion?) of the
Sinners (?) . . .
(5) . . the majesty (?) of the king of the gods,
Merodach, was wrathful over them . .
. . . . me (?), their breast
anathema (?)
. . . . in order to destroy . .
they all to the king, our (?) Lord,
. . . . of the heart of the gods were firm
Merodach, in memory of his name
. . . . . and Bît-Saggil . . to his
place may it . . .
(10) . . . . this the king my
Lord . . .

The metre seems to be the same as in the large fragment, except that in this text each line evidently contains more than two half-verses: probably, therefore, there is more matter missing on the left than is indicated in the above tentative translation. As to the subject matter, the scene of the Elamite depredations is here again laid in North Babylonia, Babylon and its chief temple Bît-Saggil being specially mentioned. One very peculiar thing about it is the name of the son of Eri-Aku,[1] viz., Dûr-mach-ilâni, *i.e.* "great wall (construct form of a word *durmachu*) of the gods." As no son of Eri-Aku is anywhere mentioned in contemporary texts, and as the name looks very like that of a place, there being absolutely no parallel to it among Babylonian personal names,[2] we are almost tempted to believe that it must be due to the creative imagination of the poet; or can it be possible that the fact of Eri-Aku being son of K*udur-M*abu*g* of D*ur-ilu* (Yamutbal) may have led the writer to invent for him a son named *Dur-m*ach*-ilani*? One thing, however, is clear, in spite of the mutilated condition of the text, and this is, that both this son of Eri-Aku's and the Tudkhul whose name occurs immediately after the second reference to plundering, must have been auxiliaries and allies of Chedor-la'omer's. On the obverse, line 15, it is not quite clear whether the words "his skull" refer to a sacrificial victim or to a Babylonian, and line 3 on the reverse is no less obscure: it might also be rendered thus: "Kudur-dugmal, his (*i.e.* some Babylonian's) son, stabbed he through the heart": it is not, therefore, necessary to argue, as Pinches does, that Chedor-la'omer was guilty of murdering his son. It is much to be regretted that the name of the town in the first line of

[1] Phonetically: Eri-E-a-ku, or Eri-I-a-ku, (*vide supra*, p. 169).

[2] The nearest approach to it is in names such as Nabu-dûrpanîa (Neo-Babyl.), Durî-Assur, Istar-dûri, Dûri-ma-itti-Rammân. But their meaning proves these names to belong to a different category from Dûr-mach-ilâni; the discrepancy would not be so great if the name were even Durmachî-ilu.

the reverse is missing; by "the land Rabbâtu," possibly either Rabbat-Ammon in the region east of the Jordan (cf. Gen. xiv.), or Khani-rabbat to the north of Mesopotamia, may be intended. If the translation "on the high-road to Rabbât" be correct, it is possible that the town whose name is missing must have been situated somewhere in Babylonia.

We now come to the last fragment, Sp. II. 987. Here again little more than an attempt at translation is possible.

. . . . band (bolt?) of heaven
which toward the four winds . .
(5) he appointed for them as a *shirtu* which in
Dintir (= Babylon), the city of renown
(is to be found)
he appointed for them the possession of Eki
(*i.e.* of Babylon) small and large.
In their everlasting decree for Kudur-
Dugmal, King of Elam
preserved (?) they . . . "Well then, what
to them seems good [will I do?]
in Eki the city of Karduniash, will I exercise
sovereignty"
in Dintir, the city of Marduk, king of the gods
laid they . . . . . .
(10) *shukullu* and dogs of Bît-Khabbâtu,[1] to whom
he is favourable
they carved . . . . . . of a flying raven
which he loves (?)

---

[1] *i.e.* House of the Robber; as the Bedûin are elsewhere described as robbers (Khablâtu), it is probable that the desert is here intended.

while a croaking raven who spits out gall,
he cannot endure,
a dog, who gnaws bones, him doth Nin(-ib?)
love
but the snake of the Bedûin which spits out
the poison, he cannot endure
(15) Who is then the king of Elam, who maintains
Bit Saggil?
. . . . the inhabitants of Eki made it
and their embassy [sent they]
the . . . . . which thou writest thus,—" I
am a king and the son of a king "
is not [true]
[who] then is the son of the king's daughter
who seats himself on the throne
of the king
Durmach-ilâni, the son of Eri-Ekua (and)
of Amat-(Istar)
(20) has seated himself on the throne of sovereignty
but before the [judges]
may [the sentence] of the king be published,
which from time immemorial . .
is proclaimed, the Lord of E-ki, they do not
confirm (?) . . .
[in] the month of Sivan, in the month of
Tammuz were made in Babylon . .
. . . .

In spite of the obscurity of many of the expressions employed in this fragment, it seems to clearly establish one fact, viz., that the Elamites had succeeded—at any rate in the opinion of the writer of the Epos—in securing a temporary foothold in Babylon. And, evidently, Chedor-la'omer had proclaimed the son of Eri-Aku king in place of Khammu-rabi. The question as to who was the son of a king's daughter, is apparently ironical, for an inscription of Eri-Aku's, published by Winckler, states that his wife Amat-Istar was the daughter of a certain Arad-Uru-ki, who, since no title is inserted after his name, was manifestly not a king.

It is thus that the mighty conqueror Chedor-la'omer is represented in the later Babylonian tradition. Now, if we assume—an assumption which has already been shown to be for other reasons inadmissible (cf. pp. 162 *et seq.*)—that some post-exilic Jew obtained the facts set down in Gen. xiv. from Babylonian sources, we must further assume that he also had before him an ancient Israelite tradition in which Abraham was connected either with Khammu-rabi or, it may be, with Chedor-la'omer. For, manifestly the Babylonian priests could not possibly have known anything about Abraham ; how then did they come to pitch on Chedor-la'omer, Eri-aku and Khammu-rabi, when questioned by this hypothetical Jew as to the political surroundings of the patriarchal epoch of his race ? There were plenty of other Babylonian kings who had made expeditions into the " countries of the West." The kings of the Tel el-Amarna period, for example, distinguished by their diplomatic embassies to Palestine and Egypt, would have been far more likely to occur to the mind of a Babylonian. Or, must we go so far as to assume that the Jew asked point-blank for information concerning the events of the period about 1950 B.C. (*i.e.* of an epoch nearly 1550 years before his time)? Even had he done so, there was little likelihood of his hearing anything about Khammu-rabi, since, as we have seen, the Babylonians of a later time, owing to their mistake in adding Dynasties A and B together, antedated this monarch by at least two hundred years (viz. 2150 B.C.). Or, as a last hypothesis—if the real object of the whole narrative in this chapter was to furnish a peg on which to hang Melchizedek's salutation and blessing, our Jew's most natural course would have been to ask about Melchizedek and any relations which may have subsisted between him and the Babylonian kings. And even assuming that the Babylonian priests knew anything at all about Melchizedek or about any of the kings of the Jordan basin contemporary with him—which is by no means probable—would not this very fact prove the existence of an historical tradition connecting a known contemporary of Abraham with Khammu-rabi.

Fortunately, however, it is not necessary to resort to indirect reasoning of this kind. The narrative in Gen. xiv. differs in some of its details not only from the account which we glean from contemporary inscriptions, but also—and to a far greater extent—from the later Babylonian tradition; it introduces into the history of Khammurabi as presented in the ancient monuments an entirely new episode, which fits into the political circumstances of the period like a missing fragment, and thus completes, and throws a most valuable light on, the knowledge of this remote epoch which we gather from the cuneiform records. The theory that the names of the

AS ILLUSTRATED BY THE MONUMENTS 191

kings, together with the fact that Chedor-la'omer had once led an expedition into "the countries of the West," were transferred from Babylonian records in *post-exilic* times, and that a campaign on the part of the four allied kings as far as Ailat and Kadesh-barnea was then *invented*, is absolutely inadmissible. The material handed down to us in Gen. xiv. is neither more nor less than genuine and ancient tradition.

In regard to the source from which Gen. xiv. was derived, the balance of probability inclines—as has already been indicated above (p. 152)—in favour of a cuneiform original. An original moreover, dating not from the post-exilic period but from Jerusalem, in or soon after the time of Abraham, a Hebrew translation of which must have been incorporated into the main stock of the Pentateuch at a very early date. We now know for a fact that the cuneiform script was employed in Palestine, and especially in Jerusalem, as early as 1400 B.C., being a survival of the supremacy previously exercised for so many years by Babylon. That this must have been so, and that Gen. xiv. must therefore have been originally inscribed on a clay tablet, follows directly from the form of the name Amraphel. Had the narrative come originally from a Hebrew source, and been written down in the West-Semitic script (*i.e.* in the so-called Phœnician alphabet) this name must inevitably have appeared as '*Ammî*-rab (with initial 'Ayin), as the earliest Hebrews were familiar with names compounded with "'Ammî"; we must not forget, moreover, that the Arabs, from whom Khammu-rabi was descended, were their near relations. The form A*m*raphel, on the other hand, can only be explained on the supposition that the original of Gen. xiv. contained the reading *Ammu*-rapal(tu). But such a reading as *Ammu*-rapaltu could not possibly occur except in a cuneiform text dating from the time of the Khammu-rabi dynasty, for at that period alone do we find the variants *Ammu*-rabi and *Ammi*-rabi side by side with *Khammu*-rabi; that the second element *rabi* was actually regarded, in Khammurabi's time, as an ideogram equivalent to *rapaltu*, is evident from the Babylonian form Eki + *rapaltu* [1] [see p. 105], with which the variants of later times, Kimtu-rapashtu and Kummu-rapaltu, are connected. But even should it be objected that the remarkable resemblance in sound between the *-raphel* in Amraphel, and *rapaltu* [2] (otherwise *rapashtu*), is a mere coincidence, there is a second and eminently noteworthy consideration which also points to a cuneiform original for Amraphel. If we assume that in the supposed Jerusalem original the name may have been written Am-mu-ra-bè (instead of Am-mu-ra-bi), then, since the symbol *bè* [3] not infrequently

---

[1] Eki = probably *Ammu*. Cf. Sumerian *ki* = earth and Semit. *ammatu* = earth.

[2] For the benefit of those who are not Assyriologists, I may explain that the feminine of *rapshu* = broad, is *rapashtu;* this the laws of Assyro-Babylonian pronunciation (especially in the common language of the people) transformed into *rapaltu*.

[3] This is really the neo-Assyrian symbol *ne*, which possessed the value *be* (or *bi*) only in the second millennium B.C. (*i.e.* in the time of the Khammu-rabi Dynasty and Tel el-Amarna period). Although in the Khammurabi records, the name of Khammurabi himself is always writ-

possesses the sound-value *pil* as well, the scribe who translated the original document into Hebrew may —especially if the name did not happen to be familiar to him—very easily have read it as Am-mu-ra-pil, which is identical, consonant for consonant, with Amraphel. Be this as it may, the first part of the name is, in any case, sufficient to prove the nature of the original source of the fourteenth chapter of Genesis, which *we*, of course, possess only in its Hebrew form.

I have already (p. 164) laid stress on the fact that the name Chedor-la'omer also points to an earlier period; for, as we have just seen, the early form in the contemporary monuments is Kudur-luggamar, while the later form which survives in the Epos is Kudur-dugmal or Kudur-luggamal.

Moreover, the ancient name for Zoar in Gen. xiv. 2 and 8, viz. *Bela'* (LXX. Βαλάκ), which nowhere else occurs throughout the whole of the Old Testament, also presupposes a cuneiform original, dating from the Ancient Babylonian Empire. Somewhere in the "countries of the West" there was an ancient city named Malkâ, also called Margu, Malgû, Malagû, Malgî or Milgia. It is probably identical with the Madga of the time of Gudêa, which is associated with a river named Gurruda (the Jordan?) as a place from which asphalt was obtained. For this reason the Babylonians came to use the word *malgû* as a synonym for brick (because it was customary

ten with the ordinary symbol for *bi*, it is quite conceivable that a Canaanite scribe may, in writing Khammurabi, have employed the other symbol for *bi*, which can also be read as *pil*.

to lay bricks with asphalt in place of mortar). In the dating of contract tablets of the Khammu-rabi dynasty reference is made to the demolition of the walls of the city of Maïr and of the city of Malkâ (Meissner, No. 27); Maïr was a famous port which gave its name to ships and textile fabrics,[1] its patron goddess being "the Mistress of the Desert," and was probably identical with Ailat (El Pa'rân, Gen. xiv). In the British Museum there is a tablet from the library of Assur-banipal (K. 3500) in which the ancient Assyrian monarch Assur-bel-kala,[2] son of Tiglath-pileser I. (ca. 1100 B.C.) calls down maledictions from deities of all degrees on the "countries of the West." I am indebted to the unselfish kindness of my old friend Pinches for an accurate copy of this important document. It runs as follows:—

(2) the goddess Ishtar . . . .
     the goddess Gula, the great healer (f.) . . .
     with destructive blindness may she their
                    (*corum*) bodies [punish]
(5) the seven (?) mighty gods, may they with
                    their weapons . . . . .
     the god (of) Baïti-ilâni (Bethel, cf. Gen. xxxv. 7)

---

[1] Cf. the analogous expressions, "Tarsis-ships" and "East Indiaman."

[2] Unfortunately the name of the king is not clearly written, and of his father's name only the first element, *Tuklat*, has been preserved. It is just possible that Assur-natsir-pal, son of Tukulti-Nindar, who flourished at the commencement of the ninth century B.C., may be meant, though, on the evidence, I consider this the less probable hypothesis; Assur-bel-kala mentions the gods of the "countries of the West" (*vide* my history of Babylonia and Assyria, p. 536).

AS ILLUSTRATED BY THE MONUMENTS 195

may he with the hands of a ravening lion . . . . .
the great gods of heaven and of the earth,
the gods of *Ébir-nâri*[1] may they with an irrevocable curse curse [them].
(10) Ba'al *samêmi* (the Baal of Heaven), Ba'al (of) Malagî, Ba'al-za-bu (*-bi* or *-na*?)
May this wind with ships from . . . .
chariots their (*carum*) names des- . . .
their (*carum*) . . . . a mighty flood with . . . . .
may them (*eas*) des- . . . . a great inundation over you [come]
the god of Milgia and he (of) Yasumûnu[2] may they your land to. . . . .
(15) Your people (may they) to spoliation hand over, from your land . . . .
the water in your mouth. the fire on your hearth
the oil when you anoint yourselves, may they destroy
the Astartu may she in the mighty combat the bow . . . . . .

---

[1] Literally, "the (far) bank of the river," meaning, probably, the Jordan. I shall have something more to say hereafter in regard to this important word, which, in the Persian era, was used of Palestine itself.

[2] Hebr. *Yeshimôn* (*i.e.* desert), in the region east of the Jordan; cf. also the personal names Isimanai (Meissner, No. 35) and Isimmanum (Meissner, No. 87), in the time of Abraham and the Arab tribe, Mar-Sîmâni (from Mar-Isîmânai?) in the time of the Assyrian monarch Sargon.

make herself to place   ...   The enemy
may he divide (your) booty
the city of Pi-a-ki (?)-li (?), the *kunnu* of
Kalu[1] king of . . . . .

This interesting tablet clearly shows that the city of Malgû must have been situated in Palestine, and very probably in the region east of the Jordan. If we add to this the fact that in the clay tablets of the time of the Khammurabi dynasty the distinction between the symbols *ma* and *ba* is often very slight, we can readily understand how the Hebrew who transcribed the Babylonian original of Gen. xiv. may have come to render the place-name Malgû or Malagî by Bela' (pronounced Belag, cf. Chedor-la'omer and Kudur-lagamar). Moreover, the earliest form of the name of the city was certainly Melakhi (from *melakh* = salt); the expressions " Salt Sea," " Valley of Salt," " City of Salt " (at the southern extremity of the Dead Sea), " Pillars of Salt," etc., are applied throughout the Old Testament to this locality. It was from this form that the Babylonians obtained their name Malagî or Malgû, etc., which afterwards found its way back into the pages of the Old Testament, in its faulty transcription Bela'.

The name El Pa'rân (otherwise Elat), Gen. xiv. 6, also probably owes its existence to a similar erroneous reading. For if Maïr—as I have shown to be probably the case—is to be identified with Elat,

---

[1] With strong *k*-sound; on the reverse, where only one or two fragmentary lines are still decipherable, in addition to the Assyrian king, a certain king of Tsur-ri (*i.e.* Tyre) is also mentioned, though, unfortunately, his name has been broken off.

there seems good reason for assuming that the symbols *ma* = ship (Semit. *elippu*) and *ir* = city (Semitic *alu*, but *eru* also, cf. Hebr. *'ir*), in the cuneiform original, may have been wrongly taken for *Elip'-ir*—a word which contains all the radical consonants of El-pa'r (ân);[1] and as the adjoining desert bore the name of Pa'rân, popular etymology would soon amplify this into El-pa'rân, especially as the added *ân* is merely a suffix, and does not form part of the actual root.

I frankly admit that what I have just said in regard to Bela' and El Pa'rân is mere conjecture, though, none the less, probable conjecture. It is, therefore, all the more necessary to lay emphasis on the fact that the name-form Amraphel for Khammurabi is in itself amply sufficient to permit—nay more, compel—us to assume that Gen. xiv. is based on a cuneiform original of the Khammurabi period, produced in Palestine. And this fact, like the other historical statements on which light has been thrown in the present chapter, goes to prove, as conclusively as possible, that Abraham was a contemporary of Khammurabi.

We now see, for the first time clearly, the obvious relation between Abraham and the conclusions in regard to the religious history of the Hebrews which we were able to deduce, in Chapter III., from the Arabian personal names of the Khammurabi dynasty. They form, as it were, an effective

---

[1] It is important to remember that the Hebrew script consisted from the outset of consonants only, so that in pronouncing a word like '*lp'r* (from Babylonian Elip'-ir) any vowels might be used.

back-ground to his history, and confirm in a manner, which is little short of marvellous, the accuracy of the details supplied by the Biblical tradition in regard to the Friend of God, and his escape from the contagion of Babylonian polytheism.

When we find that the modern critics of the Pentateuch, even in the face of such facts as these, still continue to write in the tone adopted by Wellhausen in 1889,[1] in the passage quoted below, and when we see that the ultimate outcome of the investigations of these critics is nothing more than a series of fresh variations of the old theme, that "literary criticism proves Gen. xiv. to be of very recent date" (Wellhausen, *Op. cit.* p. 312), we can only regard it as additional proof of the hopeless bankruptcy of their theories. The passage in question reads as follows—

> Nöldeke's criticism (of Gen. xiv.) remains unshaken and unanswerable: that four kings from the Persian Gulf should, "in the time of Abraham" have made an incursion into the Sinaitic Peninsula, (he forgets the history of Gudêa and of the ancient Sargon,) that they should on this occasion have attacked five kinglets on the Dead Sea littoral and have carried them off prisoners, and finally that Abraham should have set out in pursuit of the retreating victors, accompanied by 318 men-servants, and have forced them to disgorge their prey—all these incidents are sheer impossibilities which gain nothing in credibility from the fact that they are placed in a world which had passed away.[2]

[1] *Die Composition des Hexateuch's*, 2nd ed. (with Appendices) pp. 310—312: Gen. xiv.
[2] Wellhausen, *Op. cit.*, p. 311.

AS ILLUSTRATED BY THE MONUMENTS 199

At first, we were assured that the names of the four kings had been invented hap-hazard, and that Jerusalem could not possibly have been called Salem before the time of David, since prior to that date its name had been simply Jebus; the critics instead of thankfully accepting the testimony of tradition which declares that such kings *did* exist in Abraham's time, and that the name Jerusalem was even then current, had ignominiously to withdraw their false conclusions in presence of the monuments proving the kings' names to be correct, and the Tel el-Amarna tablets shewing that even in the year 1400 B.C., *i.e.* prior to the time of the Judges, Jerusalem was known as Urusalim. This last name was probably written Uru-sa-lim in the cuneiform original of Gen. xiv. (the element *Uru* being indicated by the Sumerian ideogram *uru* = city). It is possible, therefore, that the scribe who translated the document into the Canaanite idiom of Jerusalem may—as he mechanically transliterated the name—have taken the *uru* for a meaningless determinative. Or —and this is equally possible—it may have been the practice in those days to use the abbreviated form Shalem in place of Jeru-Shalem. And here I may remark that the very latest date at which this translation of Gen. xiv. can have been made, must have been just before the occupation of Canaan by the Israelites, or, in other words, some time during the life of Moses, for after that date there were no writers to be found in Canaan who were familiar with the Babylonian script and language. And now that the objections raised in regard to these points by the critics of the Pentateuch have been demolished, they will doubtless bring forward their old argument that Abraham is not an historical personage: they will assure us that monotheism of such an advanced type was unknown in pre-Mosaic times, and that Abraham must necessarily be the creation of a much later period. But even this false assumption must utterly collapse in view of the evidence afforded by the Western Semitic nomenclature of the very period in which Abraham lived. These names are absolutely free from the slightest taint of Fetishism or Totemism. On the contrary, as I shall prove in detail hereafter, they are trustworthy land-marks, which enable us to follow the evolution of the religious history of the Israelites from Abraham to Moses, and again from Moses to David. They serve to bring the truth of the Ancient Israelite tradition into an even stronger light than that shed by other external historical evidence, scant enough it is true, in so far as the Mosaic period is concerned, though even this latter demonstrates clearly and emphatically enough the absurdity of supposing the compilation of the Priestly Code to be the work of post-exilic times. I intend to bring forward conclusive proof of this absurdity in the eighth and ninth chapters.

CHAPTER VI

JACOB THE ARAMAEAN

MIDWAY between Abraham and Moses stands the figure of the Patriarch Jacob,[1] (described in Deuteronomy xxvi. 5 simply as the Aramæan), though it is true that the interval between Abraham and his grandson Jacob is a good deal shorter than that which separates Jacob from Moses. As the reader is aware, those of Abraham's kinsmen who remained behind in Haran are coupled in Genesis with the Aramaeans, and later on, we find Isaac, and more particularly his son Jacob, again associated with these Aramaean kinsfolk. Whereas the Ammonites and Moabites (*i.e.* the later stratum of the races who inhabited the region east of the Jordan) traced their descent from Lot, the companion of Abraham, and a great part of the Arabs (Ishmaelites and Keturites) from Abraham himself, the genealogical tradition refers the semi-Arabian Edomites back to Isaac, and thus makes them out to be, as it were, the brothers of the Israelites (Esau = Edom, Esau's brother Jacob = Israel). Jacob, however, as Dillmann well expresses it,[2] is allied with " a fresh strain from Ara-

[1] As to the name Jacob *vide supra* pp. 95 and 110. In the Babylonian contract tablets we find in addition to Ya'kubi-ilu, the abbreviated form Yakubu also.

[2] *Handbuch der alttestamentl. Theologie* (1895), p. 80.

maic Mesopotamia, who with the remnant of the original Hebrew settlement in Canaan went to make up the twelve tribes of the people of Israel." According to Dillmann, it was Jacob who "made his home at Padan-Aram (as Haran is called in the narrative of the Priestly Code), right in the heart of his kinsmen, so that, practically, he may be said to have drawn round him the last remnant of the Hebrews who had not yet been merged in the Aramaic stock, and to have led them into Canaan," and from thence on to Bethel; "it is only at the end of all these wanderings that Genesis places his reunion with Isaac and his people in the south at Hebron (Gen. xxxv. 27—29)". It is for this reason that Jacob, as stated above, is specially described as an Aramaean, a term which we never find applied to Abraham.

In view of this circumstance, it will not be amiss to give here a few details concerning *the early history of the Aramaeans.* In regard to their language, it was undoubtedly, in Jacob's time, merely a dialect of Arabic. What we now call Aramaic did not come into existence till a much later date. The Biblical Aramaic (sometimes wrongly named Chaldaean) and Syrian (or to be more precise, the language of the Christians of Mesopotamia) really belong to the Persian and Christian eras, and even these idioms are much more nearly related to the Arabic, in their grammar and vocabulary, than they are to the Canaanitish (Phœnician and Hebrew). The earliest Aramaeans mentioned in the inscriptions were a purely nomadic race whose personal names present characteristics exactly similar to those found in Arabian nomenclature. It is, therefore, fairly safe to conclude that at that time (*i.e.* in the second millennium B.C., and—to a certain extent —even down to the palmy days of the Assyrian Empire) they formed an integral part of the great Arabian people.

We possess three important sources of information in regard to the history of the Aramaeans. First of all, the cuneiform monuments; secondly, the Biblical tradition; and thirdly, the earliest Aramaic inscriptions. These last, however, do not date back further than the end of the 8th century B.C., and we are, for the present, concerned with an earlier period.

From the ancient Assyrian monuments we learn that as far back as the 14th century B.C., in the time of the Assyrian king Budi-ilu (Bodi-el), an Aramaic tribe called the Achlami gave the Assyrians a good deal of trouble. Salmanasar I. (ca. 1300) made more than one campaign against the Aramaeans in Northern Mesopotamia, while Tiglathpileser I. (ca. 1120 B.C.) makes pointed reference to "the Aramaic Achlami" as a race who dwelt in the desert along the banks of the Euphrates from the Shuhite country to a point northwards of Carchemish. These Achlami would seem, therefore, to have been one of the principal Aramaean tribes in the time of the ancient Assyrians. Even under Eri-Aku of Larsa, a certain Achlami (*i.e.* the Achlamite), son of Ilu-ashir, appears in the contract tablets as a witness; at that time they had evidently settled farther to the south. The name is a pure Arabic one (A'lam); in the Old Testament it is probably preserved in Achlamah, the name of one of the precious stones in the High Priest's breast-plate, and apparently also in the name of the Aramaean city Helam (2 Sam. x. 16), where the Aramaeans, who were brought out of Mesopotamia by Hadarezer from the other side of the Euphrates, were quartered. The question now arises, from which part of the Mesopotamian desert or pasture-lands were these early Aramaean collected together, and at what time did this event take place?

In answering this latter question, it is of the utmost importance to remember that in Abraham's time Mesopotamia was known simply as the region of Haran, or Aram Naharaim (Aram of the rivers, cf. Na'arim *supra*, p. 155), whereas in the time of Jacob (ca. 1750) it was called Padan Aram. It would seem, therefore, that according to Biblical tradition, the immigration of the Aramaeans into Mesopotamia must have taken place soon after the death of Abraham, or at any rate during the period between Abraham and Jacob. An important clue is afforded us by the fact that Agu-kak-rimi, one of the Kassite kings of Babylonia (p. 136), who reigned somewhere about 1650 B.C., in one of his long inscriptions styles himself " king of the Kassites and Akkadians (*i.e.* of the Babylonian Semites), king of the vast land of Babylonia, of Ashnunnak (*vide supra*, p. 168) with its countless inhabitants, king of *Padan* and of Alman, king of the Guti (Goiim in Gen. xiv)." Elsewhere, we find Arman (between the cities of Tsab-ban *i.e.*

Opis and Mê-Turnat, *i.e.* the region between the lower Zab and the river Diyâla) and Padin closely connected with one another,[1] just as the cities Tsab-ban (written Ud-ban) and Gish-ban[2] exist from the earliest antiquity; there cannot, therefore, be the slightest doubt that even in the time of Agu-kak-rimi Padan was another name for Mesopotamia, and that the name Padan-Aram (*i.e.* Padan of the Ara-maeans) in the " Priestly Code," which is first em-ployed in connection with Isaac and Jacob, rests on a genuine ancient tradition handed down from the time of the Patriarchs.

In regard to the original home of the Aramaeans, the answer to this question is furnished by a passage in the Biblical narrative, which, though hitherto misunderstood, becomes perfectly clear when viewed in the light of the cuneiform inscriptions of the As-syrian kings.

The prophet Amos, ix. 7, in speaking of Yahveh, says, " Have not I brought up Israel out of the land of Egypt and the Philistines from Caphtor (probably Crete) and *the Syrians* (*i.e. Aramaeans*) *from Kir?* " Now, in Isaiah xxii. 6, we are clearly shewn the direction in which we must look for the unknown land of Kir.[3]

We find there, as a parallel to the sentence, " And Elam bare the quiver, with chariots of men *and*

[1] Cf. W. A. I. v. 12, No. 6, Shaggan (?) of the goddess Pulala, Syn-onym W. A. I. ii. 60, No. 1, line 26, Pan-ki, *i.e.* Gishban and " Shaggan (?), which lies before mount Arman (and therefore in the plain ") = Padin.
[2] The " City of the Bow," which Hilprecht identifies with Haran.
[3] With a strong *k*-sound (*i.e.* like the Hebrew *kir* = wall).

horsemen," the supplementary clause, "and Kir uncovered the shield." From this it follows that the birthplace of the Aramaeans must have been in close proximity to Elam. And, as a matter of fact, the Assyrian inscriptions of the 8th and 7th centuries B.C. mention a whole host of nomadic Aramaean tribes who inhabited the narrow strip of desert between the Tigris and the Elamite Highlands, and who extended from the Persian Gulf in the south-east to Bagdad in the north-west—and even beyond as far as Mesopotamia. These Aramaeans would seem to have offered the same resistance to Babylonian civilization as was always displayed by the Bedûin Arab tribes in Palestine.

The more important of these Aramaean tribes seem to have been the Itu'a, Rubu'u, Charîlu, Labdudu and Chamrânu, on the north-west, and Ru'ua,[1] Li'itâu, Damunu, Chindaru, Ubulu, Pukûdu[2] and Gambulu[3] on the east. Other Aramaean tribes were the Luchu'âtu, Rabi-ilu, Nabatu,[4] Rummulûtu (cf. Arab. *ramal* = sand), Malichu, Kibrî, Rapiku (pronounced with a strong *k*-sound), etc.; one of their districts is also named *Birtu* (Veste) *sha saragîti*, which Glaser rightly connects with the Biblical

---

[1] According to Glaser, the Re'û mentioned in Genesis xi. 19.

[2] The Pekôd referred to in Ezekiel xxiii. 23.

[3] The Arabian Junbula in the morasses of the deltas of the Tigris and Euphrates—cf. Fr. Delitzsch's exhaustive comparison in *Wo lag das Paradies?* pp. 238—241.

[4] The forefathers of the Nabataean tribes who afterward migrated into North West Arabia; the Biblical Nebayoth, on the other hand, are identical with the Nabayâti of the cuneiform inscriptions, cf. GLASER, *Skizze*, II. pp. 12 et. seq., 248 and 274.

Serug (Gen. xi. 21). These names are manifestly of the same type as the personal names of the Khammurabi period, modified, to a certain extent, by later changes in pronunciation. Thus Yatu'a is practically identical with the Arabic Yathu'u;[1] Kibrî is allied with Yakbar-ilu (p. 111), Nabatu with Nabti (p. 142), Rabi-ilu with Ilu-Rabbi (p. 81), Luchu'âtu with the South Arabian Luhai-'Atht[2] and Charîlu is probably another form of Khâlî-ilu (p. 84). It seems quite possible, therefore, that these Babylonian Aramaeans of the Elamite frontier, were descendants of the Arabs who founded the Khammurabi dynasty, or at any rate of that section of them who did not become naturalized Babylonians. Even if there be a difficulty about adopting this conclusion, it is necessary to admit that they must have been descendants of near relatives of theirs. It would seem, then, that from the very earliest times onwards the desert region to the east of the lower Tigris, and also, more particularly, that part of South Babylonia which lay between Shatt-el-Hâi and the Tigris, was the resort of a race of Semitic nomads, who must have originally come from Arabia. The name Su-gir or Gir-su which appears even in the earliest Sumerian inscriptions as the title of the region east of Shatt-el-Hâi is shewn by these alternative forms—Gir-su

---

[1] Mentioned on p. 83. Cf. -yathu'a in Abî-yathu'a, pronounced Abîshu'a in Ancient Babylonian and Ancient Hebrew, while on the other hand we find Abi-yati'u as the name of the chief of the Arabian tribe of Kedar in the time of Assurbanipal (700 B.C.).

[2] Afterwards Luhai'at, just as Rabbî-Atht later on became Rabî'at, cf. also p. 79 *supra*, and [Beer] lahairoi in Gen. xvi. 14.

and Su-gir—to be clearly a compound of two—at one time independent — words, one of which (Su) has long been known as the name of the nomads who dwelt on the lower Tigris and in Mesopotamia.[1] Extended forms of this name Su are found in Suti[2] and Su-bar.[3] The first of these words Suti had, as we learn from the Tel el-Amarna texts, come to be used as a general term for the Bedûin by the middle of the second millennium B.C. In the letters written from Palestine, for instance, the Syrian Bedûin are sometimes called Sagas, sometimes Suti. Both words were borrowed from the Ancient Egyptians, the original form of the first being Sha'asu, of the second Sute (written Sutet). The other word, Subar, therefore, was used more particularly of Aramaean Mesopotamia,[4] the name of the country of Syria being probably derived from a later form Suri. In view of the facts recorded above, we need scarcely hesitate to assert that the other element of the word Sugir or Girsu, viz. Gir, must be the original form of the Biblical Kîr.

The most important point established by an examination of these facts is, that the migration of the Aramaean nomads into Mesopotamia from their original home in Kîr (or Gir), between Elam and Babylonia, must have taken place[5] in the first half

---

[1] The Assyro-Babylonian lists translate Sugir both by "Subartu" and by "Elamtu;" cf. DELITZSCH, *Paradies*, p. 234.

[2] Cf. *Guti* from *Gu*, and Goiim in Gen. xiv.   [3] *bar* = desert.

[4] Cf. *Subartu*, the name of a country, *Shubarû*, the adjective formed from it.

[5] It is at this time, too, (viz. at the beginning of the so-called "La'er

of the second millennium B.C., about 100 years before Agukakrimi, or, in other words, at the very period when, according to the Biblical tradition, the Aramaeans (Jacob and Laban) entered Mesopotamia.

In conclusion, I must not forget to point out that the journey of Abraham and his family from Ur Kashdîm (*i.e.* Ur of the Chaldees), in South Babylonia, to Haran in Mesopotamia, must be regarded as a kind of prototype of that greater migration of the Aramaic nomads which afterwards ensued from the land of Kir into Mesopotamia. Though preceding this latter in point of time, it followed a parallel route; for the road from Ur to Haran lies along the banks of the Euphrates, while that from the land of Kir to Mesopotamia, on the other hand, rather follows the course of the Tigris. Ur was the only Babylonian city of any importance on the western bank of the Euphrates. The narrow strip of country between the Euphrates and the Arabian desert, from Borsippa in the north to the Persian Gulf in the south, and the region between the mouths of the

E.npire,") that we find the name Sute applied by the Egyptians to the Asiatic Bedûin (and then to Asiatics generally), a use of the name which presupposes an advance on the part of the Sute from the lower Tigris into Mesopotamia. Under the Ancient Empire the word Sute (or Sethet) possessed quite a different meaning (cf. Max Müller, *Asien und Europa*) ; the Egyptian *Sute* = Bedûin, Asiatics, is, as Jensen points out, a Babylonian loan-word. In the time of the Middle Empire (*vide supra*, p. 50) *seti*, in spite of its application to the Bedûin of Palestine, would seem nevertheless to have been a common Egyptian word for "archers" (cf. Max Müller) ; or is it possible that the Egyptians may have first heard of the Suti at that date (possibly through the Babylonians who had dealings with Palestine in the time of the later kings of Ur, cf. *supra*, pp. 37 *et seq.*)?

Tigris and Euphrates at the lower extremity of Southern Babylonia, was known to the Babylonians as the land of Kaldu. This name, Kaldu, was originally Kashdu, then (as early as the second millennium B.C.) Kardu, from which the kings of the Kassite dynasty obtained the designation Karduniash, and finally (certainly from the ninth century B.C. onwards) Kaldu (whence the Greek Χαλδαῖοι = Chaldaeans). To this original form Kashdu we owe the Hebrew Kashdim, which is preserved in three distinct traditions, viz. in Urkasdim,[1] then in the synonymous Ar-pa-keshad (Arphaxad),[2] and finally in the name Chesed, one of the tribes descended from Nahor, the brother of Abraham, and mentioned in the genealogical table in Gen. xxii. 22. This at once furnishes us with fresh proof of the fact, that the Hebrew tradition which designates Ur-Kasdim as the original home of Abraham, dates from the beginning of the second millennium B.C., i.e. from the time of the Khammurabi dynasty and of Abraham himself; for a few centuries later, we find the name Kashdu replaced by Kardu, and at the time of the Captivity, Kaldu had long been the only term in general use. The boundaries of the land of Kashdu have already been given; on the south-east they were conterminous with those of the Aramaean tribes who dwelt in the land of Kir. For, in the As-

[1] Spelt with the letter "Sin," which was, however, originally pronounced "sh."

[2] See my note on *The Ethnological Table of Genesis* x. in the *Academy* of Oct. 17, 1896. *Ar-* (originally *Or-*?) corresponds to *Ur-*; as to the *pa* between *Ar* and *Keshad*, see what is said in Chapter ix. *infra*.

syrian inscriptions of the eighth century B.C., the city of Amlilâtu is given as the place of Bît Sha'alli, a minor Chaldaean state, while the same place (written as Amlâtu) is described as the capital of the Aramaean tribe of the Damunu; similarly Sapîya or Shapîa the capital of the Chaldaean state Bît-Amukkan, and Shapî-Bel, the capital of the Gambulu, one of the southernmost Aramaean tribes, are probably designations of the same place. And this must probably have been the case even as far back as the time of Khammurabi; to the east of Ur the pastoral districts of Kashdu must have been directly conterminous with the south-western pastoral area of the so-called Aramaean nomads of Kîr. And here again, it is necessary to lay special emphasis on the fact that these latter did not develop in Mesopotamia into what are historically known as Aramaeans, until later on, and at this time were, so far as language went, still pure Arabs, just as Abraham's people in the neighbourhood of Ur must have been at first. Moreover, the direct geographical connection is clearly established between Arabia and the ancient Kashdu territory—which latter, in its turn, was closely related with the ancient Aramaean home-land, Kir—through the so-called "country of the sea,"[1] which was regarded by the Assyrians as part of Kaldu. This "country of the sea" lay to the south-east of Ur, somewhat to the westward of the modern Basra, and extended apparently as far south as Bahrein.

The subsequent history of the Aramaeans, viz. their advance across the Euphrates into Syria

[1] Afterwards Bît-Yakin, the home of the famous Merodach-baladan.

(Damascus), belongs to the time of David, and is therefore outside the scope of our present inquiry. It was only from this later period onwards that their language began to diverge more and more from the Arabic mother-tongue. In the time of Tiglathpileser III. (eighth century B.C.), we find them advancing northwards as far as Mar'ash on the Syro-Cilician frontier; there, as the Zinjerli inscriptions discovered by F. de Luschan prove, Aramaic contended for the upper-hand with the Canaanitish language. And about 600 B.C., at Teima in North Arabia, where Euting discovered Aramaic inscriptions on monuments of a pure Assyrian type, we find the Aramaic idiom in possession of nearly all the characteristics by which the later Aramaic is distinguished.

CHAPTER VII

PALESTINE IN THE TEL EL-AMARNA PERIOD

THE Patriarchs Abraham, Isaac and Jacob were merely nomadic aliens in the land of Canaan, their stay there being but a passing visit. Their descendants migrated into the land of Goshen in the eastern portion of the Nile delta, where they dwelt four hundred years, until they were led thence by Moses, to wander for forty years through the Sinaitic peninsula and Moab; at length, in the time of Joshua, they reached and settled in Palestine, especially in the portion of it west of the Jordan, which was henceforward to be their permanent home. In regard to the long period during which the Israelites sojourned in Egypt, tradition seems to be entirely silent; only at the beginning and the end of this period does the book of Exodus vouchsafe us any information. We have been amply compensated for the absence of tradition, however, by the discovery of cuneiform records of the correspondence between a number of Egyptian viceroys of Palestine and Syria and the Pharaohs Amenothes III. and IV. (ca. 1400 B.C.). For the purposes of our investigations, it is of the utmost importance that we should learn something of the history of the land promised to the people of Israel, during the time covered by their stay in Goshen; and from these contemporary documents, which are of the highest authenticity, we are able to get a glimpse at the condition of Palestine before Joshua led his people across the Jordan.

In the present chapter we must carry our investigations into the early history of Palestine, which has been already dealt with in Chapter II., a step farther. In that chapter we explained how the Babylonian script and language came to be used as late as 1400 B.C. in correspondence with the Pharaohs, by the people of a country which, though nominally Egyptian, really belonged to the Canaanite branch of the Western Semites (cf. *supra* p. 45). Frequent reference has already been made in the present volume to the Tel el-Amarna texts and the Tel el-Amarna period (as the epoch in question is now generally termed), the last occasion being in Chapter V., when we discussed Melchizedek and the office of Priest-king (*vide supra* pp. 154 *et seq*). In this seventh chapter no attempt will be made to give an exhaustive description either of the geography of Palestine at that time or of the social condition of its people as presented in the texts in question. Those who take a special interest in these matters can obtain full information from various books and treatises on the subject, and especially from Winckler's [1] excellent

---

[1] SCHRADER, *Keilinschr. Bibl.* vol. v. (Eng. Ed. London, 1897); cf. also the instructive papers by H. ZIMMERN, *Palästina um das Jahr 1400 nach neuen Quellen, Zeitschrift des Deutschen Pal.-Vereins*, vol. xiii. (1891) pp. 133—147, and A. J. DELATTRE, *Le pays de Chanaan, province de l ancien empire Égyptien*, Paris, 1896 (extracted from the *Revue des questions historiques*, July), 93 pp. 8vo.

translation (accompanied by a reproduction of the transcribed text), which is now obtainable in both German and English. For our present purpose, our concern will be with answers to the following questions: (1) Was the language spoken in Palestine at that period, the idiom most nearly allied to the Hebrew of the Old Testament, viz. the Phoenicio-Canaanite? (2) What kind of personal names were borne by the native viceroys and princes who were tributary to the Egyptians? and (3) What was the nature of their religious belief?

In regard to the first of these questions, the Canaanisms which occur with comparative frequency in the Tel el-Amarna letters written from Syria and Palestine prove[1] conclusively that in 1400 B.C. Canaanite was a language almost identical with Hebrew. Owing to the fact that the vowels are given in the cuneiform script, we learn, among other things, that even at that time the pronoun "I" was pronounced *anôki*, with the characteristic Hebrew softening of the long *a* into *ô* (cf. Babyl. *anakû*, Hebr. *anôki*), for it was written *a-nu-ki*, which, since the cuneiform script only possesses a single symbol for both *nu* and *no*, can, of course, be read only as *anoki*. Other interesting Canaanisms, which frequently appear in the form of glosses inserted side by side with the Babylonian words, are *abîtu* = I hearken (Hebr. *abîti*, cf. *ushirti* = I send), *ôbel belet* (*vide supra*, p. 155) = Tribute-bearer, *shatê* = Field (Hebr. *sadeh*,

[1] Proof of this fact is also afforded by the Phoenician inscriptions (for the most part of later date), and by the Canaanite loan-words found in Egyptian texts of the so-called Later Empire.

written with the letter "Sin"), *khapara* and *aparu* = Dust (Hebr. *'aphar*), *yidi* = he knows, and a number of other forms beginning with the imperfect prefix *yi* (cf. p. 60 *supra*), *Shamîma* = Heaven (Hebr. *shamayim*), *rushunu* = our head (Hebr. *roshênu*), *tsaduk* = he is righteous, and many others. These forms appearing, as they do, at the end of the fifteenth century B.C., have a most important bearing on the history of the Hebrew language—indeed, it would be more correct to say on the history of the Phoenicio-Canaanite language. For it becomes clearer every day that the Hebrews of the patriarchal period, and even down to the time of Moses and Joshua, did not use the Canaanite speech—a fact which may be readily proved by a careful examination of their personal names;[1] it was not until after the conquest of the region west of the Jordan that they adopted the language of the subjugated Canaanites. This fact is brought out still more clearly by certain characteristic divergences from the ancient Arabic and Hebrew personal names, observable in the early Canaanite nomenclature of the Tel el-Amarna texts, which we will now proceed to briefly examine.

Prior to the discovery of the Tel el-Amarna tablets, we already possessed valuable information on this point, obtained from cuneiform texts of the ninth to the seventh centuries B.C., viz. from the inscriptions of the Assyrian kings. These inscriptions are of special importance owing to the fact that they give the vowels, whereas the Phoenician in-

---

[1] Cf. also what has been said above on pp. 119 *et seq.*

scriptions, which belong, for the most part, to a later period, give the consonants only. We had already obtained from the Assyrian inscriptions a knowledge of such names as Matan-Ba'al, Abi-Ba'al, Adoni-Ba'al (= my Lord is Baal), Azi-Ba'al, Budi-Ba'al (otherwise Budi-el) Ba'al-khanûnu (cf. Carthaginian Hanni-Ba'al, Hannibal)—these all come from Arvad in North Phoenicia—also Abi-milki and Akhi-milki (Arvad, Tyre and southward as far as Ashdod), 'Abdi-milkut (Sidon), Akhi-ram (Yakhir, in Northern Mesopotamia, cf. Hiram of Tyre, in the time of Solomon), Uru-milki (Gebal), Milkiuri (Melchior), Milki-ashapa (Hebr. -asaph), 'Ammi-Ba'al, Sapati-Ba'al (cf. Hebr. *shaphat* = to judge), etc., etc. Apart from the prevalence of the divine name Ba'al, these names contain elements which are either entirely foreign to the earliest Hebrew and Arabic nomenclature, such as *matan* (originally *mattan* = gift?) *adoni* (= my lord), *khanûn* (= beloved), or which, as in the case of *milk* = king (Hebr. *melek*, Arab. *malik*), occur but rarely.

An almost exactly similar view of Canaanite names is furnished us by the Tel el-Amarna letters, the only difference being that in these latter we have the great advantage of being carried back to a period as early as 1400 B.C., that is, to a time when the Hebrews were still settled in Egypt. In these letters we come upon such names as Adon (written Aduna, cf. Adoni-Ba'al *supra*), Milkuru (cf. Milkiuri), Ammu-nira,[1] Abd-milki (or -milkuti?), Abi-milki,

[1] Variant, Khamu-niri, cf. Hebr. Abî-ner and Abner = my father is light, in the time of David.

Rib-Addi (variants, Rib-Khaddi and Rabi-Addi), in which the divine name, usually transcribed as *Addi*, is represented by the ideogram of the Babylonian storm-god (Rammân or Bel), as also in the names Addu-mikhir, Pu-Addi, Mut-Addi, Shipti-Addu, Yapakhi-Addu and Yapa-Addu, Natan-Addu (or Matan-Addi?), Shamu-Addu and Shum-Addi, etc. The name 'Abd-Ashirti (variants, 'Abd-Ashrâti and 'Abd-Ashtarti), is also of special interest to the student of religious history, since it suggests that the deity Asherah, mentioned in the Old Testament, must even at that time have been worshipped in Coele-Syria (cf. p. 156); similarly we find a name, I-takkama[1] (variants, Ai-daggama and I-tagama), which presents some analogy with those [2] mentioned on pp. 115 *et seq.*; in addition, we have Dagan-takala = Dagon helps, and finally Anati (cf. Hebr. *'Anath*, Judges iii. 31), which contains the name of the Canaanite goddess 'Anat. The only thing which surprises us is that the name of Ba'al, the chief of the Canaanite gods, does not enter into a single one of these names. Fortunately, however, we learn from the Egyptian records of the Later Empire,[3] that the principal Canaanite gods of that period

---

[1] Cf. also the place-name, Ya-nuamma (Egypt. I-nu'am), with Abî-no'am, Judges v. 12, and the personal name, Ya-bi'iri (= Yah is my portion?).

[2] The Phoenician form was probably Ai-da'ama = Ai supports or sustains, cf. the name Da'am-melek, which appears in a Phoenician inscription.

[3] *i.e.* in the 18th or 19th dynasty, and therefore to a certain extent contemporary.

were Ba'al,[1] Resheph,[2] 'Anat and Astarte.[3] Now, when we come to reflect that of the above-mentioned names, compounded with the ideographic element Addu (which may also be read either as Rammân or Bel), there is only one, viz. Rib-Addi, in which it is certain that Addu is the correct reading,[4] and that the names Addu-mikhir and Ba'al-maher, Shamu-Addu and Sham-Ba'al, are doubtless identical, there seems ample ground for assuming that in many of the Canaanitish names, Addu is simply an ideogram for Ba'al, this latter name being etymologically equivalent to the Babylonian Bel. In that case we obtain the following additional equations: Shipti-Addu = Sapati-Baal, Addu-dayan = Baal-shaphat, Mut-Addi = Ish-Ba'al and Natan-Addu = Mattan-Ba'al. Hadad[5] was a special name applied to the god Ba'al, the use of which was, in primitive times, evidently confined to North Phoenicia, *e.g.* at Gebal, the birth-place of Rib-Addi; in the time of Assur-natsirpal (9th cent. B.C.), we find this appellation on the Upper Tigris, in the name Giri-Dadi (cf. Phoenic. Ger-Ashtoreth, Ger-melek, etc.), and about the same time, or even earlier, among the Aramaeans of Damascus; in the reign of Tiglathpileser, too, (8th cent. B.C.) Hadad was the principal god of Sam'al in the extreme north,

---

[1] Also in personal names, *e.g.* Ba'al-Ram, Sham-Ba'al, Ba'al-maher.
[2] The Lightning and Storm god, a manifestation form of Ba'al.
[3] Cf. W. MAX MÜLLER, *Asien und Europa*, pp. 315—319.
[4] That in this name it really is equivalent to Addi is shown by the variants, Ri-ib-Kha-ad-di, Ri-ib-Ad-da, Ri-ib-Ad-di, Ri-ib-Id-di.
[5] In the cuneiform texts it appears as Khaddi, Addu and Dadda.

where the population was a mixed Canaanite and Aramaean one. On the whole, therefore, the name would seem to have been first introduced by the Aramaeans; it is never found among genuine Phoenician names, and does not occur even in Egyptian inscriptions of the later Empire. In structure, it is undoubtedly akin to the South Arabian Wadd (p. 79), so that Hadad is probably a later form of Hôdad.

An examination of the Canaanite personal names, preserved in the Tel el-Amarna texts, leads us, therefore, to the conclusion that even as far back as 1500 B.C. the personal names of the inhabitants of Palestine presented essentially the same characteristics of form and meaning as are to be found in Phoenician names of a later period. It was only in Southern Palestine that Arabian names still prevailed, such as Yapakhi (of Gezer) = Yapa'i (cf. Yapi'u. p. 83), Zimrîda (of Lachish) = Zimrî-yada' (p. 83, note 2), Yabni-ilu (also of Lachish), Yapti'-Addu, with the, here, somewhat curious variant, Yapti-Khada,[1] and a few others. An almost precisely similar state of things is to be found among the names of the kings of Southern Canaan in the book

---

[1] Cf. the names Hadad and Be-Dad (a formation similar to Bi-'Ashtar), among the ancient Edomites (Gen. xxxvi. 35); that such names are due to Aramaean influence is rendered probable by the Aramaean origin of many of these ancient Edomite princes mentioned in Genesis xxxvi., e.g. Bela' (= Bil'am of Pethor on the Euphrates, cf. p. 152) and Sha'ûl of Rehoboth of the River (i.e. of the Euphrates). Dinhabah, too, (LXX. Δεννάβα) the name of Bela's city, reminds us of Syria (Dunib in the land of Naharaim, which was the capital of an extensive region); in that case Dinhabah and Pethor would be early variants like Bela' and Bil'am.

of Joshua, where (Josh. x. 3) we also meet with a number of pure Arabic names.¹ Another very interesting fact is that the Egyptian plenipotentiary in Palestine and Syria, who must have been a kind of governor, bears the pure Arabian name of Yankhamu (= Yan'am). Later on, in the time of the kings of Israel, a totally different state of things obtained in South-West Palestine. By that time the Canaanite element had entirely displaced the Arabian, a fact which is proved by the names of the princes of Ashdod, Gaza and Ashkelon.² From this we can see how accurate and trustworthy the tradition of the book of Joshua really is, and how little foundation there is for the distrust with which modern critics are pleased to regard it.

As to the third question propounded on p. 215, in reference to the religious belief which obtained in Palestine at this period, our survey of the personal names has already supplied an answer. Astarte and Ba'al³ hold the first place, the latter frequently appearing under his characteristic names, Adôn = Lord, and Milk or Melek (cf. later Melk-kart) = King, the former under the name Asherah, so familiar to

---

¹ *E.g.* Hoham of Hebron, Pir'am of Jarmuth, Japhi' a of Lachish, and Debîr of Eglon; cf. also Horam of Gezer, LXX. Αἰλάμ. The final *m* in this name being an instance of Arabic mimation; Hoham is identical with the Minaean name *Hauhum* (beginning with the guttural aspirate), and Pir'am with *Pir'u*, which was the name of an Arabian king under Sargon. A more correct vocalization is that in Milkom, the name of the god of 'Ammon.

² Mitinti, Akhi-milki, Khanûnu, Tsil-Bel = Tsel Pa'al.

³ In the majority of these personal names, as already indicated, the ideogram Rammân-Bel, or Addu, can only be intended for Ba'al.

readers of the Old Testament. The goddess 'Anat also occurs, and there are occasional traces of a god named Aï or Ya, who was apparently an Arabian importation, and lastly of a god Yara or Arî,[1] who is probably identical with Ari, in the O. T. Ariel.

When we compare this early Canaanite religion with that of the other Western Semites, as presented to us in the personal names of the Arabs of the Khammurabi dynasty and in South Arabian nomenclature, we are at once struck by the wide and essential difference between them. For though the composition of their personal names is evidently governed by the Western Semitic principles of formation[2] the religion of the Canaanites appears to be thoroughly impregnated by Babylonian ideas, and indeed to a far greater extent than we find to be the case with the religion of the South Arabian peoples. There, as we have seen, the element 'Astar enters into comparatively few personal names, whereas here names compounded with Ba'al (= Babyl. Bêlu) and Astarte are the rule. In Phoenician names (including those of later times), even El is almost entirely displaced by Ba'al and Adon, two divine appellations which never occur in the names of the other Western Semitic races. An explanation of this, as also of the parallel fact, viz. the persistent use of the Babylonian script and language in Palestine until shortly before the time of Joshua, has already been supplied on p. 45 (and, indeed, in the whole of the second chapter),

[1] In Sitriyara and Yishiara, written Zi-it-ri-ya-ra and Yi-ish-ia-ri.
[2] Cf. 'Ammu-nira, Ammi-Ba'al Abi-milki, Abi-Ba'al, etc.

where the fact that the land of Martu was for centuries politically dependent on Babylon is duly emphasized.

If, however, we compare the Hebrew personal names with the Canaanite, the result is exceedingly interesting. Down to the time of Joshua, these appellations present the same features as the Arabian nomenclature of the Khammurabi dynasty and of the South Arabian inscriptions. Then from Moses and Joshua onwards (*i.e.* down to the time of the Judges), names compounded with Yah came into vogue, though others containing elements, such as Ba'al and Adonî, made their way in along with them. Lastly, from the beginning of the monarchical period onwards, names formed with Yah and Yeho (the latter a direct abbreviation from Yahveh), began to displace almost all other forms, and the elements Yeho or Yahu took the place of Ba'al, even in cases where the predicate still remained Canaanitish, *e.g.* Adonî-jah, in place of Adonî-Ba'al, Jeho-shaphat in place of Ba'al-shaphat, etc. In short, these names faithfully reproduce every stage of that traditional religious development of Israel which has received such severe handling from Wellhausen and his school. First, in regard to the religion of the Patriarchal Period, the divine name is El, employed even at that date to the exclusion of other gods, which only very gradually made their way in from Babylon; it appears also in another name for God at the time, El-shaddai, in South Palestine El-'Elyôn: then we have the reform introduced by Moses in connection with the ancient divine appellation Ai or Yah[1]; the original meaning of this name had long been lost sight of, but by transforming it into Yahveh (= He Who exists, *vide supra*, pp. 100 *et seq.* and 114), it is invested, in the account given by Moses, with a new significance; next came the stormy era of the struggle between the cult of Yahveh and the Canaanite cult of Ba'al, a struggle which would probably have terminated with a compromise had it not been for the intervention of Samuel and the other prophets, who were not only enabled to preserve the worship of Yahveh from contamination, but re-instated it also on such a permanent basis, that it successfully withstood frequently renewed efforts of the kings of Israel to effect a compromise.

Before proceeding to a more detailed examination of the time of Moses and the personal names that occur in it, I should like to point out that there is also another aspect in which the fundamental bearing of the Tel el-Amarna tablets on Old Testament Tradition may be profitably considered. This correspondence between Pharaoh and the governors of the cities of Palestine, Phoenicia, and Syria, affords indirect confirmation of a fact already established by other evidence (cf. p. 125), viz., that at that epoch (ca. 1430—1400 B.C.) the Israelites were still living in Egypt, in the land of Goshen.

Before going farther, moreover, I wish to correct, as briefly as possible, a misconception which exists

---

[1] Probably = Babylonian *aï* = "Heaven," but used in the masculine, as a protest against the Babylonian feminine form, Aï.

not only in regard to the area included by the geographical term "the land of Goshen," but also in regard to the kind of life which the Israelites led there, and the degree of civilization to which they had attained. In the first place, the word "Goshen,"[1] in the Hebrew tradition, includes not merely —as is generally supposed—the Egyptian Goshen proper, but also, as is clearly indicated in Joshua x. and xi., a part of the contiguous country of Edom as far as Southern Judah; cf. Joshua x. 41, "And Joshua smote them from Kadesh-Barne'a even unto Gaza, all the country of Goshen (thus the LXX. the Hebrew reading is, "*and* all the country of Goshen"), even unto Gibeon;" and xi. 16, "so Joshua took all that land, the hill country, and all the south, and all the land of the Goshen,[2] the lowland, and the Arabah (desert) and the hill country of Israel and the lowland of the same." In a third passage (Jos. xv. 51), Goshen occurs as the name of a city, with eleven others, situate in the extreme south of the hill country of Judea, somewhere to the west of Ma'ôn (Tel Ma'in), and therefore probably at a point in the extreme north of that part of Palestine known as Goshen. In every one of the three passages quoted from Joshua, the LXX. reading is Gosom (in place of " Gesem in Arabia," the reading in Exodus). Now, at the time of the sojourn of the Israelites in Egypt, the southernmost part of Palestine was still in the undisputed possession of Pha-

---

[1] LXX. "Gesem in Arabia," *i.e.* the Egyptian province of Phakus, in the east of the Nile delta, properly Pa-kesem, abbreviated to Kesem.

[2] Cf. Egyptian Pa-Kesem, also with the article.

raoh, whereas throughout the rest of Palestine, from Hebron and Gaza as far as Syria, the Egyptian supremacy had, at any rate by the year 1400 B.C., fallen entirely into abeyance. It is instructive to note, therefore, that as the Israelite population gradually expanded and split up into separate tribes, the area allotted to it was none other than the Edomite region conterminous with the Egyptian Goshen, a district which still formed part of the Egyptian territory. Here, as we shall see later on, settled the tribe of Asser (Heb. Asher), which was the first to separate from its brethren, viz. in 1350 B.C., in the time of Seti, father of Ramses II., and migrated[1] to its subsequent home northward of Mt. Carmel in the South Phoenician *hinterland*, an example which was probably followed by some of the other tribes as well. It is extremely probable, therefore, in view of the intimate relations between Egypt and Palestine, that the Israelites in the land of Goshen maintained continual intercourse and uninterrupted contact with the latter country, throughout the whole 430 years of their stay in Egypt; the remembrance of the fact that their forefathers had once dwelt in the land of Canaan must have been carefully treasured up in the hearts of the people, and the rapidity with which, after the time of Joshua, they exchanged their Arabic idiom for the kindred language of Canaan, proves that their dealings with

---

[1] It was W. MAX MÜLLER, in his *Asien und Europa*, p. 236, who established the interesting fact that the tribe of Asser settled in Western Galilee as early as the time of Seti and of his son Ramses II., thus setting an example to the other tribes.

Palestine had prepared the way for such a transition.

In the second place, it is quite incorrect to assume that the Israelites were exclusively occupied in pastoral pursuits during their stay in Egypt. Nowhere could they have enjoyed greater facilities for acquiring the arts of husbandry and gardening than in the land of Goshen. And that they actually did combine farming with the keeping of sheep (Gen. xlvi. 34), is perfectly clear from the testimony of the Israelite tradition itself, for in Deut. xi. 10, Moses says to the people, "The land whither thou goest in to possess it, is not as the land of Egypt, from whence ye came out, where thou sowedst thy seed and wateredst it with thy foot[1] as a garden of herbs" (sc. but one which enjoys an adequate rainfall). This is corroborated by a passage in Exodus, i. 13, where we read, "And the Egyptians made the children of Israel to serve with rigour: and they made their lives bitter with hard service, in mortar and in brick and in all manner of service in the field." One of the pet theories of the modern critics of the Pentateuch—one of their accepted dogmas, in fact—is that the Israelites led a rude, uncivilized, nomadic existence in the land of Goshen, shut off from all intercourse with the outer world; some of these critics are willing, it is true, to admit that we have only the evidence of the Jehovistic narrative to prove that they lived thus, and that the Elohistic account rep-

---

[1] By means of water-wheels worked by the foot, such as are still used in modern Egypt.

resents them as intermingling with the Egyptians, and not as a mere pastoral people. The small residuum of fact underlying this theory would seem to be that in the time of the severest Oppression under Ramses II.,[1] a certain amount of segregation may have accompanied the forced labour exacted from the people of Israel: it is scarcely possible, however, that in the preceding centuries this can have been even temporarily the case.

And now to return to the Tel el-Amarna texts. Among all the numerous references to places in Palestine which occur in the letters of Rib-Addi of Gebal (Byblos), Ammu-nira of Be'erôt or Bîrûna (Beirut), Zimrîda[2] of Sidon, Abi-milki of Tyre, Pidia of Ashkelon, 'Abd-khiba of Jerusalem, Zimrîda of Lachish, etc. etc., we naturally expect to come upon some allusion to the Hebrews or to names which are afterwards associated with their history in the time of the Judges. The correspondence abounds in complaints of rebellion and sedition, and especially of the frequently recurring inroads of the Bedûin tribes, who in Syria and Northern Palestine were known as Suti (p. 211, note) and Sagas (p. 210), while in the letters from Jerusalem, on the other hand, they are described as Khabiri. Nowhere do we find a single reference to the people of Israel, or to any of the individual tribes of which it consisted.

[1] It is this monarch who is referred to in Gen. xlvii. 11, where Goshen is called "the land of Ramses."

[2] A name identical with that of Zimrîda of Lachish, and one denoting the bearer to be a native of South Palestine. The two persons are, however, quite distinct.

It is true that some scholars contend that one of
the races just mentioned, the Khabiri, who had at
that time overrun nearly the whole of Southern
Palestine, were really and actually identical with
the Hebrews, even in name. I have already quoted
a passage from one of the letters from Jerusalem (p.
155), in which reference is made to the Khabiri:
from other passages it would appear that a certain
Milki-el and the sons of Labaya had allied themselves with the Khabiri, who were at that time the
foes most dreaded by the kings of Jerusalem. They
had attacked one town after another in the land of
Shîri,[1] and the towns of Gimti-Kirmil[2] and Rub'uti,[3]
had occupied the country as far as Kilti,[4] Gimti,[5]
Ayalûna (Ajalon) and Gazri,[6] and had even—it would
seem from letter, Berl. 199—laid siege to the city of
Jerusalem itself. Abd-Khiba of Jerusalem alone remained loyal to Pharaoh to the last; again and
again he makes urgent application to the Egyptian
government for reinforcements. "If troops can be
sent before the end of the year then the territory
of my lord the king may yet be retained; but if no
troops arrive it will assuredly be lost;" it is thus
that he concludes one of his letters, and similar despairing appeals occur elsewhere.

According to Winckler, Zimmern and others,

---

[1] *i.e.* according to Zimmern, Mount Seïr, *i.e.* Edom.
[2] Gath-Carmel, now Kurmul, south of Hebron.
[3] *i.e.* Kirjath-Arba, or Hebron.
[4] Ke'îla, now Kîlâ, to the north-west of Hebron.
[5] The Philistine Gath.
[6] Gezer, now Tell Jezer, south of Ramleh.

these Khabiri are identical with the Hebrews ('I-bri), since the Canaanite *'Ayin*, with which guttural the word 'Ibri commences, is elsewhere in the texts represented by the cuneiform *kh*, and there are analogous instances of the abbreviation of an earlier form, like 'Abiri, into a later form, such as 'Ibri (cf. *maliku, milku* = king, *namiru, nimru* = panther, etc. etc.). Moreover, Winckler contends that the term Sagas (= Bedûin, Babyl. Khabbâtu = robber), which occurs so frequently in the letters from North Palestine and Syria, is merely an ideogram for Khabiri, and that, therefore, the inroads in question must have been made by the Hebrews. In my opinion, this is an entirely gratuitous and untenable assumption, even should Winckler's identification of the Kha-bi-ri of the Jerusalem letters with the 'Ibri of the Old Testament prove to be correct, an event which I regard as being in the highest degree improbable. A much more likely conjecture is that the Khabiri were the predecessors of the Israelites, but that their name, instead of being identical with the Hebraic 'Ibri (Hebrews), is connected rather with a hypothetical *Khaber;* in any case, their inroads into Palestine have nothing whatever to do with the Israelitish invasion of Canaan.[1] Had the two been

---

[1] Even though Labaya, in a letter to Pharaoh (112, l. 34), employs the general term Sagas (Sha'as = Bedûin) in a passage which, from the context, evidently refers to the Khabiri, this does not warrant us in assuming, as Winckler invariably does, the general term Sagas, in the letters from North Palestine and Syria, to be equivalent to the far more specific name Khabiri (cf. letter 199. 11, *Khabiri-ki, i.e.* the city of the Khabiri). As a matter of fact, the word Khabiri occurs only in the letters from South Palestine, written from Jerusalem.

identical, the sensational fact would lie before us that 'Abd-khiba of Jerusalem had given us really the record of such an event as the conquest of the region west of Jordan, but the existence of any such record would be a severe blow to the credibility of the Old Testament tradition. For in this latter it is not Milki-el who plays the leading part, but Joshua; the first incursion took place, not from Hebron, but from a point to the north of Jerusalem, near Jericho; the name of the king of Jerusalem attacked by the Israelites was not 'Abd-khiba, but Adoni-zedek; of the king of Gezer, not Yapakhi (Governor of Gezer, *Lond.* 49—51), but Horam (p. 220); of the king of Hasor, not 'Abd-tirshi (= 'Abd-kheres?), but Yabin; of the king of Lachish, not Zimrîda, but Yaphi'a. And then, again, there would be an amazing discrepancy between 1400 B.C., the approximate date of the Tel el-Amarna inscriptions, and *ca.* 1230, the time of Ramses, whom we have good reason for regarding (cf. p. 125) as identical with the Pharaoh of the Oppression. The theory that a section of the Israelites may have made an attempt to conquer Southern Palestine, direct from the land of Goshen, somewhere about the year 1400 B.C., which was subsequently followed by the actual effective conquest of the region west of Jordan, under Ramses III., is a somewhat different matter.

Indeed, this latter possibility is, as we shall see, the only one that will even bear examination. But, for various reasons, we may take it for granted that the name Khabiri, which has attained such prominence of late years, is not identical with that of the

Hebrews, and that the resemblance between the two names is purely accidental. On the contrary, it was from the Khabiri that Hebron (formerly known as the Four-town, or Kirjath Arba, Judges i. 10) received its later name of Khebron (originally Khabirân, *i.e.* the city of the Khabiri). In the Tel el-Amarna tablets, we find it mentioned by its old name, *i.e.* Rubûti (= Roba'ôt), meaning "the four quarters [of the city]." It is expressly stated in one of the letters from Jerusalem, that Milki-el and a certain Shuardat[1] had hired the people of Gezer, Gath, and Ke'ila as mercenaries, and with their help had captured Rubûti, and that, as a consequence, the territory of Pharaoh passed into the hands of the Khabiri, Milki-el being elsewhere described as one of their partisans; 'Abd-khiba declares in one passage that Milki-el and the sons of Labaya had delivered the land of Pharaoh into the hands of the Khabiri (L. 103. 29) and in another letter (L. 105. 5) that Milki-el, who had originally been an Egyptian official, had gone over to the sons of Labaya, the ringleader of the rebels. Milki-el and Labaya,[2] therefore, are the personages most prominently connected with the Khabiri, and it was these latter who captured Rubûti (Roba'ôt = Kirjath-Arba). Is

---

[1] In another letter, the names given are those of Milki-el and his father-in-law Tâgi. Shuardat, from its formation, seems to be a name similar to the Hebrew Shu-thelah (Num. xxvi. 36), or to the name Shutatna (elsewhere Za-tatna and Zi-tatna ; cf. Dothan?) which occurs in the Tel el Amarna tablets ; cf. also the name Zi-shamîmi (literally = He of Heaven). The name Tâgi reminds us of Tô'î in 2 Sam. viii. 9.

[2] Variant, Lab'a, cf. the place-name, Leba'ôt in S. Palestine.

it a mere accident that, from the time of the Judges onwards, Kirjath-Arba bears the name of Khebron, and that in the Israelitish pedigrees [1] (which so frequently preserve the memory of past events under a genealogical garb), the names of Heber and Malkiel are coupled together as grandsons of Asher? In another pedigree (Exodus vi. 18), Hebron is mentioned as a grandson of Levi, whose name bears a remarkable resemblance to that of Labaya (pronounced *Lavaya*). In my opinion, these facts tend to prove beyond a doubt that the Israelites possessed some inkling of the events in question—and that we have here another instance of the great historical importance of personal names occurring in those seemingly arid wastes, the Old Testament pedigrees. But if, as is clear from the evidence just adduced, the Khabiri were thus intimately connected with Hebron, and have actually survived in the Old Testament lists under the name of Heber [Kheber], it follows, as a matter of course, that there can have been no identity between their name and that of the 'Ibri (Hebrews).

For our present purpose, it matters little what the original meaning of the word Khabiri may have been. Some scholars regard it as a generic term for an ally, or confederate (cf. Hebrew *khaber* = companion), and possibly they are right. If so, this merely furnishes us with a fresh argument against identifying it with 'Ibri. Others suggest that it may be another form of Khabirai (written Kha-bir-ai), *i.e.* the Khabiraeans, a term used to indicate the inhabitants of

[1] Num. xxvi. 45 and Gen. xlvi. 17, and cf. 1 Chron. vii. 31.

Elam, *i.e.* the Kassites ; thus we find reference to a Kassite named Kudurra, son of Tushur,[1] in a sale-contract of the time of King Marduk-akhi-irba (ca. 1065 B.C.), and also to a certain Kharbi-Shipak in another document of about the same date. In view of the fact that in this latter inscription the town of Zakkalû (*i.e.* the Philistine Dor, the city of Zakkal mentioned in the Egyptian inscriptions), and the Phoenician town of Irikatta (Arka) are mentioned,[2] I was at one time prepared to accept the identification of Khabiri with Khabirai, but I have since come to the conclusion that the similarity between the two names is purely fortuitous. Khabirai really means an inhabitant of the land of Khapir,[3] or Apir,[4] and Khapirai would, therefore, be a more correct transcription of it ; Khabiri, however, is identical with Kheber, in Gen. xlvi. 17.

On the other hand, this latter passage, in which Kheber and Milki-el are made out to be descendants of the Israelite tribe of Asher (Asser), affords us a clue to the real origin of the Khabiri of the Tel el-Amarna tablets. This clue opens out such a vista of interesting discoveries in other directions, that it deserves the honour of a chapter to itself.

[1] Written Ud (?) -ush-shu-ru, therefore the reading cannot be Batsish (Scheil) ; cf. Hilprecht's Edition, B. E., No. 149.
[2] Cf. my *Assyriological Notes*, § 9, in the *Proceedings* of the Bibl. Arch. Soc., May 1895.
[3] Cf. JENSEN, *Zeitschr. der D. M. Ges.*, vol. 50 (1896), p. 246.
[4] Ophir, *i.e.* originally, that part of Elam which lay over against East Arabia, afterwards used of East Arabia itself.

CHAPTER VIII

THE LAND OF SHÛR AND THE MINAEANS

WE have just seen (p. 226) that the tribe of Asher had, after various migrations, settled down in West Galilee, as far back as the time of Seti I. and Ramses II., *i.e.* about 1350 B.C., or only fifty years later than the period to which the Tel el-Amarna tablets belong. It has been shown further, by the evidence of the Biblical tradition, taken in conjunction with the Tel el-Amarna letters from South Palestine, that the Khabiri, who had forced their way in from the south, belonged to this tribe of Asher. They came in the first place from Edom, and the Biblical narrative tells us that the strip of country between Egypt and Judah, that is, the western portion of Edom, somewhere in the vicinity of the region generally assigned to the Wilderness of Shûr and the territory of the Amalekites, was looked upon as an integral part of the land of Goshen. It may, therefore, be assumed that even before the time of Moses a part of the tribes of Israel had either settled down, or possessed pasturage, in the country between Egypt and Judah. Now, if we put all the above facts together, we are led—indeed, I might almost say, forced — to the conclusion that Asher was one of these tribes who had encamped in the north of Goshen, and that the Khabiri invasion of South Palestine marks the initial stage of its subsequent advance northwards.

But, quite apart from the above considerations, there is a good deal of other evidence of various kinds to prove that, even prior to the Tel el-Amarna period, the extreme southern portion of Palestine between el-'Arîsh and Gaza (or Beersheba) had been inhabited by the tribe of Asher. This evidence comes to us from three different sources, which are all the more worthy of credit because they happen to be entirely independent of one another; these are (1) various passages in the Old Testament which have hitherto never been rightly understood, (2) the Egyptian monuments, and (3) the Minaean inscriptions, which last have already been noticed on pp. 76–80, though only in general terms.

Let us first of all examine the passages in the Old Testament somewhat more closely.

In Gen. xxv. 3, there is a genealogical table in which a number of Arab tribes are said to be descended from Abraham, viz. Zimrân, Jokshân, Medân, Midiân, Ishbak and Shûah. While 'Ephah[1] and Abîda'[2] are given as descendants of Midiân—a race frequently mentioned in Biblical history—the sons of Jokshan, on the other hand, appear as *Dedan* and Sheba' (Saba), and the three sons of Dedan figure under the tribal appellations, Ashûrîm, Letûshîm

---

[1] Properly 'Ayappa, the Khayappa Arabs of the time of Tiglathpileser III. and Sargon.

[2] *i.e.* the Minaean king, Abî-yada'," who will receive fuller mention later on.

and Le'ummîm. As the two latter do not appear again, we may dismiss them from our minds and concentrate our attention on Ashûr, the direct descendant of Dedan—indeed his first-born son. The fact that he is affiliated to Dedan is in itself sufficient to prove that Ashûr cannot be identical with the celebrated Assur, or Assyria, a name which is, moreover, introduced elsewhere (in Gen. x. 22). For, according to the Old Testament account, Dedan's dwelling-place was in the immediate vicinity of Edom; the boundaries of this latter region are always described in the stereotyped phrase "from Teman (in the South) unto Dedan," indeed, in early times, Dedan seems to have included the northern extremity of Edom, and it was not until a later period that the caravans of the Dedanite merchants withdrew farther into the Arabian interior. Even in the time of Gudea, alabaster was obtained from the mountains of *Tidanu* (p. 34), and king Gimil-Sin of Ur (p. 37) built a "wall of the countries of the West" (or Martu) which he calls *murîk-Tidnim* = "the wall that wards off the Tidnu."[1] Glaser tells us[2] that in one of the longer Minaean Temple Records discovered by him, there is a reference to the female slaves from Egypt (*Mitsr*), Gaza, Moab, Ammon, Kedar and Dedan, who were consecrated to the service of the deity; three of these Dedanite slaves bear the remarkable names, Bi-mahali-'Uzzâ =

[1] F. Thureau Dangin in Halévy's *Revue Semitique*, 1897, p. 73, note 3.
[2] Cf. my treatise: *Aegypten in den südarabischen Inschriften* in the *Festschrift zu G. Ebers' 60 Geburtstag, Leipzig*, 1897.

by the patience [or favour] of the goddess 'Uzzâ,[1] Kharshu-hâ-na'imat = her sun is lovely, and 'Al-kheresh = over the Sun (?) and a Medanite[2] slave named Maphlitat.[3]

It is evident from this that the Ashûrîm (plural of Ashûr) of Gen. xxv. 3, must have lived somewhere near Dedan — *i.e.* in Northern Edom. There are, moreover, other passages which indicate still more definitely the locality of this land of Ashûr—a name, it should be noted, representing a so-called "broken" or internal plural form of the singular Asher (cf. Arab. A'shûr, *infra*).

In Gen. xxv. 18, we are told of the Israelites that "they dwelt from Havilah (according to Glaser, Central and North East Arabia) unto Shûr that is before Egypt," to which an explanatory gloss in the margin adds, "(*i.e.*) as thou goest towards Assyria [Ashûr]." A later copyist, who evidently knew nothing of an Ashûr lying between Egypt and Palestine, endeavoured to explain the words "unto Ashûr," which he evidently took to mean Assyria, by the further gloss, "that is before Kelakh;" from this arose (owing to association with Gen. xvi. 12, *koll ekhâv*) the meaningless clause, "he abode [fell] in the presence of all his brethren"—a clause which

---

[1] Cf. the man's name Bi-mehal in i. Chron. vii. 33, a grandson of Kheber [Heber], and consequently a great-great-grandson of Asher.

[2] Unless, indeed, the correct reading here also is Dedan, for the first symbol is not very clear.

[3] Cf. the equally Asherite name Japhlet, in i. Chron. vii. 32, and the place-name Japhleti, in Joshua xvi. 3, both of them Arabic in form, for in the Canaanite language the word would be Jiphlat.

has occupied its present place in the text since the time of Ezra. From this, it is clear that Shûr is merely a popular abbreviation of the longer form Ashûr. The ordinary meaning of the word *shûr* in Hebrew being "wall," the name was explained by identifying it with the "Wall of Egypt"; from the position of this "wall" (originally near Tel el-Kebîr, afterwards in the vicinity of the modern Isma'ilia), which consisted of a line of strongholds shutting out the Wady Tumîlat, it is evident that this application of Shûr is mistaken. In regard to the other fortresses situated more to the north-east (to which Zar or Sela belonged), the Egyptians never applied to them the official title, "Wall of the Princes."[1]

In 1 Sam. xv. 7, we find an expression almost identical with this gloss in Gen. xxv. 18, applied to the territory of the Amalekites, viz., "from Havilah as thou goest to Shûr, that is before Egypt," the only difference being that in Genesis the gloss has "Ashûr," instead of, as here, "Shûr." We may, therefore, regard it as certain—especially as the fact is further supported by other passages as well—that the "land of Shûr," to which such frequent references occur, has nothing whatever to do with the Hebrew word *shûr* = wall, for the simple reason that it is an abbreviation of Ashûr. Whereas in

---

[1] Cf. W. Max Müller's exhaustive dissertation on the Egyptian "Wall," in *Asien und Europa*, pp. 43—46. Müller suggests that Zar, the name of the frontier fort, may be an Egyptian transliteration of Shûr: from the way in which it is written, however, it seems more likely that Zar (or Sar) is rather identical with a Canaanite word *sal* = wall (cf. Babyl. *sillu*, Hebr. *solalah*).

2 Sam. ii. 9 (where we find the reading ha-Ashûrî, instead of the more usual ha-Asheri), it is evidently the later territories of the tribe of Asher which are intended. In two other passages (viz. 1 Sam. xxvii. 8 and Jos. xiii. 2), however, where the present Hebrew text has ha-Geshûrî, the earlier and original reading would seem to have been ha-Ashûri (= the Asherites), used as a synonym for the Amalekites. No one now disputes that the Geshur here referred to is not the kingdom of Geshur in Bashan, but another place of the same name in South Palestine; Eduard Glaser was the first to divine this (*Skizze*, ii. p. 458), when he proposed to read ha-Ashuri in place of ha-Geshuri, in both passages.[1] In Joshua xiii. 2 we read, "all the regions (*gelîlôth*) of the Philistines and all the land of the Geshurites, from the Shikhor [Shihor] which is (flows) before Egypt, even unto the border of Ekron northward," where the phrase, "from the [river] Shîchor[2] which is (flows) before Egypt," exactly corresponds with the expression " Shûr which is before Egypt," employed elsewhere. The translators of the Septuagint seem to have read Shûr, or *midbar Shûr* (= wilderness of Shûr[3]), instead of Shîchor, since they render the passage, "from the uninhabited region which lies before Egypt." The name Shîchor, which is here applied to the Wady el-'Arîsh is also of considerable

---

[1] Cf. also my *Aufsätze und Abhandlungen*, p. 9, note 1.

[2] Viz. "the brook of Egypt," or Wady el-'Arîsh, the actual boundary between Egypt and Palestine.

[3] This is the name given in the Old Testament to the desert which lies between el-'Arîsh and the Suez Canal.

AS ILLUSTRATED BY THE MONUMENTS 241

interest, since the Asherites, after their arrival in their new home to the north of Carmel, gave the stream which marked the southern boundary of their territory, the name of Shîchor Libnat (Joshua xix. 26), just as they probably called Mount Carmel after the place designated Gath-Carmel, in their former home in South Palestine. The history of every age furnishes similar instances of emigrants bringing their old place-names with them, and applying them to their new surroundings.[1]

In the other passage mentioned, 1 Sam. xxvii. 8 (as also in 1 Sam. xv. 7, which has already been discussed above), it is the Amalekites who are referred to. We there read that "David and his men went up and made a raid upon the Geshurites and the Gizrites[2] [*al.* Girzites] and the Amalekites: for those *nations* were the inhabitants of the land, from Telam [Marg. Reading R. V., cf. Josh. xv. 24] as thou goest to Shûr, even unto the land of Egypt." The parallel passage in the LXX. is thus to be restored, the only change required being that of $\Gamma \epsilon \lambda a \mu\ \Sigma o \nu \rho$ into $T \epsilon \lambda a \mu\ \Sigma o \nu \rho$, *i.e.* "Telam (which is) in Shûr;" $\Gamma \eta \lambda \omega \mu$ (Hebr. *Gillo*, Josh. xv. 51) having probably suggested $\Gamma \epsilon \lambda a \mu$; as both these places, *i.e.* Telam and Gelom (or Gillo), are situated in the southernmost extremity of Judah.

In both passages, therefore, these southern Geshurites are closely associated with the land of Shûr, and even if we cannot see our way to adopt Glaser's hypothesis that the name is a clerical error for

---

[1] Cf. EDUARD GLASER, *Abessinier*, pp. 17 *et seq.*

[2] This word (= the men of Gezer) does not appear in the LXX. and might very well be omitted.

16

Ashurites, we are not likely to be far wrong in recognizing in the initial guttural the word $gê=$ "lowland"; in that case Geshur would be simply a contraction of Gê-Ashûr or Gê-Shûr. Moreover, we must not overlook the fact that David's raids against the Geshurites and Amalekites are again referred to, in 1 Sam. xxvii. 10, as raids against "the South" of Judah, Jerahmeel and Kain (cf. also 1 Sam. xxx. 29, and in regard to Kain, Josh. xv. 27).

Any doubt which might still remain as to the fact that the land of Ashûr or Shûr extended from the "Brook of Egypt" (Wady el-'Arîsh) to the region between Beersheba and Hebron, is completely removed by an examination of two further texts, viz. Gen. xvi. 7, taken in conjunction with xvi. 14, and Gen. xx. 1, taken in conjunction with Gen. xxiv. 62 and xxv. 11. In the first of these passages, we find Hagar "in the wilderness by the fountain in the way to Shûr," and a few lines later on we are told that the well in question, Lahai Roi, was situated between Kadesh (*i.e.* Kadesh Barne'a) and Bared. Now though, it is true, we do not know the exact position of Bared,[1] yet we learn from the history of Abraham (Gen. xx. 1), that he journeyed into the *Negeb*, or "land of the South," and "dwelt between Kadesh and Shûr," in Gerar, three hours' journey south of Gaza; here, too, dwelt Isaac (xxiv. 62), hard by this same well of Lahai Roi (xxiv. 62 and xxv. 11), near his father Abraham, who died there (xxv.

---

[1] It is probably identical with Berdan in the territory of Gerar, LAGARDE, *Onom.*, 145. 3.

8). It is evident, therefore, that "between Kadesh and Bared," and "between Kadesh and Shûr," are parallel expressions, and that Shûr, from which Gaza cannot have been far distant (cf. *infra* A'shûr and Gaza), must, therefore, have been situated to the north of Kadesh, somewhere in the neighbourhood of Be'er-sheba.

Unquestionably, the most noteworthy of all the passages in the Old Testament which contain a reference—hitherto unsuspected, but none the less indisputable—to the ancient Ashûr in South Palestine, is the " parable" of Balaam against the Kenites (*i.e.* the people of Kain mentioned above), and against Og, king of Bashan; Num. xxiv. 21—24. It runs as follows: "(21) And he [Balaam] looked on the Kenite and took up his parable, and said—

 Strong is thy dwelling place,
 And thy nest is set in the rock.
(22) Nevertheless Kain shall belong to the 'Eber[1]
         ["be wasted," R. V.]
 And however long it may last, Ashur shall
         carry thee away captive;
[and when he saw Og of Bashan (LXX.)], he took up his parable, and said—

 Jackals (*iyyîm*) shall come from the North[2] and wild-cats (*tsîyyîm*) from the coast of Kittîm,

---

[1] I am indebted to Klostermann for this ingenious conjecture (*le-'Eber*, in place of *leba'er*); it completes the parallelism with verse 24, in which the names Ashur and 'Eber already occur.

[2] *missem'ol*, an ingenious emendation suggested by D. H. MÜLLER, in *Die Propheten*, p. 215, though he adopts the translation "from Sam 'al," and evidently has the Zinjerli inscriptions in view.

and they shall afflict (the land of) Ashûr and
(the land of) 'Eber,
and he also (viz. Og) shall come to destruction.

It is clear that Assur, as an equivalent of Assyria,[1] cannot be here intended, and the context makes it equally evident that the relation between the terms Ashûr and 'Eber was of the very closest nature, and that Ashûr here represents that earlier form of the name of the land of Shûr in South Palestine already indicated in other passages—a fact which has been made sufficiently obvious in the course of the last few pages. Under the term Kenites we must include a part of the Amalekites, who are mentioned a few lines earlier. The threatened invasion of the tribes of the North—to which, by the way, allusion is also made in Deut. xxviii. 49 and 50—refers to the so-called "Peoples of the Sea," who, at the very moment of Balaam's prophecy, were setting out from Asia Minor, to invade Syria and Palestine, in the eighth year of the reign of Ramses III. (about 1232 B.C.), a proceeding which threatened dangerous consequences to Egypt. They had made a previous inroad in the time of Minephtah, but now they came accompanied by a number of new tribes, among others by the Pulasati (Philistines) and the Zakkal

---

[1] In the clause "Ashûr shall carry thee away captive," Ashûr evidently refers to the next-door neighbours of the Kenites, and probably also to the subsequent masters of Ashûr, or Southern Judah, the Israelites of the time of the Judges and of David, (cf. *supra*, the passage in 1 Sam. xxvii. 10). By the time of the Kings, the obsolete term Ashûr, as a name for Shûr, was no longer intelligible, and it was naturally taken as applying to Assyria.

(see p. 234), and not merely in ships,[1] but in caravans as well, bringing their wives and children with them on ox-waggons—in short, constituting the migration of an entire people. " No country was able to resist their arms, from Kheta-land, Kode[2] and Carchemish, unto Arvad and Alasia (Cyprus); they annihilated them, and pitched their tents in the heart of the country of the Amorites, whose inhabitants were plundered and whose land was as though it had never been; they came armed and threatened Egypt"—(they must, therefore, have made their way through Palestine as far as the frontier province of Shur)—so runs the Egyptian account of the affair. Egypt itself was in imminent danger of invasion, and Pharaoh promptly made up his mind to join battle with the invaders on the frontier. With the help of his Sardinian mercenaries, he succeeded in repelling the enemy both by sea and land, and seizing the opportunity, he made a predatory incursion into the country of the Amorites, which had already been harried by the " Peoples of the Sea," and was therefore unable to offer any serious resistance. This was the last time for many a long day that a Pharaoh set foot in Syria.

These, then, were the foes whose coming was foreseen by the inspired Balaam, and who were eventu-

---

[1] In Balaam's prophecy there is a play upon this ambiguous word *tsiyyîm*, which is used for " beasts of the desert," or "wild cats," as well as for a kind of ship. Kittim is the familiar term for the Hittites (var. Chittim), and was afterwards specially applied to Cilicia and Cyprus.

[2] District, *i.e.* the territory round the gulf of Issos, cf. Letter Berlin 79 rev. 13; Kuti in a letter of Rib-Addi of Gebal.

ally to penetrate as far as the territories of Ashûr and 'Eber, bringing ruin and devastation in their train. Indeed, this whole prophecy owes all its significance to the fact that it was delivered in the Mosaic period. If we try to apply its predictions even to the time of the kings of Israel, and their political surroundings, they at once lose all meaning; the "parables" of Balaam in general, and this prophecy in particular, are no less deeply impressed with the stamp of authenticity than is the Song of Deborah in Judges v., and they are fully entitled to rank as contemporary records, which—apart from certain obscurities on minor points, due mainly to copyists' errors—have been proved by external evidence to be unquestionably both ancient and trustworthy, thus fulfilling the conditions laid down on p. 25. As a further piece of external evidence, the following may be adduced.

In one of the inscriptions of the Minaean kings, the same indeed which has already been briefly dealt with on pp. 76 et seq. and p. 89, viz. Hal. 535 and 578 —or rather Gl. 1155, since the text now accepted is based on a cast brought home by Glaser—we find a similar parallel drawn between Ashur and 'Eber.

The beginning of this very interesting monument reads as follows:[1]

"'Ammî-tsaduka, son of Hama- (or Himi-) 'Atht of Yapî'ân and Sa 'd, son of the Walig of Dzapgân, the two great ones (kabris or governors) of Mutsrân

---

[1] Cf. GLASER, *Abessinier*, p. 74, and my notes in the *Proceedings* of the 10th Congress of Orientalists, Section II. p. 110; also in the *Zeitschrift der Deutschen Morgenl. Gesell.ch.* 49, p. 527, note 2.

and (of ?) Ma'ân of Mutsrân[1] under the protection (?) of Egypt—and there were engaged with them both in trading operations Egypt, and *A'shûr* (so-called internal plural of Asher) and *'Ibr-naharân*, while of the Kabirate (governorship) of . . . . . . of Ridâ' whose Kabirate precedes (*i.e.* precedes that of the two authors of the inscription in rank)—consecrated and built to the god 'Athtar the platform of Tan 'am, etc."

The *raison d'être* of the inscription is given in the following sentences:

" on the day in which 'Athtar, etc., delivered them and their goods and their emir (leader) from the hosts of [the tribes of] Saba' and Khavilân,[2] by whom they and their goods and their camels were attacked, on the Caravan route between Ma'ân and Ragmat, and during the war which took place between the Lord of Yamnat and of Sha'mat.[3]

" and on the day in which 'Athtar, etc., delivered them and their goods, as they were half-way on their road home from Egypt during the hostilities which took place between Madhai[4] and Egypt, while 'Athtar delivered them and their goods safe and sound as far as the boundary of their city Karnâvu

[1] Or, "and the Minaeans of Mutsrân (*i.e.* probably of Midian).
[2] Cf. Job i. 15 and 17; in the LXX. the reading is, Sabaeans and Khavîlah; in the Hebrew, Sabaeans and Kashdîm; the latter are the Arabs of Bahrein, (cf. p. 211).
[3] *i.e.* of the South and North countries, which Glaser takes to mean the kings of Upper and Lower Egypt, who were then at war with one another.
[4] According to Glaser, these must be the Mazoy or Egyptian patrols on whom the king of Upper Egypt mainly relied.

(which must have been in their native South Arabia, unless some North-west Arabian town of the same name is meant).

The inscription terminates thus (cf. GLASER, *Abessinier*, pp. 74 *et seq.*):

"By 'Athtar, etc., and by Abî-yada'a Yathî'u (cf. *supra*, p. 236), the (reigning) king of Ma'ân, and by the two sons of the Ma'dii-kariba, son of Ili-yapi'a, and Ma'ân their tribe and the Lord of Yathil,[1] and the two great ones of Mutsrân, Ammî-tsaduka and S'ad (the aforesaid authors of the inscriptions); and Ma'ân of Mutsrân (the Minaeans of Mutsrân) have placed their possessions and their inscriptions under the protection of the (above-mentioned) deities of Ma'ân and Yathil (viz. of 'Athtar, etc.), and of the king of Ma'ân before (or against) every one who shall cause their inscriptions to be taken away, removed and carried off from their place. By the (Lord) of Ridâ'[2] and by 'Ammî-sami'a of Balâh, the great one (or viceroy) of Yathil."

If Glaser is right in his very plausible explanation of the term "king of Yamnat and Sha'mat," and of the race-name Madhai,[3] then this inscription, which by its association of *Ashûr* and *'Ibr-naharân* throws

---

[1] The second capital of the kingdom of Ma'ân, now Barâkish.

[2] *Bi-dhi-Kidâ* ; this word seems to have been accidentally omitted by the inscriber.

[3] That Madhai cannot possibly be intended for Media is evident from the fact that the country of Cambyses—who must, in that case, have been the monarch referred to—would necessarily have been described as Parsu (Persia); just as the Bible calls his father Cyrus "king of Persia," so too, the Egyptian inscriptions always refer to Cambyses as "the Persian."

a remarkable light on the words Ashûr and 'Eber in Balaam's "parable," most probably dates from about 1250 B.C., at which time the sway of the rightful Pharaoh Set-nekht, the predecessor of Ramses III., was confined to Upper Egypt — a Semitic usurper, named Irsu, or Ilsu (*i.e.* probably Ilî-yasu'a or Ilîshû'a), having made himself master of Lower Egypt. At any rate, it cannot be much later than the twelfth or eleventh century B.C. — a remark which applies to a considerable number of the Minaean inscriptions. This is sufficiently proved by the history of the word Ashûr, a term which was certainly not used later than the Israelite monarchy, except in the abbreviated form Shur.[1] Further proofs are supplied by the arguments advanced some years ago by Glaser, in support of his theory, as to the high antiquity of the Minaean kingdom, by the evidence of such passages[2] as Judges x. 12, where reference is made to the people of Ma'ân,[3] by Job ii. 11,[4] and finally—last but not least—by the testimony of the personal names of the Khammurabi dynasty, which has been fully dealt with in Chapter III. Taking all these things together, we have, in my opinion, an overwhelming body of evidence

---

[1] It is assuredly something more than mere accident, that the word never occurs again either in the Books of the Kings or in any of the prophetic writings.

[2] Cf. my *Aufsätze und Abhandlungen*, p. 3 and note.

[3] LXX. "Midian," evidently an explanatory gloss on Ma'ân.

[4] Tsophar [Zophar], "king of the Minaeans," according to the original and sole possible reading; cf. as Mordtmann suggests, Gen. xxxvi. 11 and 1 Chron. i. 36, Σωφαρ.

in favour of Glaser's theory in regard to the Minaeans.

In another Minaean inscription, Gl. 1083 (= Hal. 187 + 188 + 191), of the time of king Ilî-yapi'a Riyâm (probably the father of Abî-yada'a), we read that "on the day in which he (the author of the inscription) had business dealings (*i.e.* in incense; *irtakala*, cf. Hebr. *rokel* = trader) with Egypt and Ghazzat [Gaza] and A'shûr,"[1] an association of names which at once reminds us of the phrase, "Egypt and A'shûr and 'Ibr naharân," quoted above.

The question now arises as to what was the geographical or political significance attached, in the thirteenth century B.C., to this term *'Ibr naharân*, which is so closely connected with A'shûr, both in Balaam's prophecy (in the abbreviated form 'Eber), and also in the inscription of the reign of Abî-yada'a, just translated, an enquiry which naturally leads to the further question, as to what was its original meaning. In endeavouring to answer this latter question, our first concern will be to ascertain the sense which Babylonian and Hebrew usage attributes to such a word as *nâru*, or *nahar* (or with the article, *ha-nahar*, South Arabian *ha-naharan* = stream).

Leaving parallel expressions in Hebrew and Babylonian on one side, for the moment, and working on purely mechanical lines, we will, first of all, simply place the two assertions in the South Ara-

[1] Ed. Glaser, *Abessinier*, p. 75.

bian inscriptions in parallel lines, side by side, thus:

> They carried on a trade in incense with
> Egypt, Gaza and A'shûr
> "   A'shûr and 'Ibr naharân

From this we may conclude that to the Minaeans Gaza and 'Ibr naharân were interchangeable terms, or, at any rate—assuming that 'Ibr naharân included a much larger territory than that of Gaza—that they undoubtedly regarded Gaza as forming part of it. A certain amount of light is thrown on the question by a passage in 1 Kings iv. 24 (LXX. 3 Kings, iv. 24,) where we are told, " For Solomon had dominion over the whole of 'Eber ha-nahar [gloss: 'from Raphi,[1] unto Gaza'], and he had peace on all sides round about him." The gloss " from Tiphsah (Thapsacus) even to Gaza," in the present Hebrew text, is probably post-exilic;[2] in most MSS. of the Septuagint, no explanatory gloss appears here, and there is only one variant on the Septuagint, cited by Klostermann, which gives the interpolation, " from Raphi unto Gaza," already mentioned. A few lines earlier we read (1 Kings iv. 21), that " Solomon ruled over all the kingdoms from the River (*i.e.* as usual, the Euphrates) unto the land of the Philistines, and unto the border of Egypt,"

[1] *i.e.* Raphia between 'el-'Arîsh and Gaza.
[2] The Syrian version has "Takhpîs (a transliteration elsewhere employed for the Egyptian frontier for Tahpankes, Jer. xliii. 7, etc.) unto Gaza, which, if it be the original reading of the gloss of which Tiphsah is a later corruption, furnishes a most striking parallel to "from Raphia unto Gaza." In that case both glosses would mean " from Egypt unto Gaza."

which shows that 'Eber ha-nahar (literally = "Beyond the River") in iv. 24 cannot refer to Mesopotamia, a country which lay outside Solomon's dominions. Nor must it be forgotten, that iv. 24 is introduced as an explanation of the statements in iv. 23, in reference to the daily supply of game for Solomon's table, viz. wild goats, or harts, gazelles, yachmûr—antelopes, and fatted fowl; Mesopotamia was too far off to be able to provide such things; they were probably brought from Negeb (the country of the South), which lay close at hand, and perhaps, too, from Tahpanhes (Daphne), near Pelusium, where birds were plentiful. A correct interpretation of 1 Kings iv. 24 would seem to indicate, that in Solomon's time the term 'Eber ha-nahar was applied to the littoral from Pelusium, or the "Brook of Egypt," or even from Raphia, as far as Gaza, *i.e.* the westernmost portion of the land of Ashûr, or Shûr, on the sea-board. Whereas the Minaeans draw a clear distinction between A'shûr and Gaza, and also between A'shur and 'Ibr naharân,[1] in 1 Kings iv. 24—if we are to place any reliance on the glosses dealt with above—Gaza is mentioned as one of the boundaries of 'Eber ha-nahar. It would seem, therefore, that in the Minaean inscriptions, 'Ibr naharân is the littoral, and A'shûr the hinterland, while, under Solomon, 'Eber ha-nahar includes the same area as the Minaean 'Ibr naharân, and probably the territory of Ashûr, which lay beyond it, as well.

Be this as it may, an examination of the inscrip-

---

[1] So too, in Balaam's prophecy, we have "Ashûr and 'Eber."

tion translated on pp. 194 *et seq.*, which belongs to the time of Assur-bel-kala, king of Assyria (ca. 1100 B.C.), will help us to arrive at a better understanding of the geographical term in question. For there the word Ebir-nâri (= Hebr. 'Eber ha-nahar, and Minaean 'Ibr naharân) includes Malgî and Yeshî-môn, *i.e.* the region east of the Jordan as well, and either Ekron (south of the modern Ramleh) or else the country east of Pelusium, accordingly as we adopt the reading, Ba'al-zabubi, or Ba'al-Tsapûna, at the end of line 10. Seeing that Ba'al-zephon means literally, " Ba'al of the north wind," and that in line 11, immediately after Ba'al-Zabu- [. . . . .], or—another possible reading—Ba'al-Tsapu- [. . . . . .] we have a reference to "this wind," and to ships and waggons, I consider Ba'al-Tsa-pu [na] to be much the more probable restoration of the two. And as this Ba'al-Tsapuna lay between the Ba'al of Ma-lagî (*vide* p. 196) and the Ba'al of Yeshîmôn, it can scarcely be identical with the mountain Ba'al-tsa-puna, mentioned by Tiglathpileser III. as part of the territory of Hamath, in spite of the fact that the king of Tyre is named at the very end of the inscription. Or, is it possible that this Ba'al-Tsapuna was the god of Zaphon in Gad, mentioned in Josh. xiii. 27, which, like Yeshîmôn, was also situated in the country east of the Jordan, though, as is generally assumed, much farther north?[1] But as, in this case, we should naturally expect the sequence to be Malagî, Yasimûn, Tsapuna, I prefer to adhere to my

[1] The enumeration in Josh. xiii. 24 is evidently from South to North.

original interpretation, given above. Still taking this Assyrian inscription as our guide, it would seem that 'Eber ha-nahar must have extended as far as the Egyptian frontier—not merely to Raphia or to the Brook of Egypt (Wady el-'Arîsh)—but right up to the chain of forts on the Egyptian frontier in the North-East of the Delta; for even in the time of Moses, it is there that we find the "Ba'al of the North" localised in the name Ba'al-Zephon (near Migdol and Pi-ha-hiroth), a place mentioned in the history of the Exodus.[1]

And now to enquire further into the original meaning of Ebir nâri, or 'Eber ha-nahar (literally, "the far bank of the stream or river"), we find in the first place—quite apart from the passage in 1 Kings iv. 21—that in the Old Testament *ha-nahar* (= simply the Stream, the River) is used to indicate the Euphrates, and *'Eber ha-nahar* for Mesopotamia.[2] The Jordan is never called *ha-nahar*, but always ha-Yarden, *e.g.* 'eber ha-Yarden, which was used by the Moabites as a name for Judah, and by the Judeans as a name for Moab. Similarly, the Wady el-'Arîsh is never referred to as a *nahar* or as *ha-nahar* (= simply, the River); it is scarcely possible, therefore, that the term 'ibr naharân (the Babylonian *ebir nâri*, the *Eber* of Bala'am and *'Eber ha-*

---
[1] Cf. also a certain Ba'ilat Tsaṭûna among the deities worshipped at Memphis in the time of the later Empire (W. MAX MÜLLER, *Asien und Europa*, p. 315).

[2] Cf. Josh. xxiv. 2 *et seq.* and 14 *et seq.*, 2 Sam. x. 16, and 1 Kings xiv. 15. In all these cases, down to the time of the Captivity, the point of view is assumed to be that of a resident in Palestine.

nahar of Solomon) can have been derived from this stream, which formed the boundary between Egypt and Palestine, even apart from the fact that, had this been so, the form of the name must have originated in Egypt, for the territory to which it was applied lay to the north of the Wady el-'Arîsh. On the other hand, the name invariably given in the Old Testament to this stream, is *nakhal Mitsrayim*, "the Brook of Egypt." The Assyrian monarch, Esarhaddon, also employs this form (Assyr. *nakhal Mutsur*), and to guard against any possibility of mistake, he adds *ashar nâru lâ ishu*, " where no river is " (*i.e.* no continuous flow of water). Moreover, in Assyro-Babylonian, as in Hebrew, *nakhlu* = ravine or Wady; and finally, the Egyptians of the later Empire also mention a Nakhalu to the south of Raphia and Gaza[1] which, since it is accompanied by the determinative used to indicate " water," obviously refers to " the Brook of Egypt." This Wady, therefore, cannot help us to explain the source of the term *'Ibr naharân*.

The origin of the term 'Eber ha-nahar in the sense of Palestine, used more particularly of South Palestine, is of considerable importance historically, for the designation must have come into use in Palestine at a time when this country was a province of Babylon, or, in other words, in the time of the Khammurabi dynasty, when Abraham, the Hebrew (ha-'Ibrî), migrated " from the other side of the River " (*'eber ha-nahar*, *ebir nâri*), *i.e.* from Mesopotamia, into

[1] W. MAX MÜLLER, *Asien und Europa*, p. 134.

Canaan. This accounts for the fact that the earliest mention of the name "Hebrew," in the narrative portions of the Old Testament, is to be found in a chapter based on a cuneiform original, viz. Gen. xiv., and is there applied as a cognomen to Abraham, an emigrant from Mesopotamia.[1] That the term Ibrî (Hebrew) presupposes the existence of the name Eber, is evident from the genealogical table (Gen. x. 24), where Kainan (LXX.), Shelah and Eber are named as descendants of Arphaxad (Ur-kasdîm, *vide supra*, p. 210), and from the statement in Gen. xi., where Abraham is described as a descendant of Arphaxad and Eber; and that this name Eber must be an abbreviated form of Eber ha-nahar has already been made clear, by the identification of Balaam's "Ashur and Eber" with the Minaean A'shûr and 'Ibr naharân. Moreover, it is a well-established fact, that elsewhere in the Old Testament the expression 'Ibri is never used of the Israelites, except where it is put in the mouth of non-Israelite, or where an Israelite is speaking to the Egyptians about his fellow-countrymen, or, finally, where the writer wishes to draw a distinction between the Israelites and some other race. In the majority of these latter cases, it is by the Egyptians of the time of Joseph or Moses, or in contrast with the Egyptians, or occasionally with the Philistines, that the Israelites are called Hebrews. It is, therefore, a matter for serious consideration whether, even thus late in the day, we ought not to adopt the

---

[1] Cf. *supra*, pp. 191 *et seq*., for full details.

AS ILLUSTRATED BY THE MONUMENTS 257

almost exploded theory, according to which the name 'Apri, or 'Epri[1]—which occurs so frequently in Egyptian monuments of the later Empire — is made out to be merely an Egyptian transliteration of 'Ibri. The principal objection to this identification, first proposed by F. Chabas and afterwards supported by G. Ebers, lies in the difference between the labials employed; yet attention has already been drawn (on p. 109, note 1) to an obvious instance in which the Canaanite *b* has been represented by the Egyptian *p*. A further objection lies in the circumstances that, even under Ramses IV., *i.e.* some considerable time after the Exodus, we find it recorded that 800 'Epriu (Egypt. plural of 'Epri), drawn from the foreign residents of 'An,[2] were employed in compulsory labour at the quarries of Wady Hammamât. But just as the Israelites were accompanied in their Exodus by a number of aliens (Ex. xii. 38), it may equally well have happened that many Israelites remained behind and mingled with the foreign population of Egypt. In this case, the Egyptians would naturally apply to them the generic name of 'Epri, which, according to the Old Testament view, rightfully belonged to all the descendants of Abraham [*e.g.* even to the inhabitants of South Arabia]; the inscription recently discovered by Flinders Petrie (*vide* p. 264) has now

---

[1] Applied to a Semitic race who dwelt in the East of the Delta, and who were occasionally called upon by the Egyptians to supply compulsory labour.

[2] The eastern portion of Goshen, in the Heroopolitan Nome at the eastern extremity of the present Wady Tumilat.

made it certain that, in the time of Mînephtah, the Pharaoh of the Exodus, the Egyptians knew the Israelites by their special name Isir'il (*i.e.* Israel).

One thing I am firmly convinced of, and that is the uselessness of trying to make out that there is no sort of connection between *ebir nâri*, the Ancient Assyrian name for Palestine (which must, of course, have come originally from Babylonia), the *Eber* of Balaam, the Eber ha-nahar of Solomon, the Ibr naharân of the Minaean inscriptions—for all these expressions originally served to indicate the same thing —and the race-name Ibri, which, by the way, also occurs (Gen. x.) under the form Eber.[1] Moreover, the retention of the term Ebir nâri—suggested in the first instance by the migration of Abraham—as an official name for Palestine, by the Babylonians who ruled there under the Khammurabi Dynasty, was rendered all the easier by the fact that this name, once it had been introduced and accepted, could be construed in any of the various ways which the necessities of the moment might require. Thus, from the Babylonian point of view, the term " Be-

---

[1] Some years ago, Glaser (*Ausland*, 1891, p. 47, note 1) made a tentative suggestion to this effect, "Or must we, in the end, translate 'Ibr nahaiân as the Hebrews of the (boundary) river;" and later on Nathaniel Schmidt expressed himself still more definitely on the subject, in a paper entitled " The external evidence of the Exodus," which appeared in *Hebraica X*. (1894), pp. 159 *et seq.*, and is well worth reading. In this paper I notice that Morris Jastrow, jun., has anticipated me by drawing attention to the connexion between Gen. xlvi. 17 (Heber and Malchiel), and the Khabiri and Malki-el of the Tel el-Amarna tablets; he failed, however, to appreciate the significance of the fact that they may both be traced to Asher.

yond the River" must, at first, have meant the whole of Syria (including Palestine); it was the official name used for the province of Syria under the kings of Persia, and perhaps even in the time of the Neo-Babylonian Empire as well,[1] when it was probably unearthed from the Ancient Babylonian records, and re-introduced by Nebuchadnezzar, who had a mania for imitating the institutions and expressions of Khammurabi.[2] The elastic character of the term "Beyond," naturally led to its being assigned different meanings, fitting in with various political changes. If, for instance—and the thing is quite conceivable—the Babylonians, before they finally surrendered Palestine to the Egyptians, retained for a time their hold on the eastern bank of the Jordan, while the Egyptian aggression was mainly confined to the western bank, it is perfectly possible that *ebir nâri* may, at a pinch, have come to be equivalent to *eber ha-Yarden* (= the country on the other side of the Jordan), and thus have been applied to the region either east or west of the Jordan according to circumstances, and finally to both together. Nay more, when Jacob and his people crossed "the Brook of Egypt," on their way to settle

[1] Cf. *Keilinschr. Bibl.* IV. p. 269. Ebir nâri in a contract tablet dating from the third year of Cyrus, and p. 305 Ushtanni, viceroy of Babylon and Ebir nâri, in a tablet dating from the third year of Darius.

[2] After what has been said on pp. 210. *et seq.*, in regard to the original nationality of the Chaldaeans (or rather Kasdaeans), to which race Nebuchadnezzar belonged, the reader will easily understand that this was something more than a mere accident. It was not necessary that Nebuchadnezzar should have been an Arab himself—the fact that his earliest ancestors were these Chaldaean Arabs, is sufficient in itself.

in the land of Goshen, the term Eber must have followed them, and must occasionally have been used of Goshen in its wider sense, viz. the whole area between the isthmus of Suez and Gaza.

And now, after this exhaustive analysis of the terms "Eber of the River," and "Hebrew," I may perhaps be allowed, before concluding the present chapter, to return for a moment to the land of Ashur. The Egyptians of the Ptolemaic period, who had a weakness for introducing into their inscriptions archaic and obscure terms borrowed from earlier epochs, have, in one instance, inserted the gloss *Eshru* in connection with the well-known land of Menti, the name applied to the Sinaitic peninsula from the time of the later Empire. It need scarcely be said, that the term *Eshru* cannot here refer to the sacred lake of that name, which plays a part in Egyptian mythology and is localized at Karnak and also at Bubastis. On the contrary, the allusion here must be to the land of Ashur, or, in other words, to the wilderness of Shûr. Moreover, in view of all that we have learnt in regard to Ashur and Shur, the question arises whether the land of Shêri or Shîri, which we find mentioned in the Tel el-Amarna letters from Jerusalem, and which must evidently have been situated somewhere in the far South (*vide* p. 230), may be—not Seïr, but rather a Babylonian transliteration of Shur. It is true, that such a transliteration would be inaccurate, since we should expect to find the word written Shuri; on the other hand, the identification with Seïr [Se'îr] also lies open to objection, even though the form Kilti = Ke'ïlah (an equation, by the way, which is not absolutely certain) seems to afford a precedent for the omission of the *Ayin*. The description in the text, viz. " The countries of Shiri [-ki] unto Gimti-Kirmil" (el-Kurmul, to the north of Tel-Ma'in), is, geographically, much more applicable to the land of Ashur than to Mount Seïr, since this latter lies too far south.

As, in talking of Mount Seïr, we have come as far as the land of Edom, the former home of the Horites, I may be allowed to quote in this connexion one of the Tel el-Amarna tablets (L. 64 = Winckler, No. 237), which is of considerable interest both from a geographical as well as an historical point of view. It should be noted beforehand that, according to Deut. ii. 12 and Gen. xxxvi., the Horites had either been driven out, or absorbed by the sons of Esau, or, in other words, by the Edomites. The letter reads as follows—

" To Yan'am, my lord (the viceroy of Yerimôt and nominal governor of Egyptian Palestine), Mut-Addi, thy servant: I prostrate myself at the feet of my lord. As I told thee by word of mouth, Ayab (cf. the name Job) has secretly fled, even as the king of Bikhishi (Pe'ish ?), fled before the officers of the king, as my lord the king liveth. As my lord the king liveth, if Ayab is in Bikhishi, then is it two months (that he is there). Lo, there is Bin-inima,[1] inquire of him; lo, there is Tadua (= Dadu'a?), inquire of

---

[1] A name similar to Benjamin, only in a semi-Egyptian form, the Egyptian equivalent of the Hebrew *yamin* = on the right hand, is *wanim*, which in the cuneiform script appears as *inim*.

him; lo, there is Yashuya (Washuya or Pishuya?), inquire of him. While he from .... the city of Astarti is expelled, at such time as all the cities of the land of Gari[1] arose in revolt: Udumu (Edom), Aduri (Addar, Josh. xv. 3?), Araru (Ar'ar or Arôer) Mishtu, Magdal, Khini-anabi (= En-anab, 'The Spring of Grapes'), and Zarki (cf. Zereth, Josh. xiii. 19?), then were the cities of Khapini (or Khawâni, Khayâni) and Yabishi (Jabesh) taken. Moreover, after thou hadst written a letter to me, did I write unto him (viz. Ayab) to tell him that thou hadst returned from thy journey. And, lo, he has reached Bikhishi and has received the order."

In view of the names of these Edomite cities, it is a question whether we ought not to restore Gen. xxxvi. 39 as follows: " and his (Hadar's) cities were Pa'îsh (in the Massoretic text, Pa'û, var. Pa'i, LXX. Phogor), Me'eshet (cf. *supra* Mishtu), Mehêtab-el, Bath Matred[2] and Mê-zahab." It is quite possible that the land of Khar, or Gari, included, in addition to Edom proper, a part of the territory of Ashur as well; especially if we remember the wide meaning occasionally attached to the term " land of Khar," in the Egyptian texts of the later Empire, where it is

---

[1] Winckler takes this to mean Edom. I feel no hesitation in identifying this name with the Egyptian Khar, Hebr. Khor; Khôrî = Horites, which means, of course, not cave-dwellers, but the people of the land of Khar.

[2] Probably the correct reading is Bêt-Matred. The next word, Mêtsahab (cf. Mê-deba, and on the other hand Dî-zahab), is, in any case, much more lik- the name of a place than of a person.

frequently used to describe the whole of Southern Palestine, from the Egyptian frontier onwards. Both the letter quoted above, however, and Hebrew tradition in regard to the Horites, show that originally it was used of Edom alone.

In dealing with Deut. xxviii. 68 (on p. 11), I have already had occasion to point out that Hosea ix. 3 is merely a quotation from this passage. When, however, Hosea, after giving the words of Deuteronomy, viz. " But Ephraim shall return to Egypt," adds, "and they shall eat unclean food in Ashur [Assyria]," it seems extremely probable—in view of the facts brought forward in the present chapter—that this supplementary clause formed part of the original text of Deuteronomy, and was only omitted later owing to its having been confounded with Assyria. The principles of parallelism require that the Ashur in question—even though Hosea may have understood it as equivalent to Assyria—should be some region in the immediate vicinity of Egypt, and there is, of course, no other locality which complies with this condition except the land of Shur, which even the compiler of the Book of Joshua regarded as equivalent to that part of Goshen which lay in South Palestine;[1] it was there that the tribe of Asher, and probably certain other tribes of Israel, had settled long before the exodus of the remaining tribes from Egypt; indeed, they had already set out on their

---

[1] Another passage in which Ashûr originally indicated the region to the north of the "Brook of Egypt," though later the reference was taken as applying to Assyria, viz. Gen. ii. 14, will be briefly dealt with at the end of the 10th chapter of the present volume.

journey further north before that time. The early stages of this migration of the tribe Asher from the land of Ashur were indicated by the advance of the Khabiri (about 1400 B.C.), while by the middle of the fourteenth century B.C., in the time of Seti I. and Ramses II., we find them safely installed in their subsequent home to the north of Carmel.

When we find Minephtah, the Pharaoh of the Exodus, concluding the recently-discovered inscription—which forms a pendant to another inscription dealing with the defeat of the Libyans and Peoples of the Sea—in the following boastful strain, it is quite possible that by Israel he means the territory of Asher, of whose dependence on Israel the Egyptians cannot have been ignorant—

> "Libya is laid waste, Kheta (the Hittite region from whence came the "Peoples of the Sea") has been pacified, Canaan with all its ill-disposed ones has been captured, Ashkelon has been led away captive, Gezer taken, I-no'am (to the east of Tyre, and therefore in the territory of Ashur) has been annihilated, Isir'il[1] has been laid waste and its seed destroyed, Khar has become even as the widows (*khar*) of Egypt, all lands are, together, at peace. Every man that roameth about hath been chastened by the king Minephtah."

This inscription is dated in the fifth year of Minephtah (1277 B.C.); on comparing it with its companion

---

[1] Written with the determinative "people," so that it is evidently a nation and not a place that is meant. Cf. later (in the inscriptions of Salmanaser II.) Ahab of Sir'il = Israel.

text, the so-called Karnak Inscription, we find that Minephtah was not in Palestine or Syria at the time, but he must have considered himself fortunate in having been able to drive back his enemies from the Egyptian frontier; moreover, these enemies prove to have been merely the Libyans and the Peoples of the Sea (Lycians, Achivi, Tyrrhenians, Saklus and Sardinians), who were, however, supplied with munitions of war by the Phoenicians. The Israelites under Moses could hardly have chosen a more opportune juncture than this for their departure out of Egypt, and, as their exodus was indirectly connected with the barbaric invasion, Minephtah mentions them by name in the highly poetic account which he gives of the affair.[1] The territory he assigns to them, however—inferentially at any rate—is that of Asher (to the east of Acre and Tyre), since it occupies a place on the list between I-no'am and Khar.

As has already been pointed out on a previous page, it is probable that other tribes of Israel besides that of Asher had settled in South Palestine before the time of Moses. Prominent among these apparently were the tribes of Simeon and Levi, both of whom began to emigrate at an early date, and seem soon to have almost passed out of memory. A comparison of the blessing pronounced by Jacob,

---

[1] The statement in Exodus xii. 38, "And a mixed multitude went up also with them," may perhaps be taken as an indication of a certain cooperation with the enemies by whom Egypt was then assailed. If this be so, we can all the more easily understand the mobilization of the Egyptian forces who were sent in pursuit of the fugitives (Exodus xiv. 6 *et seq.*).

in Gen. xlix., with that of Moses, in Deut. xxxiii., clearly proves that besides the priestly tribe of Levi, there was another tribe of the same name, which had ceased to exist long before the time of Moses; in the first of these two passages, Levi, and Simeon as well, are cursed as murderers and violent men, and are threatened with division and scattering; while in the second, on the other hand, Simeon is not mentioned at all, and the tribe of Levi—evidently a later and fundamentally different body from the first-named tribe of that name—are blessed as the guardians of doctrine and prophecy. It is evident that a stirring page of history must have intervened between the dates of these two documents, and the events recorded in the Tel el-Amarna Letters seem to offer the only satisfactory explanation of the discrepancy observable between them. It is by no means impossible that this earlier tribe of Levi, which had already disappeared in the time of Moses, may have been connected in some way or other with Labaya and his sons, of whom we hear so frequently in the letters from Jerusalem (*vide supra*, p. 232). In that case, it is needless to point out Jacob's blessing must have been composed before the time of Moses; in the period after Moses, such an execration of Levi would have been not only meaningless, but absolutely inconceivable.

In conclusion, let us consider, for a moment, the practical effect of all the evidence which we have gleaned from the Tel el-Amarna tablets—dating from the period between 1430 and 1400 B.C.—and from the Minaean and Egyptian inscriptions. Far from obliging us to modify in any way the traditional view of Old Testament history, or from placing a weapon in the hands of its opponents, it tends, on the contrary, to confirm—indirectly it is true—the accuracy of the Old Testament narrative, and at the same time to fill up a gap in it, by enabling us to reconstruct the history of the period which preceded the conquest of Palestine by Joshua, about the year 1230 B.C. The ancient Hebrew tradition—and more especially that part of it which deals with the earliest times—has, in many instances, come down to us in a merely fragmentary and mutilated condition. But even isolated references and allusions, such as those which occur in regard to the land of Ashur, Heber and Malki-el, Hebron, etc., etc., when supplemented by the external evidence that lies to our hand, are shewn to be ancient and authentic tradition, and thus supply further testimony to the existence of *pre-Mosaic* records. In the next chapter, I propose to bring forward a number of fresh arguments in favour of this view, which is so diametrically opposed to the theories at present upheld by Wellhausen and his school. The most important and decisive of these arguments is based on personal names occurring in the book of Exodus, although the remainder are scarcely less cogent.

CHAPTER IX

THE TIME OF MOSES

FROM a very early date, a regular trade in incense together with other drugs and spices of the Hadramaut, was carried on by the Minaeans—a nation of South Arabia to whom we have more than once had occasion to refer—with North-west Arabia, Southern Palestine and Egypt. In order to place this trade with the countries which lay outside their own territory upon a stable basis, they must naturally have done their best to secure the ancient caravan route which led from South Arabia to Gaza, by the establishment of fortified stations along its course. As there would seem to have been a second caravan route, extending from the Hadramaut across East Arabia as far as Babylon—in addition to a number of branch routes similar to that which led through the country east of the Jordan to Damascus—it is manifest that for countless ages there must have been a brisk intercourse between Arabia and the nations on its frontiers, such as is clearly reflected in the Egyptian and Babylonian legends regarding the interior of Arabia and the Elysian incense-bearing shore. The first authentic historical evidence of this intercourse is furnished by the representation of an embassy on a monument of the twelfth

Egyptian Dynasty, bearing a gift of antimony (*vide supra*, pp. 52 *et seq.*); and the next occurs in the narrative (Gen. xxxvii.) of the sale of Joseph to a band of Arabian incense-merchants. In one passage, these traders appear as Ishmaelites, in another, as Midianites, as the following parallel extracts clearly show—

(25) And they sat down to eat bread: and they lifted up their eyes and looked, and behold, a travelling company of Ishmaelites came from Gilead (*i.e.* from the country east of the Jordan) with their camels bearing nek'ôt (tragacanth gum) Styrax[1] and ladanum (or Myrrh) going to carry it down into Egypt.	(28) And there passed by Midianites, merchantmen
(28 *b*) and they (his brethren) drew and lifted up Joseph out of the pit and sold Joseph to the Ishmaelites for twenty pieces of silver.	they brought Joseph into Egypt. (36) And the Midianites sold him into Egypt unto Potiphar.

So, too, in the account of Gideon's victory over the Midianites, we find the names Midianite and Ishmaelite used interchangeably (cf. Judges viii. 24, " because they were Ishmaelites," with the rest of the narrative). Again, in Genesis xxv., the genealogies of Ketûrah[2] and Hagar run parallel with one another; by the former Abraham became the father of

---

[1] In regard to this article, cf. my *Aufsätze und Abhandlungen*, where it is discussed at length.

[2] *i.e.* incense, cf. Basmat, Kets'îah, and other feminine names of similar import.

Jokshan and Midian (*vide supra*, p. 236), by the latter of Ishmael, from whom Nebayôth, Kedar, etc., were descended, just as Dedan was descended from Jokshan and Abída' from Midian.

The fact that under the Minaean king Abiyada'a[1] the Minaeans had a governor stationed in the territory of Mutsrân, is explained by their anxiety to guard the north-western portion of the caravan route to Gaza and Egypt, which at that point skirted the borders of South Palestine and Egypt. Glaser tells me, by way of supplementing the information contained in the inscription Gl. 1155, of which he was the first to publish a correct version, that in another as yet unpublished inscription of this same king Abi-yada'a (Gl. 1302), it is explicitly stated that " on the day, on which Sa 'd (probably identical with the author of Gl. 1155) appointed (*kabbara*) two men over the Minaeans of Mutsrân (Ma'ân Mutsrân) as princes (or governors), and they remain safe and uninjured, because (?) Sa 'd and his tribe wished well (showed favour) to these two men." Now this land of Mutsrân is probably identical with the region situate on the Aelanitic Gulf in North-west Arabia, which is generally known as the land of Midian. The gloss " Midian," for Ma 'ôn (*i.e.* Ma 'ân) which appears in the Greek translation of the Hebrew text of Judges x. 12, the part played by the Midianites in the history of Joseph and the Hebrew Tradition, which makes out king Abi-yada'a to be the son of Midian, all combine to prove this. Its capital was

---

[1] *Vide supra*, pp. 246 *et seq.*, the inscription Gl. 1155.

the Arabian Ma'ân, which retains its ancient name down to the present day, and has been from time immemorial an important halting-place for caravans and pilgrims. It was at the same time the northernmost point of this region, which, in the inscriptions, is invariably referred to as Ma'an Mutsrân (the Minaeans of Mutsrân), while Waga' (on the Red Sea), el-Oela (where Euting discovered a number of Minaean inscriptions), and Yathrib (Medina) formed, respectively, the western, eastern and southern boundaries. It is by no means an insignificant fact that the Minaeans procured their female slaves from Waga' and Yathrib, as well as from the countries adjoining Mutsrân, *i.e.* from Mitsr (Egypt), Gaza, Moab, Ammon, Dedan and Kedar (*vide supra*, pp. 237 *et seq.*). Moreover, as their inscriptions clearly show, the Minaeans not only carried on a trade in incense with Egypt, Gaza, Ashur and 'Ibr naharân (*vide* Chap. viii.), but must also have exercised for centuries an influence on the country east of the Jordan—whence the Midianites in the Story of Joseph came—a fact which is demonstrated by the large number of South Arabian place-names, dating from the time of the Judges, at latest, which recur in that region.

To begin with, the name of Ma'ân itself is repeated in the Ma'ân to the south of Petra mentioned above, then in Ma'ôn near Hebron, and finally in another Ma'ôn in the region east of the Jordan (*vide supra*, p. 76, note 1). The name (which appears as Magan in the cuneiform texts) was originally applied to the north-eastern part of Arabia (Yemâma and Bahrein), the Babylonian[1] "country of the Sea," the cradle of South Arabian civilization;[2] Hadramaut (including Katabân) and the South Arabian Ma'ân marked the further stages of its growth, while Ma'ân near Petra, and the two Ma'ôns in Palestine, were the latest tendrils thrown out towards the North-west. The name of the Hadramautic and South-west Arabian city Shibâm is found in Sebâm (originally pronounced Shebâm) and Sibma near Hesbon, while the name of the Minaean capital Karnâvu is recognized in Ashteroth-Karnaim in Bashan; with Ashtoreth we may compare the interesting variant, Be-Eshterah, in Josh. xxi. 27, a form which cannot be rightly explained except by a reference to the South Arabian personal name Bi-Athtar (= by or with Astar).[3] Yathîmât, a district belonging to the tribe of 'Akib re-appears in Yeshimôth (Num. xxi. 20), the Hadramautic Mêpha'at, in Mêphaat in Moab,[4] the Katabanian capital Tamna' in the name of the Edomite tribe Timna' (Gen. xxxvi. 40), the Katabanian district of Tsinnat (which Glaser declares to have

[1] The Arabic designation Bahrân, which later on was mistaken for a dual form (hence the modern name Bahrein), was originally nothing more than an Arabic translation of the Babylonian term *mât tâmti* = "country of the Sea ;" cf. also the name Tihâma = Sea, applied to the west coast of Arabia.

[2] Cf. EDUARD GLASER, *Skizze*, ii. p. 250, where a similar view is clearly expressed, though, at the time Glaser was writing, attention had not yet been drawn to the intimate relations which existed between the Arabs and Babylonians in the time of Khammurabi.

[3] Cf. also the names Ba'Anah (= by Anat), Be-Dad (= by Hadad), and Ba-'Asa (= by Asît ?).

[4] Cf. from the same, the root Yapa', which occupies a very large place in the South Arabian language, Yap'ân (or Yapî'ân), and the Hebrew place-name Yapî'a.

been the site of a celebrated temple), in the name of the Wilderness of Tsinnah. Moreover, the names of Mount Nebo and Mount Sinai, as also of the wilderness of Sin, are probably of South Arabian rather than Babylonian origin, for the inhabitants of the Hadramaut and Katabania had borrowed the gods Sin and Nebo from the Babylonians:[1] besides the Arabic tribal name Nebayôth comes from Nebo, for it was a favourite practice to throw the names of deities into the feminine plural as a sign of majesty.[2] And lastly, it is to be noted in this connection, that in Ashtar-Kamosh, the deity who occupies the chief place in the Moabite Pantheon, we have the same form of this divine name as that found in South Arabia, the feminine termination being absent from both (cf. on the other hand, the Canaanite Ashtoreth or Astarte).

In the Mesa inscription (ninth century B.C.) the Moabites seem to have fallen completely under the influence of Canaan; the language used by them is almost identical with Hebrew, and their script is— not the Minaeo-Sabaean—but the Canaanite. Their spelling, however, has, in places, a strong affinity with that of the Minaean inscriptions. These latter differ from the Sabaean, among other things, in the frequent use of the letter h to denote a long $\bar{a}$ and short $\bar{\imath}$, just as in German h is used to indicate the

---

[1] The former under the name Sîn, the latter as Anbai—the original Babylonian name being Nabiu.

[2] Cf. Baalôth, Ashtarôth, Anatot; in Babylonia the forms Sinâtu, Shamas-hâtu, also occur, the two last as masculine personal names in the contract tablets of the Khammurabi Dynasty.

lengthening of a vowel;[1] so too, in Hebrew, in certain cases, the letter *h* is used for a long *a* (*e.g.* Milkah for Milkâ, originally Milkat), Debôrah for Debôrâ, *banah* = he was building, for *banâ*, a contraction from *banaya*) and for a long *e* (*e.g. yibneh* = he builds, for *yibnê*, a contraction from *yibnai*). The Moabite language shares this peculiarity in spelling, *of which there are no instances in Phoenician*, but it sometimes employs it in cases where Hebrew does not, *e.g.* in the place-names Mehdeba' (Hebr. Mêdebâ') and Neboh (Hebr. Nebô); Moabite therefore, as far as spelling is concerned, is more akin to Minaean than to Hebrew. The only possible inference which can be drawn from this is that both the Moabites and Hebrews, during the period prior to their adoption of the Canaanite language, that is, while they still spoke a pure Arabic dialect,[2] must have originally employed the Minaean script in place of the so-called Phoenician or Canaanitish; for in no other way can this remarkable fact be satisfactorily ex-

[1] It may serve to reassure critics of the present volume who have read the strictures in MORDTMANN'S *Beiträge zur minäischen Epigraphik*, pp. 78 *et seq.* (published at Weimar in January 1897), and are inclined to doubt this fact and to regard the deductions I make from it as unconvincing, if I state that I have gone into the whole matter *de novo*, and find that there is not the slightest doubt about the purely graphic character of the form in question; cf. my paper, entitled *Das graphische* h *des minäischen*, in the *Mitth. der vorderasiat. Gesellsch.* of Berlin.

[2] That this must have been so in the case of the Hebrews is evident, not only from the form of the earliest Hebrew personal names, but from many other peculiarities of their language. Cf. in Ex. xvi. 15, the question *man hû* = "What (really 'who') is that?" for which in Canaanite (and therefore in post-Mosaic Hebrew also) would be said *mi hû* (*e.g.* Gen. xxvii. 33).

plained. The period in question was, in the case of the Hebrew, and probably in that of the Moabites as well, the interval which elapsed between Abraham and Joshua. This serves to account for the alternative forms of the name of Abraham, which was originally Abrâm, though the spelling Abrhm (pronounced Abrâm) also occurs. Afterwards, when this spelling (which when applied to the internal elements of words has no parallel outside the Minaean inscriptions) came to be no longer understood, the name was changed into its present form, Ab-raham, a word which it is absolutely impossible to explain by any ascertained principle of Semitic name-formation, and the passage in Gen. xvii. 5 seems an interpolation intended to account for the alteration. This fact is of the utmost importance to the study of the origin of the earlier Hebrew literature, since it permits us to assume confidently that a certain, and not inconsiderable, portion of the tradition on which Genesis is based had already been reduced to writing in the time of Moses. When, therefore, the Israelites, after taking permanent possession of the region west of the Jordan, came to adopt the Canaanite language and script,[1] these sacred documents, which had increased in number during the time of Moses, owing to the addition of the law and of the account of its origin, were naturally subjected to the processes of paraphrasing, translation, and—

[1] There is nothing to prevent us from assuming that the Canaanite (or so-called Phoenician) script was in use in Palestine during the Tel el-Amarna period; at that time, however, it had not yet been officially employed as the medium of diplomatic correspondence with Egypt.

it is needless to deny—of recension as well. These facts naturally place the whole question of the distinction of the sources in a new light.

And now let us leave Moab and return to Midian. This region, which is mentioned in the Minaean inscriptions under the name of Mutsrân, plays an important part in the history of Moses and of the Mosaic Priestly Law. As we have seen, the geographical position of Midian coincided with that of the Minaean Mutsrân (Ma'ân, Mutsrân), and the Midianites who appear on the scene in the story of Joseph were identical with the Minaean incense-merchants. But this is not all. Here, too, dwelt Regu-el Jethrô,[1] the " Priest of Midian,"[2] with whom Moses took refuge, whose son-in-law he became, with whom, later on, Moses solemnly "ate bread before God" (Ex. xviii. 12), and to whom Moses was indebted for detailed advice as to legislation for the Israelites (Ex. xviii. 19 *et seq.*). If we add to this the fact, that it is in the Minaean inscriptions found in Mutsrân—viz. in the fragments discovered by Euting at el-Oela—that we find references to priests and priestesses of the god Wadd (cf. p. 79), in which the word *lavi'u* (fem. *lavi'at*)[3]—a term identical with

---

[1] In Minaean the name appears as Ridsvu-il Vitrân.

[2] *Kohen Midyan.* Cf. in reference to *kohen* my remarks on p. 17 *supra*.

[3] See my *Aufsätze und Abhandlungen*, pp. 30 *et seq.* In the revised edition of the Euting Inscriptions recently published by J. H. Mordtmann, which, by the way, is really the first edition worthy of the name, since it is the first which complies with the requirements set forth on p. 13 of my *Aufsätze und Abhandlungen*, even Mordtmann admits (p. 43) that I am right in identifying *lavi'u* with Levi.

the Hebrew Levi or Levite—is employed, it will be readily admitted that quite a new light is thus thrown on the intimate relationship which subsisted between Moses and "the Priest of Midian"—a relationship which has hitherto received far less attention than it really deserves. The probability is, therefore, that if we were to submit the ideas and language (and particularly the ritual terms) of the "Priestly Code" to a more systematic examination, we should find many other traces of early Arabian influences, all of them naturally attributable to Moses' residence in the land of Midian. The altar of incense, for instance, seems from the description we get of it, in Ex. xxx. 1 *et seq.*, to have been little more than a replica of the Minaean altars, but on a somewhat larger scale;[1] the use of incense, which plays such an important part in the "Priestly Code," is another point of contact, which is further evidenced by such direct Arabic words as *tamîd* (cf. p. 17), *'ôlah* = Burnt-offering,[2] *azkarah*, etc. This last expression, which is usually translated as the "sweet savour" (of the meat-offering, or Minchah), really means, as a reference to Levit. ii. 9 and 16 will shew, the combustible part of the meat-offering (consisting of the finest meal and incense), which gave forth a partic-

[1] Cf. for instance, the illustration given in Glaser's *Mittheilungen* (Prague, 1886), p. 75. The "crown of gold round about" (Ex. xxx. 3) is here represented by the projection on the top of the altar, and even the "horns" are suggested by the bullock's head (with a sun between the horns) which can be distinguished on one side of the projection.

[2] Arab. *ghâliyat*, a kind of incense, a cognate form is *ghalwâ*; cf. also the verb *ghalâ*, used of the bubbling of a pot of meat, and *ghâlî*, a participle from it which means "fat" of meat.

ularly agreeable odour; it cannot be rightly explained except through the Arabic. The word is not even Hebrew in form; it is a broken plural form (*azkár*) from zakar (Arab. dhakar), and means the "male" (or best) kinds of incense, full particulars of which may be found in the dictionaries compiled by native Arab scholars. Even the ceremonies observed on the great Day of Atonement (Lev. xvi.) serve to remind us of early Arabian sacrificial usages and early Arabian ideas; the demon of the Wilderness Az-azel [Lev. xvi. 10] translated in the A.V. "scapegoat," finds a counterpart in Uzzâ, a divinity who, the Minaean inscriptions inform us, was known to the ancient Dedanites (cf. *supra*, p. 238), and, on the other side, in the Arabic root *azala*, which embodies the ideas of barrenness and infinity associated with the desert.

But, undoubtedly, the most striking feature in the history of the Mosaic Code—especially at the present time, when emphasis is laid on the fact that it originated "in the wilderness," and was thus only meant for a nomadic race—is to be found in the magnificent appointments of the tabernacle and of the high-priest, and in the elaborate ritual prescribed by it. And it is remarkable in this connection, that it is from the so-called "Priestly Code," which is held by Wellhausen and his school to have been first composed in post-exilic times, that we receive the fullest details on both these points. When we come to reflect, however, that Moses (whose name even is of Egyptian origin) grew up and was educated in a country where he had every opportunity for observing the gorgeous ceremonial daily practised at the court of Pharaoh's daughter, and that afterwards he had spent years among the Minaean priesthood, in the house of the high priest Jethro in the land of Midian, it surely need not surprise us to find him endeavouring to introduce the observance of a similar elaborate ritual among his fellow-countrymen. The time of Moses was, of all others, the most opportune for the inauguration of such a ritual, whereas it would have been scarcely possible to select a less favourable period than that of the Babylonian Captivity or the years immediately succeeding it. The chief characteristic of the Judaistic movement which took place under Ezekiel and Ezra, was not that it created a new Law and put it forward as the sole and sufficient dogma to which members of the Jewish faith were henceforth to conform, but that it harked back beyond the teaching of the Prophets, by a single step, to primitive ages, and strove, in a one-sided fashion, to artificially galvanize into life long-forgotten ordinances. As might have been expected—since no man can hope to set back the hands of time with impunity—the result was a sort of fossil-form of religion.

The following remarkable and surprising fact furnishes direct evidence that Moses was not only influenced by Jethro, but that he also adopted many of the forms of Egyptian worship.

Every one will remember the instructions given by Moses in regard to the ouches of gold, and two chains of pure gold in the form of twisted cords, which were to form the shoulder-pieces of the high-priest's dress, and the so-called khoshen (literally "ornament," "beauty"), or breastplate of judgment, which was to be set with precious stones, in four rows of three stones each, symbolical of the twelve tribes of Israel (Ex. xxviii. 13 *et seq.*). Now, Adolf Erman, in his magnificent and scholarly work, *Aegypten und ägyptisches Leben im Altertum* (Tübingen, 1885), on pp. 402 *et seq.*, assures us that: "In the time of the eighteenth and nineteenth dynasties (*i.e.* shortly before the time of Moses) the chief-priest of Memphis still wore as his distinctive sign of office the same wondrous neck-ornament which had been borne by his predecessor under the fourth dynasty."[1] On the next page he gives, without further comment, a cliché of this neck-ornament; from the shoulders or neck two parallel rows of cords descend obliquely to the breast; the cords cross one another, and at every point of intersection there is a little ball, or a small ornament in the shape of a cross (in reality intended to represent the Egyptian *ankh*, or symbol for life). If we examine the picture carefully, we can make out that from top to bottom there are four rows of these ornaments, each of which is composed of precious stones, and that (again reckoning from top to bottom) there are

[1] Cf. also Erman's short paper, entitled "*Aus dem Grab eines Hohenpriesters von Memphis*," in the *Zeitschr, für ägypt. Sprache und Alterthumskunde*, vol. xxxiii. (1895) pp. 18—24, where an illustration is given (p. 22) of this interesting breast-ornament, which was called by the Egyptians *se'eh* (pronounced *se'ekh*); but neither in this paper, nor in the larger work quoted above, does Erman notice its obvious similarity to the breast-plate of the Israelite priests.

three crosses and three balls, then three more crosses and three more balls, an arrangement which very nearly resembles that prescribed in Ex. xxviii. 17—20. Moreover, on both right and left of this ornament, which was worn by the Egyptian priests in the centre of the breast, there are two symbolical figures, also attached to the ouch, which was invariably made of the same precious metal as the cords which were attached to them, but more massive; on the right is a sparrow-hawk, on the left a jackal. The two latter were sacred to Horus and Anubis, who play an important part in the Egyptian cult of the dead; as figures on the priestly badge, however, they were apparently symbolical of prophecy, and were probably worn during the giving of oracles. In Ex. xxviii. 30 we read, "And thou shalt put in the breast-plate of judgment (*khoshen*) the Urim and the Thummim (R. V. margin, "the Lights and the Perfections"); and they shall be upon Aaron's heart when he goeth in before the Lord; and Aaron shall bear the judgment (oracle) of the children of Israel upon his heart before the Lord continually." In regard to the names of the twelve gems, one of them at any rate is an Egyptian loan-word, viz. *leshem* = hyacinth or opal, Egypt. *neshem*, and probably *achlamah*, also (= jasper or amethyst, Egypt. *ekhnôme*).[1]

---

[1] In this case, the hypothesis put forward on p. 204, viz. that *achlamah* was connected with the name of the race Achlamu must be abandoned, unless we are prepared to assume that *ekhnôme* was also originally named after the Achlamites, and that the Israelites borrowed the word from the Egyptians.

The almost absolute similarity between the breast-ornament of the Egyptian priests of the later Empire, and that of the Israelites described in the so-called Priestly Code, affords food for reflection, and can scarcely be explained except by assuming that it was borrowed from the Egyptians in the time of Moses. And where a high-priest stands at the head of affairs, we naturally infer from this the existence of an inferior clergy; similarly, an elaborate ritual—such as Moses evidently had in view, and in a great measure actually brought into use, in so far as the conditions of life in the desert permitted — naturally pre-supposes a sanctuary and a numerous staff of attendants. The relations between the priestly class and the ordinary Levites or servants of the Temple, furnish the modern critics of the Pentateuch with their main argument in favour of arranging the chronological sequence of the different sources in the following order : (1) the Jehovist narrative, (2) Deuteronomy (seventh century B.C.), and (3) Priestly Code (post-exilic), the Ideal Law, propounded by the priest Ezekiel (Ez. xliv.—xlvi.) in the time of the Captivity being adduced as the obvious connecting link between Deuteronomy and the Priestly Code. The critics tell us that in Deuteronomy no distinction is drawn between the Levitical priests and the ordinary Levites who belonged to the lower grade of temple ministrants; and that even a provincial Levite when he came up to Jerusalem was permitted to " minister in the name of the Lord his God even as all his brethren the Levites do which stand there before the Lord " (Deut. xviii. 6 *et seq.*). Then, we are assured that in 572 B.C. (or about twenty-five years after the Israelites had been led away captive to Babylon), Ezekiel came forward with a totally new pretension, viz. that as a punishment for their transgressions, the Levites were not to be (any longer) allowed to approach the temple for the purpose of performing their priestly duties there, this privilege being specially reserved for those Levitical priests who, at the time when the Israelites went astray after idols, protested against it and ministered unto Yahveh in the sanctuary, namely the sons of Zadok (Ezekiel xliv. 9 *et seq.*); in fact, the Levites were reduced to the status of mere underlings and servants of the temple. In the Priestly Code, however, this distinction between Priests and Levites, which—so the critics inform us—was first introduced by Ezekiel, is thrown back into Mosaic times; the sons of Aaron, moreover, (who, like Moses himself, were descended from the tribe of Levi,) are represented as set apart for the priesthood from the beginning, while the (other) Levites were made to be mere bearers and underlings. According to this view, there is, so they say, a clear historical progression from Deuteronomy to Ezekiel, and from Ezekiel's programme on to the Priestly Code, in which Ezekiel's aims find their ultimate realization. In order to make the position quite clear, I should like to point out that Zadok and Abiathar were high-priests in the time of David, and that after the rejection of Abiathar in the reign of Solomon, the office was vested in Zadok alone; Zadok is described as the son of Ahitub, who is probably identical with the

Ahitub, son of Phinehas, son of Eli, mentioned in 1 Sam. xiv. 3, whereas the later, official genealogies of the high-priests trace the descent of Zadok, son of Ahitub, direct from Amariah, the eighth in descent from Aaron. Probably, therefore, the real fact was that Zadok, though a descendant of Aaron, did not spring from the direct line. If this was so, it is probable that Ezekiel designedly describes those who were to be henceforward alone eligible for the office of priest—not as sons of Aaron—but sons of Zadok, especially as there must at that time have been other descendants of Aaron in existence besides the sons of Zadok.

Though the above line of argument may, at the first glance, seem quite unanswerable, yet an unprejudiced consideration of Deuteronomy will speedily reveal the fact that even there a distinction is clearly made between the Levitic Priests of the central Holy Place—with "the Priest" (Deut. xvii. 12, xx. 2) at their head—and their lesser brethren, the so-called provincial priests, who were distributed over the whole country. Indeed, the 18th chapter of Deuteronomy (1—8), which specially deals with the status of priests, gives one, by its very meagreness and brevity, the impression of being merely a recapitulation of directions which had been set forth in greater detail on some previous occasion. If this be so, and if Deuteronomy really refers to an original distinction between the "Levite Priests" (= "the Sons of Aaron" of the Priestly Code) and "the Levites," then Wellhausen's line of argument not only loses a great deal of its force, but the main pillar of the theory he has erected comes tumbling about his ears. For, in that case, Ezekiel's pretensions appear in a totally new light; a closer examination reveals the fact that Ezekiel merely follows Deuteronomy when he seeks to enforce the original distinction between the Levites and Levite Priests, the latter being attached to the Central Holy Place at Jerusalem. Seeing that the Levites had usurped priestly functions in the high-places, it was inevitable that an enforcement of the provisions of the Priestly Code—with which Ezekiel, in his capacity as priest, must have been perfectly familiar, and which he now wished to set in operation—should bring upon them signal punishment and degradation. Moreover, in Ezekiel's prophetic vision of the new temple and its arrangement, we can trace from the beginning (Ezek. xl. 3) an almost unmistakable allusion to Moses himself; in his dream Ezekiel finds himself on the top of a high mountain, from whence he has a view of the ruins of Jerusalem, and there a man, whose "appearance was like the appearance of brass, with a line of flax in his hand and a measuring reed," gives him the dimensions of the new temple; does not this at once remind us of Moses, who from the summit of Mount Nebo was allowed to take one look at that holy land which he himself was never to enter? The man of brass is none other than Moses, whose "eye was not dim, nor his natural force abated," when Yahveh shewed him from the hill-top the whole country that had been promised to the Israelites. No modern critic will ever succeed in permanently dislodging this venerable brazen figure from his lofty watch-tower, in spite of all triumphant assertions to the contrary. For if we refuse to credit him and his generation with the Priestly Code, with Deuteronomy and its touching valedictory oration, with the Jehovistic Book of the Covenant, or even with the Decalogue, what is there left of Moses beyond a mere empty unsubstantial shadow?

The fact that the Mosaic Law in its most complete form, as set forth in the Priestly Code, was not fully enforced until after the Babylonian Captivity, cannot possibly be regarded as a proof that it did not come into existence until this later period. After Moses and Joshua came the turbulent transitional period of the Judges, a time, however, which possesses a special importance for the question before us, owing to the fact that it was then that the Israelites adopted a new language—the Canaanite—a tongue which was, it is true, nearly allied to their old idiom, but still a new tongue to them. It was at this time, too, that the foreign element Ba'al first made its appearance in Israelitish personal names, and that the ancient traditions of the race were translated into Hebrew, and subjected to what would seem to have been a more or less thorough recension.[1] It was not

---

[1] Cf. p. 274, where this point is briefly dealt with. By " Hebrew," I mean here the language which we find presented to us in the pages of the Old Testament, and which was essentially identical with Phoenician, its points of difference from Phoenician representing survivals from the earlier idiom of Israel. Did we but possess a fuller knowledge of Phoenician, we should be able to determine with greater exactitude how much of Hebrew is genuine Canaanite and how much is Arabic. I must

until the time of Samuel and David that things began to grow more settled. The first king to find himself in a position to insist on the observance of the Mosaic Code was Solomon, but the temple which he had built was scarcely finished, when, led away by the influence of his wives, he allowed sacrifices to be offered unto strange gods, and immediately after his death came the deplorable political schism which resulted in the permanent separation of the little province of Judah, the seat of the new central Holy Place, from the rest of Israel. And, be it noted, it was in the northern kingdom that the final recension of both the Book of Judges and the Jehovistic narrative was carried out. These two books, according to the modern critics, contain little or no evidence to show that the Priestly Code was then in operation, and this fact is regarded as one of the main arguments in favour of their theory as to the post-exilic origin of the Code. It must not be forgotten, however, that the priests of the northern kingdom had only too often good reasons for either modifying or entirely suppressing portions of the traditions which would otherwise have become a standing reproach to themselves. For instance, the oft-quoted passage in Ex. xx. 24, "An altar of earth thou shalt make unto me, and shalt sacrifice thereon thy burnt offerings and thy peace offerings, thy sheep and thine oxen: in every place where I record

insist, however, on the fact that the only persons whom I can recognize as competent to decide questions of this kind are those who are equally familiar with Arabic (including the Minaeo-Sabaean and Aethiopic dialects), Babylonian, and Phoenician.

my name I will come unto thee and bless thee,"[1]—is evidently a recension attributable to the laxer practice which obtained among these northern priests, who though they condemned the calf-worship introduced by Jeroboam, yet were not prepared to deprive the people of the blessings of the national God who sat enthroned on Sion. Did we but possess a more complete and detailed tradition in regard to the time of the Judges and the period of the Kings,[2] I am firmly convinced that Wellhausen's whole theory—even apart from the fact that it is contradicted by the testimony of the monuments—would at once collapse like a house of cards. Unfortunately, however, the historical tradition of the Old Testament has come down to us only in fragments. And the "popular" character of the Jehovistic narrative, out of which Wellhausen tries to make so much capital, is in a great measure due to a circumstance which for a long time past has not received all the attention it merits, viz. the fact that this source owes its distinctive character to the northern kingdom (*i.e.* to Israel rather than to Judah). Although this primitive popular element

[1] As opposed to the phrase, "the place which the Lord your God shall choose," which is so often and so emphatically repeated in Deuteronomy. But such a petty alteration as that involved in the substitution of "the place" for "every place," is of little importance compared with the many biassed interpolations with which Wellhausen delights to bolster up his theory.

[2] Such as that which probably furnished part of the material for "the Midrash of the Book of Kings," quoted in the Books of the Chronicles, though there the facts may have been presented in a more imaginative guise.

may appeal more strongly than any other to our imaginations, it is scarcely an adequate vehicle for the transmission of a lofty and abstract conception of the Godhead such as that which Moses—whose aim was misunderstood by his contemporaries—was commissioned to, and actually did, impart, though in doing so he was obliged to employ as an accessory an elaborate system of sacrificial and ritual observances. As we have already had ample opportunity for observing, these two opposing principles (popular and priestly religion) have existed side by side in Western Asia from time immemorial. Characters such as Melchizedek of Salem in the time of Abraham, or Jethro of Midian, and Balaam in the time of Moses, suggest no taint of anachronism to any one who remembers the religious import of the earliest Western Semitic personal names, and of the earliest literary monuments of Egypt and Babylonia. Of course the free-thinker who looks at all such matters from an "enlightened standpoint," may, if he chooses, describe them as mere "religious humbug," or "priestly trickery," even though the evidence of the inscriptions constrains him to ac knowledge that they date back to the time of Abraham or of the Pyramids; this, after all, is a question of taste, and with such persons it would be useless to argue further. When, however, we find that a whole school of evangelical theologians do not hesitate to declare that a passage was at a later date composed or interpolated, simply because they are unwilling to recognize the existence of any high moral teaching or lofty conception of the Godhead prior to the time of the prophets of the eighth or seventh centuries B.C., then, in view of the facts adduced in the present volume, we cannot but regard their attitude as a deplorably mistaken one, and hope that it may soon become a thing of the past. It was once the fashion to declare that all passages in Arabian poetry of the period prior to Muhammed, in which the word Allah (= God, properly al-ilâhu = the God, *i.e.* the one God) occurred, must *ipso facto* be classed as later interpolations. At present, however, when—thanks to the evidence of the later Sabaean inscriptions—it becomes every day more certain that hundreds of years before the time of Muhammed, both Judaism and Christianity had taken root and found acceptance in various places in Arabia, scholars are beginning to abandon the hasty conclusions of ten years ago in favour of the accepted opinion of the day. The same thing will happen in connection with the criticism of the Pentateuch. Had the beginnings of the Israelite religion really been a mixture of Fetichism and ancestor-worship, these beginnings would have left their impress upon the language and could have been detected by the method of comparative philology. It becomes, however, clearer every day that the Semites—and more particularly the Western Semites—had from the beginning a much purer conception of the Deity than was possessed by any of the other races of antiquity, such as the Sumerians or Aryans, for instance, and critics of the Old Testament can no longer afford to shut their eyes to this fact.

In regard to the influence of Egypt in Mosaic times—an influence of which the priestly breastplate affords such a striking illustration—it should further be pointed out that there are quite a number of Egyptian loan-words to be found in the laws of the Priestly Code. Under this head may be mentioned such words as *sheti* = warp, from the Egyptian *seta'* = to spin, or heckle (BONDI, *Zeitschr. für ägypt. Spr.*, vol. xxxiii. p. 1); *zereth* = span, from Egyptian *tsert* = hand (BONDI, *ibid.*, vol. xxxii. p. 132); *sol'am* = locust, from Egyptian *senhem;* names of gems such as *achlamah* and *leshem* (see p. 281), *peshet* and *pishtah* = flax, linen (Egyptian *pesht*), *ephah* and *hîn*,[1] and probably a number of other names for units of measurement, together with various personal names of the Mosaic epoch, *e.g.* in the first place, the name of Moses himself (cf. *mose* in Thutmosis [originally Tehut-mose] and similar names); then the names Phinehas, Puti-el (half Egyptian, half Semitic, cf. Poti-ph-re) [Potiphar] and many other words, including probably the much-debated *Pesakh* (Passah). In the case of no other religious festival do we find so much stress laid upon its *memorial* character as in this, (cf. Ex. xii. 14), and there must be something more than mere coincidence in the fact that the Egyptian word *sacha'*[2] means "to call to mind." This shews that the initial *pe* must be a form of the article which was in general use in the time of the

---

[1] Egyptian, *ipt* and *hin;* the former borrowed in primitive times from Babylonian *pttu*, and the latter from Babyl. *gin*.

[2] Radically related to the Babylonian *sakhâru* = "to seek, to reflect upon," and the common Semitic element *zakâru*.

later Empire, and that, therefore, the word was originally *pe-sakh*.[1]

This brings me back once more to the identification of Arpakeshad [Arphaxad] with Ur Kasdim, which has already been touched upon on p. 210. These two words are essentially and absolutely equivalent; both are used to denote the original home of the Hebrews. Now it is clear, on *à priori* grounds, that just as Keshad is equivalent to Kasdim, so too Ar- is equivalent to Ur-, especially when we remember that in the Western Semitic script the consonants only are given; the sole distinction between the two expressions in their earliest written form lies in the element *pa* introduced between *Ar-* and *Keshad* in the former name, and in the plural termination *im* affixed to the second element of the latter. Since tradition, both in Gen. x. 22 and 24, as well as in Gen. xi. 10 *et seq.*, and 1 Chron. i. 17 and 24, points to the vocalization Arpakeshad (LXX. Arphaxad), we need not hesitate to accept this as correct. Now the fact that Elam and Assur appear

---

[1] My friend Glaser, after reading my note on *Arpakeshad*, in the *Academy*, and before he was aware that the Egyptian word *sakha* meant "to remember," drew my attention to the fact that *pesakh* might be divided into *pe-* (the Egyptian article) and *sakh*, an analysis which seems to me to be unassailable. Glaser, whose opinion in regard to my explanation of *Arpakeshad* is all the more deserving of respect, because he has never adopted a partizan attitude on questions of Old Testament criticism, after carefully weighing the alternative interpretation proposed by Cheyne (which will be discussed later on), boldly supports my analysis *Ar-pa keshad*. His example is likely to be followed by all those who refuse to be blinded by the prejudices which obscure the vision of modern critics of the Pentateuch.

in place of Babel and Assur[1] (which are the names we should have expected to find), points to a time when Babylonia was under Elamite rule; that is to say, to the epoch of the Kassite dynasty (ca. 1700— 1183), or, in other words, the period of the children of Israel's sojourn in Egypt, and the time of Moses and Joshua. In that case, however, the *pa* inserted between *Ar* (originally Ur) and *Keshad*, can be nothing else but the Egyptian article,[2] since it cannot be explained in any other way, and our only alternative would be to strike it out as meaningless. One tradition, therefore, which is probably to be attributed to the Jehovist writer, calls Abraham's native place Ur Kasdîm (Ur of the Chaldees, apparently in order to distinguish it from Uru-shalem = Jerusalem) while the other tradition — strange to say, that of the Priestly Code—employs a semi-Egyptian expression, Ur-pa-Keshad (Ur of the Keshad, *i.e.* of the Chaldees). That Egyptian forms of this kind were common enough, especially in the case of geographical terms and of expressions applied to the Egyptians themselves, among a race who had spent over 400 years in Egypt, is evident from the presence of such names as Puti-el (Ex. vi. 25), "Eleazar, Aaron's son, took him one of the daughters of Puti-el to wife"

---

[1] The Elam mentioned here as one of the sons of Shem cannot possibly be identical with Elam proper; the ethnological and linguistic differences between the Elamites and the Semitic Babylonians (the Sumerians had already been merged with the Semites long before the time of Abraham) must have been familiar to Semitic peoples from the very earliest antiquity.

[2] *i.e.* "Ur of the Keshad;" cf. Keshed, Gen. xxii. 22.

(cf. Potiphar, Potosiris). It is interesting to note that the son of this marriage also received the Egyptian name of Phinehas.

This variant, Arpakeshad for Ur-kasdîm, affords us a striking proof of the fact that the Israelites, during their stay in Egypt, had not forgotten the original ancestor of their race, or the name of the place from whence they had first sprung. Nay, more, I confidently assert, that all the traditions concerning the period before Joseph (*i.e.* of the Patriarchs, including the primitive records which Abraham brought with him from Chaldaea), which have been handed down to us in Genesis, in various recensions, were even at that time current among the Israelites, and that, too, in a written form. That it was impossible for them to have borrowed these traditions from the Canaanites at a later date is conclusively proved by the evidence of their names. For the names of the Patriarchs, as well as those of the Israelite contemporaries of Moses, from the stage of religious development which they reveal, present so strong a contrast with those of the Canaanites that, on this ground alone, it is impossible to believe that Abraham can have been a Canaanite Weli or Saint, whose worship the Israelites appropriated after their conquest of Hebron. In regard to the place-names, Ya'kob-el and Yashap-el, referred to on p. 110, note 1, these have all the appearance of having been originally formed from personal names, and were either survivals from some epoch long gone by before the Western Semites of Northern Palestine had as yet become generally subject to the influence of the Babylonian religion, or else Ya'kob-el was a direct reminiscence of the patriarch Jacob, dating from the time when he dwelt in the vicinity of Bethel; in the latter event, Ya-shap-el must either have been founded by or received its name from a relative of one of the patriarchs.

Compared with my explanation of Arpakeshad, the theory recently put forward by Professor Cheyne of Oxford[1] can only be described as distinctly infelicitous—based, as it is, on assumptions of far too sweeping a character. He suggests that Shem must have had six sons instead of only five, viz. Elam, Assur, Arpak = Arrapach on the lower Zab, Keshad, Lud and Aram, and, in spite of the fact that the conjunction "and" appears between each of the five names both in the original Hebrew text and in the Greek translation, and that, therefore, at the very least, we should expect "and Arpak and Keshad," he proposes to read "Arpak, Keshad," instead of "Arpakeshad." Unfortunately, the circumstance that we should in that case be obliged to strike out the element "Arpa" from Arpakeshad, in Gen. x. 24 and Gen. xi. 10, where the name occurs as that of an ancestor of Eber's, renders this conjecture of Cheyne's—in itself ingenious enough—quite inadmissible, even apart from the fact that, both in the Tribute-lists of Thutmosis III. and in the cuneiform texts, Arrapach is always written with the strong aspirate kh, and

[1] Cf. Cheyne's paper, *Professor Hommel on Arphaxad*, in the *Expositor*, Feb. 1897, pp. 145—148.

never with a *k*. The reluctance of Wellhausen's supporters to adopt my obvious analysis of Arpa-keshad into Arpa-keshad (or, since the vowel points are merely a later addition, Ur-pa-keshad) can be readily understood, since were they to do so they would naturally be obliged to accept the conclusions which result from it — conclusions which demonstrate the absurdity of their theories. Professor Cheyne is unable to conceal the fact that if it were really possible to assign the Priestly Code to a very early pre-exilic date, such as the Mosaic period, for instance, there would be nothing astonishing about a hybrid formation such as Ur-pa-Chesed, since it is well-known that the Egyptians of the later Empire borrowed largely from the Semites,[1] and the Semites doubtless returned the compliment; he adds, moreover, that the matter would stand on quite a different footing if I were really in a position to prove " that the personal names in the Priestly Code are to any large extent primitive (*i.e.* ancient and genuine), as is generally assumed "—an assumption which he is strongly inclined to question.

Before concluding the present chapter, however, I propose, in fulfilment of the promise made on p. 26, to briefly show that the personal names assigned to the time of Moses by the Priestly Code, and more particularly the lists of names in the Book of Numbers, possess precisely the same features as the Arabian personal names of the second millennium

---

[1] Cf. more particularly *pa ba-'al* (W. MAX MÜLLER, *Asien und Europa*, p. 309), instead of *ha-ba-'al*, an absolutely analogous hybrid used by the Egyptians.

B.C., referred to in Chapter III. Fortunately, the Arabian personal names of the Khammurabi dynasty, and the Canaanite names of the Tel el-Amarna period dealt with in Chapter VII., furnish two definite bases of comparison by which we may test the earlier Hebrew personal names. They enable us to divide these latter into two main groups; one containing the still almost purely Arabic names of the Mosaic period; the other, the nomenclature of the time of the Judges with its strong admixture of Canaanite elements.

In the first place, let us see whether Wellhausen is in the right when he says, "The long lists of names in Num. i., vii., and xiii.[1] are nearly all cast in the same mould, and are in no way similar to genuine ancient personal names;"[2] or whether this assertion is of the same hasty and dictatorial character as that other assertion of his, in regard to the Greek origin

[1] With these, of course, the names in Num. xxxiv. should also be classed. This list Wellhausen assigns to the Persian epoch, because it contains the name Parnak.
[2] *Prolegomena*, 2nd ed. p. 371, from which I copied the above sentence. Similarly in the 1st edition, a copy of which is in my own possession, we read on p. 334, "that these names have no parallel in ancient times, and look very much as though they had been manufactured." Such names, we are told, "can scarcely have been taken from Mosaic records, especially those in which the verb is in the perfect tense." And again, "the unquestionably ancient and genuine compounds Ishmael, Israel, Jerahmeel, Eliezer, Othniel, Bethuel, Kemuel, are all of them names of peoples or nations," whereas, so Wellhausen argues, personal names compounded with El do not occur in the Jehovistic tradition dealing with the time of Moses, nor indeed up to the time of Samuel— all of which statements have already been shewn by the evidence adduced in Chapter III. to be inaccurate.

of most of the Arabian names of the constellations, which appear in his *Reste arabischen Heidenthums*.[1]

In the lists in question we find a large number of names with which Chapter III. has already familiarized us ; *e.g.* Abî-dan = my Father judges, and Elî-ab = my God is a Father, Elî-dâd = my God is a Relation, Akhî-'ezer = my Brother is Help, Akhî-ra' (originally Akhî-rû'a = my Brother is a Friend, or Akhî-Rê' = my Brother is Ra?) and Akhî-hûd (from Akhî-yehûd), Shemû-el (*vide* p. 98), Ammî-el = my Uncle is God, Ammî-hûd (from Ammî yehûd, cf. Yehûda), Ammî-nadab = my Uncle has given, and Ammî-shaddai = my Uncle is Shaddai (*vide supra*, pp. 108 *et seq.*), to which may be added the allied forms Gaddî-el = my Grandfather is God, Tsûrî-Shaddai = Shaddai is my Rock, Tsûrî-el = my Rock is God, Pedah-Tsûr = He (the Rock) has redeemed ; cf. Pedah-el and Eli-Tsûr = my God is a Rock.[2] The following names, compounded with El, may also be mentioned: Eli-tsaphan = my God hath borrowed (cf. also Num. iii. 30), Eli-shama' = my God hath harkened, El-yasaph = my God hath increased (from Eli-yasaph), Mî-ka-el = Who is as God (cf. Mî-sha-el, Ex. vi. 22, and *supra*, pp. 71 and 141), Gamlî-el = my recompense is God, Hannî-el = my Grace is God, Nethan-el = God gave it, Paltî-el = my redemption is God (cf. *supra*, p. 238), Shelûmî-el

---

[1] Cf. my exhaustive contradiction of this statement based on ancient Arabian poetry, in a paper entitled, *Ursprung und Alter der arabischen Sternnamen*, in the *Zeitschr. der D. M. Gesellsch.* vol. xlv. (1891) pp. 502—619. Cf. also the Appendix, pp. 319—320.

[2] For S. Arabian names with Tsuri, cf. Appendix, pp. 319, 320.

= my peace is God, etc. To these may be added the abbreviated names, which are especially numerous in the list of the spies given in Num. xiii., such as Bukki, Gaddi, Gemalli Palti, (cf. Paltî-el and Yaphlet), Shelômi (cf. Shelûmi-el), etc.; to this class also belong Zimri, Num. xxv. 14 (*vide supra*, p. 83, note 2), and other similar names occurring in the Priestly Code. To complete our list, we may note names of one element like 'Akrân, 'Azzân, Shiphtân, 'Enân (from 'Ainân), Kislôn, Nakhshôn,[1] Tsû'ar (another pure Arabic formation, cf. S. Arabian Tsai'ar), Kaleb (cf. *supra*, p. 113), Nûn (cf. the name Nûnîa in a contract tablet of the time of king Zabium), Raphû'a (cf. p. 81, Ilî-rapa'a), Shaphat (cf. Shiphtan and the name Yeho-shaphat = Yahveh judgeth, as also En-Mishpat, p. 148), and a few more. The verb *shaphat* = to judge, seems, it is true, to be peculiar to the Canaanite language, the genuine Arabic name-formation preferring to substitute *din* (cf. *supra*, Abi-dân),[2] but in view of the constant intercourse between Canaan and Egypt in the time of the later Empire, it is by no means surprising that words of this kind—to which may be added others, such as *tsaphan* = to save (cf. *supra*, Eli-tsaphan and the Phoenician Tsaphon-Ba'al)—should have gained

---

[1] The termination *ôn* shows that the true Arabian termination *ân* (*e.g.* in 'Akrân) was already being assimilated to Canaanite.

[2] It is indeed an open question whether the word *shaphat* was not originally spelt with a "Sin," and whether there may not have been two nearly allied verbs *shaphat*, one spelt with a Shin (modified *s*), the other with a Sin (originally = *sh*), in which case the S. Arabian *shuphata* = to determine, promise, grant (spelt, it is true, with a different *t*), would apply here.

currency among the Israelites. And lastly, in regard to the name Parnak, which Wellhausen declares to be of Persian origin, Friedr. Delitzsch (*Wo lag das Paradies?* p. 265) has already found a parallel to it in Barnaki, a territory near Tel Assur on the Middle Euphrates, mentioned in one of Esarhaddon's inscriptions—a name which might also be transcribed as Parnak.[1]

Now, if all these names had been made to pattern, either during or after the Captivity,[2] we should naturally expect to find them prominently represented among the numerous personal names which occur in Ezra and Nehemiah. This, however, is by no means the case. Even such characteristic names as those compounded with 'Amm, Tsûr, and Shaddai, are never found in post-exilic times; names compounded with El, on the other hand, appear in a curious medley with those compounded with Yah, these latter being, however, by far the more numerous of the two. And though, it is true, that names like Be-zal-el = under the protection of God, Ex. xxxi. 2,[3] recur under Ezra, this was of course due to the mania for imitating Mosaic institutions, which, after reaching the last stage of decay, had just then been revived in an unparalleled manner.

---

[1] As a matter of fact, this word, like many other so-called Quadriliterals, may possibly have been formed from a pure Arabic Pannaku (cf. Arab. *fanaka*), by the insertion of an *r* (dissimilation); many analogous instances are to be found both in Arabic and Aramaic.

[2] It would be interesting to know something more of this "pattern," which was available in post-exilic times.

[3] Cf. Zal-munna' and Zal-pachad, LXX. Sal-paad, and the Ancient Babylonian Tsili-Istar and similar names, p. 71.

It is quite certain, therefore, that the names contained in these lists in the Book of Numbers cannot be rightly assigned to any other period than that of Moses. In spite, therefore, of the presence of some names (especially in Numbers xiii.) which seem to indicate that the text is corrupt in places, these lists have been shown, by the external evidence of the tradition preserved in inscriptions of the second millennium B.C. (*vide supra*, Chapter III.), to be genuine and trustworthy documents,[1] before which historical theories built up by modern critics of the Pentateuch must "collapse irretrievably."

---

[1] The names in 1st Chronicles (to say nothing of those in Joshua) contain much ancient material, a fact sufficiently proved by such names as Yaphlet, Yamlek, Yish'î and many others. On some future occasion I hope to deal more fully with this point.

CHAPTER X

FROM JOSHUA TO DAVID

RETROSPECT AND CONCLUSION

EVEN if we possessed no other details in regard to the history of Israel from the conquest of the region west of the Jordan (*i.e.* from the time of Joshua) down to the reign of David or Solomon, beyond the personal names of the period in question, and a sort of skeleton outline of the various wars and victories, written something after this fashion, " Gideon (Ye-rub-Ba'al) defeated the Midianites," we should still be able by their aid alone to secure the recognition of one fact which has a most important bearing on the religious history of the people. I refer to the infiltration of Canaanite elements into the nomenclature of Mosaic and pre-Mosaic times, which up to the time of Joshua had been almost entirely free from such admixture, being still essentially Arabian in character. Names like Jerub-Ba'al (son of Saul), Merib-Ba'al (son of Jonathan), and Be'el-yada' (son of David, afterwards changed into Eli-yada'), speak for themselves, and prove that by that date the Israelites had proved unfaithful to their ancient traditions, and had allowed themselves to be deeply influenced by the religion of the conquered Canaanites.[1] Even names compounded with Adônî = my Lord (cf. *supra*, p. 217), such as Adônî-râm, betray this influence. The frequent recurrence in the Book of Judges of passages in which we are told that the Israelites forsook Yahveh, and followed after Ba'al and Astarte (*c.g.* ii. 11 *et seq.*), or that they intermingled with the Canaanites and served the gods of their wives or of their sons-in-law (iii. 6), harmonise in every way with the conclusions to be drawn from a study of the personal names. These names compounded with Ba'al clearly shew that these laments over the apostasy of Israel, during the time of the Judges, are in no way due to the pen of a later "Deuteronomistic" editor.

That this apostasy was, however, merely partial and transitory, and that Mosaic principles always managed to get the upper hand in the end, is evident from the steady increase in the number of names compounded with Jo, Jeho (from Yahveh) and Jah, such as Joash, Jotham, Jeho-natan (Jonathan), Abi-jah, Joab, Zeruiah, Shephat-iah, Adônî-Jah, Uri-jah, Jeho-shaphat, Benâ-iah, Jehoiada. Although a son of David bore a name containing the element Ba'al, viz. Be'el-iada'—which was, however, afterwards, and probably during David's life-time, altered to Eli-iada'—we find from this period forward no other instance of a Hebrew personal name con-

[1] To this list may be added the name 'Ebed-Ba'al = servant of Ba'al, Judges ix. 26. In the Hebrew text the name appears simply as 'Ebed; the LXX. variant, Io-Ba'al = Yahveh is Ba'al, proves, however, that this name must originally have been compounded with Ba'al, and in that case must naturally have been 'Ebed-Ba'al.

taining Ba'al—not even a single example during the time of the Kings of Israel—a circumstance we may well be allowed to attribute to the permanent influence of such men as Samuel. Not even a king like Ahab dared in later times to give to his son an appellation involving Ba'al. On the contrary, it is manifestly apparent from the names of the Israelite kings, from Solomon onwards, that Yahveh was the prevailing element in all personal designations. How, we may well ask, could the Mosaic Priestly Law come into general usage at a period when, owing to intercourse with the Canaanites, and the appropriation of their language, there was such an assumption of heathen ideas as to almost swamp the pure worship of Yahveh? The Priests and Prophets who remained true to their faith, must have felt no little satisfaction at having been able to transfer faithfully, by paraphrase or translation, the Holy traditions into the lately-cultivated speech[1] and newly-adopted characters of Canaan. In their actual surroundings, and amid the prevailing confusion this must have been their first desirable object. They must have endeavoured, moreover, to secure a wider recognition of the claims of Yahveh, as opposed to the cults of Baal and Astarte, in order to prepare for the introduction of His worship, which

---

[1] This was the Old Testament Hebrew, which although really essentially identical with the ancient Canaanite speech, must have taken over much from the earlier language (Arabic) of the Israelites ; see pp. 274 and 286. I have not hesitated to express my belief, that the linguistic peculiarities of the Priestly Code especially preserve evidence of ancient Arabic survivals.

was already bound up with the Mosaic Code. In this they were successful, and Solomon was the man who was called upon to complete the task which they had begun. The temple was there ready for the purpose, but the worship of Strange Gods, introduced by foreign Princesses, threatened to ruin everything. Solomon died, and it was left to his successors to fulfil the neglected duty; but the unfortunate political schism took place, and with it a further departure from the faith. There still remained, however, at Jerusalem a sacerdotal body to hand on the legacy bequeathed by Moses, and to continue their work throughout the time of the Kings, as we may readily gather from what is related of Jehoshaphat, Hezekiah, and Josiah.

If we were in possession of the *Book of the Wars of the Lord*, or of the *Book of the Upright* (*Sepher ha-jashar*, in which we may see an allusion to Jeshûrûn-Israel), we should doubtless see many things in a clearer light. Still, there is enough material in the personal names involving the name of God, and in the continuous external testimony to the true tradition, furnished by inscriptions to make manifest for all time the falsity of the reconstruction of history associated with the Wellhausen School. Think for a moment of the new horizon opened to us by the Arabic names of the Khammu-rabi dynasty! Who would have dared but a short time ago to have presumed that, as far back as 1700 B.C., Ai or Ya, Shaddai and Shemu (Sum-hu), were in currency as expressions of the religious life of the early progenitors of the Hebrews, and that such names as " Ya is

Priest" (Ya-Kaleb, shortened into Kaleb), "my Uncle (or Father) is Shaddai" ('Ammi-Shaddai), "his name is God" (Samuel), reach back into that definite early period reckoned by the disciples of Wellhausen as mythical! We have seen, from the evidence of personal names, and of inscriptions also, that personalities such as those of Abraham and Melchizedek have nothing of the nature of anachronisms about them, but rest upon traditions which had been put into writing long before the time of Moses. We have learned from the Tel el-Amarna tablets the history of the period prior to the Exodus, and have been able to follow the raiding expeditions into the then semi-Egyptian Canaan, undertaken by the tribe of Asher and the Khabiri, at a time considerably before Moses. Lastly, we gather from the South Arabian inscriptions materials for completing our knowledge of the Sacerdotal system of the Midianites—a system which plays such an important part in the Mosaic history. And how much further material lies still buried in the soil of Babylon, Arabia, and Egypt, with promise of new surprises and further confirmation! Let us in the meantime, in thankful acknowledgment of the Providence of God, rejoice in the treasures already brought to the surface. The contemporaneous monuments, illustrating the religious and secular history of Abraham's time, are indeed worth their weight in gold, and deserve, in an aspect not yet touched upon in the previous chapters, to be still more fully appreciated.

If Abraham were in reality, as both the Bible and the monotheistic names of his people and contemporaries found in the inscriptions prove, the upholder of a concept of Deity which, though simple and childlike, was at the same time a profound recognition of the Divine Unity, then we are put in possession of a new light on *Primitive Biblical History* (Gen. i., ii.).

As the Israelites did not borrow their "Patriarch Legends" at first hand from the Baal-worshippers of Canaan, they did not in manner become possessed of the primitive history of mankind. A people with such a past religious history as the children of Israel, would certainly have no need to rely upon the subjugated peoples of Palestine for accounts of the Creation of the world, the Fall, the Deluge, and of their early progenitors; seemingly mythological traces—the so-called anthropomorphisms—in the Jehovist source, which from a linguistic point of view shews much fewer evidences of an Arabic original than the Priestly Code, may at most have been owing to Canaanite influences.[1] In other respects, the first eleven chapters of Genesis show, as is well known, the closest relationship with the corresponding traditions of Babylonia—with this important exception, that while the latter is inter-penetrated with Sumerian Polytheism, the Bible exhibits nothing but the purest Monotheism—the anthropomorphism ascribed to the Jehovist reflecting only in a superficial

---

[1] It is not at all impossible that the clearly distinguishable Jehovist portions of Genesis represent generally a recension of the ancient traditional material made in the time of the Judges. In this case we should not be obliged to look (as on p. 287, where we hazarded the hypothesis) to the period of the Kings for this recension.

manner, if at all, anything of a polytheistic conception. We have, it is true, the usual explanations offered us, either that the Babylonian traditions were introduced from Assyria in the time of King Ahaz —an utterly untenable hypothesis—or, what has more plausibility about it, the theory that these traditions were brought into Canaan in the Tel el-Amarna epoch, and became known to the Israelites in later times. On either hypothesis, the Israelites must then for the first time, under the influence of the Prophets of the time of the Kings, have rejected the polytheistic element.[1]

The whole affair appears naturally in quite another light once we recognize the monotheism of Abraham—the "Friend of God," who emigrated from the confines of Babylonia into Palestine. While in 1890, in treating of the account of Creation given in Genesis i., I brought myself under the displeasure of Wellhausen by speaking "of the ingenuity of the last recension as being equivalent to a Revelation,"[2] I now no longer hesitate to say that the Monotheistic concept of the Biblical text, and especially of the "Priestly Code,"[3] must, compared with the Babylonian polytheistic version, be regarded as

---

[1] Cf. H. Gunkel's *Schöpfung und Chaos in Urzeit und Endzeit, mit Beiträgen von H. Zimmern, Göttingen*, 1895, in which important book the second hypothesis is put forward.

[2] *Inschriftliche Glossen und Exkurse zur Genesis und den Propheten*, II. (Neue Kirchliche Zeitschrift, vol. I. pp. 393—412) p. 407.

[3] Or, perhaps better, the Elohist portions. For the narrative portion, and especially in Genesis, which modern critics ascribe to the "Priestly Codex," belongs to material of the original Elohist, the Source E of Wellhausen, and the B of Dillmann.

the original. Gunkel's remark, on p. 149 of the book referred to in note 1 of the preceding page, that it was the "*dilettanti*" who "gave themselves up to visions in regard to the religious conditions of that primitive period when Abraham dwelt in *Ur-Kasdim*," is in this respect characteristic. Twenty pages further on he himself even dares to face the ticklish question whether we should not "go back to a still more ancient period, and connect with Abraham the introduction of the Babylonian Creation myth among the Hebrews" (p. 167). He comes to the conclusion, that "even if there were no reason to regard the tradition itself as unhistorical (that is, that Abraham was an emigrant from Babylonia), it would not apparently be advisable to leave the sure footing of history and transfer ourselves into a distant period of which Hebrew tradition had at most given only a few scattered details." We have seen, however, in the present volume, how near that "distant period" has been brought to us by the Ancient Babylonian contract tablets, what an important influence the section of the West Semites to which Abraham belonged had already at this time managed to assert in Babylonia, and how trustworthy and true Hebrew tradition, dealing with pre-Mosaic times, had shown itself to be. Gunkel's book, therefore, is in many parts—notwithstanding the author's contrary intention—only a further confirmation of the position which I have taken up in regard to the Wellhausen hypothesis.

Among important things which the Hebrews brought from Babylonia, may also be reckoned a copious borrowing of the poetic art in its formal aspect. Zimmern in 1893, following a hint of Gunkel's, had already made the important discovery that the Babylonian metres consisted of a regular arrangement of accented syllables, which by means of the cæsura placed at the end of every half-verse,[1] were made up frequently into distichs, tristichs, or tetrastichs. Gunkel makes, in the work referred to, an application of this law, with the happiest results, to ancient Hebrew Poetry, of which he gives many translated examples. I append an example, which illustrates at one and the same time this metrical form, and the well-known parallelism of members (*Parallelismus Membrorum*).

Righteousness and judgment are | the foundation of Thy Throne,
Mercy and truth | go before Thy face.
                                         (Ps. lxxxix. 14.)

The following is another instance, which Franz Delitzsch, at least in his German version, either accidentally or intentionally, cast into its proper rhythm.

He that dwélls in the wárd of the Híghest
And abídes in the sháde of the Míghtiest.   (Ps. xci. 1.)

With which we may compare the lines from the Babylonian Creation Epos:

---

[1] H. Zimmern *Ein vorläufiges Wort über babylonische Metrik*, Zeitschr. f. Assyriologie, vol. viii. pp. 121—124. Cf. the later treatise, *Weiteres zur babylonischen Metrik*, ibid. vol. x. 1895, pp. 1—24. Cf. also p. 183, where the metre of the Kudurlugmal fragment is dealt with.

Naught shall be reformed | what ever I furnish,
Ne'er be taken back | the word of my mouth!

or (from the same):

After he thus his opposer | subdued and thus vanquished,
The haughty contradictor, | to shame thus had brought him.[1]

This metrical arrangement in strophes had, it is true, been imported from Babylon into Canaan during the long period when the latter country was under Babylonian rule and influenced by Babylonian culture. We find traces of this even in the Tel el-Amarna tablets. That the Israelites did not borrow it in the first instance from the Canaanites, but from Abraham's time forward (when they were still Arabs) obtained it like many other things direct from Babylonia, is clear from the following circumstance. We find in the earliest forms of Arab poetry, namely the so-called Ragaz (Rejez) Poems, a marked instance of imitation of the Babylonian strophe.[2] The Ragaz forms the connecting link between the latter and the various Arab metres, such as Kâmil, Wâfir, etc., which are distinguished by a regular alternation of long and short syllables. That the connection here mentioned goes back to Abrahamic times is manifest from the expressions *hagawa, saga'a* (Arabic, *sag'u* [sej'] = rhymed prose; Babylonian, *shegû* = song of mourning), which were

[1] Cf. also the citation on p. 63 from Ishtar's Descent into Hell.
[2] I have called attention in my Assyriological Notes, § 16, *Proceedings Bibl. Arch. Soc.* Jan. 1896 (where I have given an example), to the fact that rhyme is here occasionally employed. It is always used in the Arabic Ragaz verse.

employed both in Hebrew and Arabic when it was necessary to infuse a stirring element into poetical and prophetical pieces.[1]

To return to early Hebrew history after this digression into the domain of metre, it would be well worth the trouble to deal—from the new standpoint furnished by the researches and results of the present work—more fully with the entire material of the first eleven chapters of Genesis, and to illustrate it from Babylonian parallels. There would in such a case be much to say about the lofty concepts of Deity held by the Northern Babylonian Semites (cf. p. 74, twelfth line from the foot), a concept which makes itself clearly apparent in many examples of the religious literature of the Babylonians, all interpenetrated as it was by Sumerian polytheism.[2]

But I must defer for a future occasion the consid-

[1] A more artistic reproduction of the strophe, such as that pointed out by D. H. Müller in several portions of the Prophets, Father Zenner in various Psalms, and F. Perles in certain other songs (*e g.* Deut. xxxii.), depends upon the introduction of a certain rhetorical element into poetry, of which, in spite of D. H. Müller's assertion to the contrary (*Die Propheten in ihrer urspr. Form*, Vienna, 1896), no instance has yet been discovered in Babylonian poetry. It is impossible to admit that the observations of D. H. Müller and Zenner (who are dependent on each other), in regard to the form of the strophe and to the antiphonal arrangement, can be referred back to early Semitic times, as D. H. Müller most earnestly insists on p. 212 of the work referred to. Perhaps I may be allowed, in face of the ostentatious manner in which Müller's book was introduced to the world, to point out that many kindred points are hinted at, or expressly dealt with, in Franz Delitzsch's *Commentary* on the Psalms, especially his translations of the same.

[2] Cf. what is said on p. 86 of the system of name-giving which obtained among the Babylonian Semites; also the deep piety of the Babylonian Psalms of penitence, etc.

eration of this, as of many other points, on account of the limits of space, and will content myself in conclusion with drawing attention briefly to a section of the primitive history which clearly indicates the Old-Chaldæan (*i.e.* according to pp. 210 *et seq.*, the Arabo-Babylonian) origin of the Hebrews. I refer to the description given in Genesis ii. 10—14 of the geographical position of Paradise—(v. 8) " And the Lord God planted a garden eastward, in Eden, (*i.e.* in the desert, Babylonian *Edin*, and thus over against Babylonia, *i.e.* in Arabia). . . . (v. 10) And a river went out . . . thence it was parted, and became four heads. (v. 11) The name of the first is *Pishôn;* that is it which compasseth the whole land of Khawîlah (Havilah), where there is gold. (v. 12) And the gold of that land is good ; there is the Bedolakh [Bdellium, R. V.] and the Shohamstone [Onyx or Beryl stone, R. V.]. (v. 13) And the name of the second river is *Gîkhôn* [Gihon] ; the same is it that encompasseth the whole land of *Kûsh*. (v. 14) And the name of the third river is Khid-dekel [Hiddekel]; that is it which goeth in front of Ashur [R. V. Assyria] ; and the fourth river is the Phrat [Euphrates]."

Now E. Glaser has already shown, in several passages of his *Skizze*, that by Pîshon and Gîkhon the two great central Arabian Wadys, er-Rumma and Dawâsir, were possibly meant; furthermore, that by Khavîla (Havilah) the *hinterland* of Bahrein, in ancient times productive of gold and precious stones, was intended (see pp. 211 and 272 of the present work, for the relation of the latter to the " Country of the Sea" of the cuneiform inscriptions), and that Kush is a known Biblical designation of Central Arabia[1];—for the corroboration of which I refer my readers to my fuller treatment of the subject in the second volume of the *Neue Kirchlichen Zeitschrift*.[2] As for the Khiddekel [Hiddekel], which had, on account of a similarity of sound, been identified later with the Tigris (Idignat, Diglat, cf. Dan. x. 4), it also has a manifest Arabian application. It is only by the Arabic word *Khadd*, an expression for Wady, that the first element in this river-name, which has hitherto been uniformly misunderstood, can be explained: it is the "Wady of Diklah" (Gen. x. 27), or the Wady of Palms. By the latter, however, the Wady el-'Arish is not perhaps intended, but rather, according to the hydrographical deductions of Glaser (*Skizze* II. 343),[3] the Wady Sirhân, or the Northern Arabian Jôf, which flows into the Euphrates, and to the river-system of which a complete network of Wadys, tò the eastward of the S. Palestinian land of Ashur, belong, thus corresponding with the Biblical description ["Khadd-

[1] Cf. for instance 2 Chron. xiv., and my commentary on it [Zerach of Kush, a Sabaean prince] in the *Acts of the 10th Oriental Congress* (Geneva), 3rd part, Leiden 1896, pp. 112 *et seq*.

[2] *Inschrift. Glossen und Exkurse*, 4th vol. of the *Neue Kirchliche Zeitschrift*, pp. 881—902.

[3] Glaser thus writes: "It is also to be noted that the Northern Jauf does not carry its waters towards Jebel Shammar, but in the direction of the Euphrates, or probably, like the Wady er-Rumma, straight to the northern part of the Persian Gulf . . . . These Wadys hardly ever reach the sea, but their course is recognisable by fruitful spots here and there, spots which engendered the belief at all times that these were stages in the course of the Wadi er-Rumma."

dekel] that is it which goeth in front of (that is, to the eastward of) Ashûr [*i.e.* E. of Edom, and not Assyria, as in R. V.].

Thus the Paradise of the Hebrews, according to their early, if not earliest conception, lay between the Euphrates on the east and the land of Ashur on the west (cf. p. 238, where the boundaries of Gen. xxv. 18 are dealt with); it was watered by the Pishon (the Faishân or Saihân of the Arabs) and the Gîkhon (Geï'hân) and its most glorious portion, to judge by the emphasis laid upon its products, was Khavîla [Havilah] or North-eastern Arabia. This conception could have been formed only at a time not very far removed from that in which the Hebrews had left their ancient father-land—probably soon after Abraham's journey from Ur to Haran— and in no case so late as a post-Mosaic period. Consequently, we have clear evidence that Abraham must have brought the primitive traditions with him, and that they were not borrowed for the first time from the Canaanites after the conquest of the region to the west of the Jordan.

With this reference to the Paradise, I bring my investigations to a conclusion. These investigations will result in recovering, I trust, for Biblical Science a territory which has been regarded by many of late as a long-lost Eden, upon which they had nothing but regretful sighs to bestow. I have not much hope of converting quickly to my views the advanced critics, to whom the slightest attempt to invest Abraham and his time with reality must appear as the child-like efforts of *dilettanti*, only worthy of a pitying smile. My highest reward shall be attained, however, if I can restore to many younger theologians, and many of the cultured laity too—who have allowed themselves, with some impatience, it is true, and half-hearted opposition, to be bewitched and confused by the daring of Wellhausen's scientific demonstrations—the ancient Biblical Paradise of their faith, which they had already begun to mourn as irrevocably lost.

APPENDIX

(a) THE LAND OF YADI'A-AB

ON p. 82, the appellations Yada'a-abu, Yada'a-ilu, Yada'a-sumhu and Sumaida' (as to which latter cf. p. 98) are mentioned, together with a number of other South Arabian personal names. With Yada'a-ilu may be compared Yedi'a-el, a name which occurs in the genealogical tables in the Books of the Chronicles. In regard to Yada'a-ab, however — a name which we find in the South Arabian inscriptions applied to several kings of the Hadramaut[1] — Father Scheil has just published (*Recueil*, xix. p. 21) a very interesting contract-tablet date, of the time of Samsu-iluna, one of the kings of the Khammurabi dynasty (*vide supra*, p. 68), which runs as follows—

"In the year in which Samsu-iluna, the king, (in) Ya-di-kha-bu and Guti, the mountain-forests (*khurshâna*) caused stems (Ideogr. *ul*, Semitic *elbu*) of date-palms (*mis-uk-a-na*) and of *gam*-trees to be cut (or felled)."

The *gam*-tree, or *kiddatu*,[2] is the *laurus Cassia*, so that evidently both Yadikhabu and Guti must have been situated in Arabia. This latter name is else-

[1] Cf. MORDTMANN, *Z.D.G.M.* xxxi. p. 80, and more recently, GLASER, *Abessinier*, p. 34 etc.

[2] Pronounced with a strong *k*-sound cf. Hebrew *kiddah*.

where applied to a region which lay to the east of Assyria, but it is evident from the context that it is here used of some place either between or on the wooded plateaux of Arabia; the name appears to be identical with the Arabic Gawwat, for the Arabian geographers mention the fact that Yemâma was formerly known as Gaww.[1]

It is quite clear, therefore, both from the Hebrew Yedî'a-el and from this word Yadikhabu, that the Arabian names in question ought to be pronounced Yadi'a-ilu and Yadi'a-abu respectively (instead of Yada'a-ilu etc.).

(b) THE DIVINE NAME TSÛR

In regard to the ancient Hebrew name Tsûr (rock), which came to be employed as a Divine appellation (*vide* p. 297), special prominence being given to it in the Song of Moses (Deut. xxxii. 4, "The Rock, his work is perfect;" v. 37, "the Rock in which they trusted"), as well as in other passages in the Old Testament (*e.g.* 1 Sam. ii. 2, in the Song of Hannah; in Ps. xviii. and 2 Sam. xxii. etc.), and which occurs as a place-name in Beth-Tsûr (cf. Beth-el), near Hebron, I have just come upon this in a South Arabian votive inscription from Harim, where it occurs in the name

---

[1] Even in the South Arabian inscriptions we find the Gaww as the name of a district near Saba (*vide* my *Südarab. Chrestomathie*, p. 111), in which Dhû-Alam, a sanctuary of Sin in the Hadramaut, would seem to have been situated. Probably, too, the king Tudkhul (of Goi, Gen. xiv. 1), mentioned above on p. 184, ought to be referred to this territory, rather than to Guti, which lay to the east of Assyria.

AS ILLUSTRATED BY THE MONUMENTS 319

of a female slave, or temple hand-maiden, apparently of Midianite origin.[1]

As I had occasion to point out some time ago (*Aufsätze and Abhandl.* p. 29, note 1), the names in the inscriptions Hal. 144—146, 148, 150, 151, 153—159,[2] which occur after the Divine name Môtab-Natiyân,[3] are not attributes applied to this deity, but personal names. Moreover, when we come to compare them with similar names — often very much alike in sound — in the Minaean temple records, referred to on p. 237, we find that they are *feminine* personal names. Side by side with such names as Abi-hamaya = my Father protects, Abi-radsawa = my Father is well pleased, Abi-shapaka = my Father gives freely, Abi-shawwara = my Father consents (?), Ili-hail (cf. the Hebrew female name Abi-hail), we also come across the female name Tsûri-'addana,[4] which in Hebrew must have been written Tsûri-'addan.

In the Zinjerli inscriptions, again, (N. Syria, 8th century B.C.,) we find Tsûr in the name of king Bir-tsûr (= the god Bir is a Rock) of Sam'al, who is the adversary of a certain king Azri-Ya'u (a name compounded with Yahveh) of Ya'udî, a district of N. Syria. As I have elsewhere [5] pointed out, these

---

[1] Cf. Num. xxv. 15, where a prince of the Midianites bears the name Tsur—an abbreviation from Tsûrî-el.

[2] These inscriptions date from the time of the Sabaean priest-kings, *i.e.* from the 8th century B.C. at latest, or perhaps a good deal earlier.

[3] Cf. the name of the Nabataean deity, Mautebah.

[4] Cf. Hebrew Yehô-'addan, 2 Kings xiv. 2, the mother of king Amazlah (= my rock, *i.e.* God, is pleased).

[5] *Das graphische* h *im minäischen* (*vide supra*, p. 273, note 1).

inscriptions come down to us from races who were originally natives of Edom or Midian.

Now, since this name Tsûr crops up in the 8th century B.C., as a divine appellation employed both in South Arabia and in Sam'al, and in both cases as an importation from N.W. Arabia (thus indicating a common source), it is evident that its first introduction into the land of Midian must have taken place at least some centuries earlier, a fact which is of decisive importance in determining the antiquity of Hebrew names compounded with *Tsûr* (*vide supra*, p. 298).

The female names Abi-radsawa, Ili-hail and Tsûri-'addana, in the votive inscriptions dating from the time of king Yadhmur-malik of Harim (according to Glaser, a contemporary of Kariba-ili Watar, priest-king of Saba), correspond to the female names in the Minaean temple records; viz.: Abi-radsawa (of Bausân), Abi-hail (of Gaza), and Abi-'addana (of Gaza), the meaning of this last name being "my Father is pleased," instead of "my Rock is pleased."[1] The fact that both the Hebrew Yeho-'*addan*, and the S. Arab. Abi-'*addana* and Tsûri-'*addana*, are female names, is very interesting, and shows once again the very close relationship which existed between the ancient Hebrew and South Arabian (more especially the Minaean or Midianite) nomenclature; nor can

---

Of course, it is only the *names* that are identical, their owners being different in each case. These female slaves consecrated to the deity, most of whom came from Midian—some of them, however, from Katabân and Hadramaut as well—seem to have performed the same functions as the *lavi'ât*, or female Levites, mentioned on pp. 276 *et seq*.

it be a mere accident that the same element *hamaya* = to protect, appears both in the Hebrew female name Hami-tal (written Khami-tal, cf. Abi-tal) and in the Minaean female name Abi-hamaya, or that the element *hàil* is employed in both the female names Ili-hail (Minaean) and Abi-hail (Hebrew).

In this connexion—and as a further illustration of my remarks on pp. 277 *et seq.*—I may be allowed to draw attention to another interesting votive inscription (Hal. 681), the author of which is a woman, and which runs as follows—" Muraggila (or Margûla), daughter of Thaubân, the Hanakitess, has offered up a thank-offering and vow (*tanakhkhayat wa- tan-adhdhharan*, cf. Hebrew *minkhah*[1] and *neder*) to the lord (*ba'al*) of the house of her god, Su'aid, because she had prayed to him for forgiveness,[2] that he might again be pacified; then laid he a penance on her, she, however, offered a *sin-offering* (khatta'at, Heb. *piel*, *e.g.* Lev. vi. 19) and paid forfeit (?) and humbled herself; may he (the god) in mercy reward her for it." These and similar inscriptions (cf. also Hal. 147, 149, and 152 from Harim), though they cannot be classed with the Ancient Sabaean, undoubtedly belong to the era before Christ, at a period when the Jewish influences which afterwards (from about 300 A.D. onwards) came into operation

[1] In this case *minhah* = bloodless sacrifice, and *minhah* = gift, must be etymologically distinct.

[2] Similar bronze tablets from Harim contain, in place of this expression, the words "because she, on the third day of the festival (cf. Ex. xix. 15) and moreover during the time of her impurity, had come near unto a man," (Gl. 1054, Vienna Museum), or "because she had transgressed (*ha-khata'at*) in the sanctuary" (Hal. 682).

in South Arabic cannot have yet been in operation; this is sufficiently proved by the references found in them to heathen deities, such as Dhu-Samway, Halfân (god of oaths), and Athtar. The ritual term *khat'at* = sin-offering, must, therefore, have been indigenous to South Arabia from the time of the ancient Minaeans.

(c) THE LAND OF EBER

An article by Eduard Glaser (dated March 13, 1897), dealing with the antiquity of the Minaean inscriptions, which has just appeared in Berlin, in the *Mittheilungen der vorderasiatischen Gesellschaft*, may be usefully compared with what I have said on pp. 251—259. Glaser, who looked through the proof-sheets of the present volume, and whom I have to thank for his kindness in allowing me to see the article in question before it was printed, suggests an extremely probable explanation of the parallel references (dealt with on p. 251) in regard to

Egypt, Gaza and A'shûr,

Egypt, A'shûr and Ibr naharân,

which, in my opinion, throws for the first time a full light on the original position of the Land of Eber. Glaser's conclusions are briefly as follows—

(*a*) The sequence in question is a purely geographical one, viz. first Egypt, then Gaza, then the territory of A'shûr lying further to the south-east of Gaza, and lastly Ibr naharân. Gaza is not specially mentioned in the second enumeration, and ought probably to be taken as forming part of Ashur, but

in any case it is certainly not identical with Ibr naharân, which must rather be looked for somewhere
beyond Gaza and Ashur; to the Minaeans it meant
either the region east of the Jordan,[1] or the territory situated to the northward of Ashur (*i.e.* Palestine proper and Syria), or even both of these together.

(*b*) A close examination will show that the expression Eber ha-nahar, in the Old Testament, is *nowhere*
used of Mesopotamia, but always of the *western*
bank of the Euphrates.[2] Even in 2 Sam. x. 16, it
is much more probable that the region referred to
is that of Aleppo and Mambidji, rather than, as
has hitherto been assumed, Haran.

(*c*) The name originated in Babylonia, not in Palestine, but (as I also assumed) at an early period of
Babylonian history. The Canaanites named the inhabitants of the land of Eber (which latter region
must have included Ur, Borsippa, the Shuhite country—in short, the whole of the territory on the western bank of the Lower and Middle Euphrates), Ibri
(or Hebrews), because they came from this region.
The geographical term Ebir nâri (Eber ha-nahar,
Ibr naharân) must have travelled westward with the
Hebrews (Abraham) and the races allied to them
(mentioned in the Bible as descendants of Abraham).
A parallel case is that of the term Meshriki (= native of the east), which was originally applied to the

---

[1] In this connexion, I may point out that the Minaeans undoubtedly had relations with Ammon, Moab, and Dedan (cf. *supra*, p. 271 *et seq.*).

[2] On p. 254, note 1, I have advanced a contrary proposition; following in this all who had previously attempted to explain the name.

inhabitants of Eastern Yemen, by the Western Yemenites, but which came in time to be used of the former even by the Arabs inhabiting the regions still further eastward. The fact that the Biblical genealogy personifies the land of Eber as one of the forefathers of Abraham, can only be explained on the assumption that Ibri (= inhabitant of the land of Eber) was a designation applied to Abraham by his contemporaries; in any case, however, the term Ebir nâri must have been applied to the western bank of the Euphrates long before the time of Abraham.

In view of these conclusions of Glaser's, it will first of all be necessary to modify what is said on pp. 251 *et seq.*, in reference to the passage in 1 Kings iv. 24. No importance need now be attached to the glosses " from Raphi to Gaza " and " from Takhpis to Gaza," while in the Massoretic text the gloss " from Tiphsah to Gaza," even though it may be a later interpolation, seems to represent the view entertained as far back as the time of Solomon. Similarly the Ba'al-Tsapûna (pp. 253 *et seq.*) of the inscription of Assur-bel-kala refers rather to the Ba'al of Lebanon.

Moreover, on p. 255, Mesopotamia, as the second, if merely temporary, home of Abraham, must be entirely abandoned. Ebir nâri was rather originally the region between Borsippa and Ur, including the adjoining " Country of the Sea " to the southward, and was therefore at once the original home of Abraham and of all the Western Semitic tribes whose descent is traced from him in Genesis. This is very clearly indicated in Josh. xxiv. 2, where we read : " Your fathers dwelt of old in Eber ha-nahar, even Terah, the father of Abraham and the father of Nahor, and they served other gods. (3) And I took your father Abraham from Eber ha-nahar and led him throughout all the land of Canaan." This passage furnishes an exact parallel to Gen. xi. 31 (generally assigned to the Priestly Code) : " And Terah took Abraham his son, etc., and they went forth with them from Ur Kasdîm to go into the land of Canaan ; and they came into Haran and dwelt there." In the first of these two passages, Haran in Mesopotamia is not mentioned at all, even as a temporary haltingplace on the journey from Ur to Canaan, while in the second it is only added at the end of the sentence. The parallel expressions are, " from Eber ha-nahar to Canaan," and " from Ur to Canaan." In Josh. xxiv. 2, therefore, the term Eber ha-nahar cannot be intended for Haran in Mesopotamia, since even according to Gen. xv. 7 (Jehovist), Ur Kasdîm was the earliest home of Abraham ; cf. moreover, the further evidence in favour of Ur afforded by Arpakeshad (Urpakeshad = Ur Kasdîm), and the collateral fact that in the Hebrew genealogy (Gen. xi. 14, and cf. x. 24 *et seq.*) the name of Eber occurs between Arpakeshad and Terah. There can no longer be the slightest doubt, therefore, that Eber ha-nahar (shortened into Eber) was originally merely a synonym for Ur Kasdîm ; in the time of Assur-bel-kala (ca. 1100 B.C.) Ebir nâri was already used as a name for Palestine,

---

[1] In regard to the text K. 3500, published for the first time in its entirety on pp. 194 *et seq. supra*, I may say that my attention was first drawn to it by a brief reference in Winckler's *Geschichte Israel's*, p. 223,

and finally, in the time of the Captivity, for the whole region between the Euphrates and the Mediterranean, then more particularly of Palestine. The changes undergone by this term, which first originated in Babylonia (not in Palestine as is wrongly assumed on p. 255) at a very early period of Babylonian history, is intimately bound up with the migration of the Hebrews from Ur into Canaan.

These researches of Glaser's, outlined above, leave the arguments I have advanced on pp. 235—250, in regard to the position of the land of Ashur in Southern Palestine, and the close connexion between the parallel expressions, " Ashûr and Eber," in Balaam's prophecy, and " A'shûr and Ibr naharân " in the Minaean inscription, Gl. 1155, entirely unaffected.

note 1, where Baal-za-bu [. . .] alone is in question as one of the gods of *ebir nâri*, a name which Winckler had already restored as Baal-tsa-pu-[na]. Prior to this, Bezold in his *Catalogue K*. 3500, had published in the cuneiform script, but without any transcription or translation, the passages, " the gods of Ebir nâri, may they curse you with an irrevocable curse, Baal-sa-me-me, Baal-ma-la-gi-i, Baal-za-bu-bi-i," and " Astartu in the mighty battle the Bow." . . . Neither Bezold nor Winckler, however, made any attempt to identify the name of the king or the date at which the inscription was composed ; Bezold simply calls it "Prayer (?) of Assyrian king (?) for the destruction of his enemies ; mention is made of various gods of foreign countries," the two passages cited above then follow as an indication of the tenour of the inscription.

In conclusion, I must again lay emphasis on the fact that in my *Aufsätze und Abhandlungen*, p. 7, note 8 (cf. also p. 123, *Ibru naharan* in the translati n of the Hebrew Inscription), I had already, owing to an erroneous geographical conception, identified *eber ha-nahar* with *ibr naharân*, but that Winckler (in the note quoted above from his book) was the first to identify *ebir nari* with *eber ha-nahar*, though on the other hand he has, as I think quite wrongly, up to the present, denied that either of them are identical with the Minaean *ibr naharân*.

INDEX

Aaron, 281, 283, 293
-ab, 84, 298, 303
Abatia, 111
Abd-ashirti, 155, 218
Abd-ashrâti, 218
Abd-ashtarti, 218
Abd-el, 105
Abdi-milkut, 217
Abd-kheres, 231
Abd-khiba, 154 ff, 228, 229, 231
Abd-milki, 217
Abd-tirshi, 231
Abi- (in S. Arab. names), 84
-abi, 97
Abi-'addana, 320
Abi-ali, 84
Abi-amara, 84
Abiathar, 283
Abi-baal, 217, 222
Abida', 118 n., 236, 270
Abi-dan, 298
Abi-dhamara, 84
Abi-dhara'a, 84
Abi-hail, 319
Abi-hamaya, 319
Abijah, 303
Abi-kariba, 84
Abi-milki, 217, 222, 228
Abi-ner, 217 n.
Abi-noam, 218 n.
Abi-radsawa, 319, 320
Abi-ramu, 72 n., 94 and n., 101
Abi-sami'a, 84
Abi-shapaka, 84, 319
Abi-shawwara, 319
Abi-shu'a, 53, 68 (King), 75, 91, 92, n., 107, n., 207, n.
Abi-tal, 321
Abi-wakula, 84

Abi-yada', 84, 236 n., 248, 250, 270 f.
Abi-yashukha, 107 n.
Abi-yathu'a, 53, 84, 207
Abi-yati'u, 207
Abi-za'ada, 84
Abner, 217, n.
Abraham (Abram), 45, 69, 72 n., 94, 95, 109, 116, 125, 132, 139, 146 ff., 189, 197, 199, 209, 236, 242, 269, 275, 293, 306 f., 308, 309, 315
Abu-Ai, 143
Abum-kima-ili, 71
Abu-rama, 142
Achaemenides, 23, 31, 179
Achivi, 261
achlamah, 204, 281 n.
Achlami, 203 f.
adda, 166, 175
-'addana, 320
Addi, Addu, 218, 219
Addu-dayan, 219
Addu-mikhir, 218, 219
'Adhara-ilu, 82, 111
Adôn, 222, 223
Adoni, 217, 223, 302
Adoni-baal, 217
Adonijah, 223, 302
Adoni-râm, 302
Adoni-tsedek, 231
Aduna, 217
A-Ea-kalamma, 121
Ælanitic Gulf, 148, 270
Agamis, Agavis, 168 n.
Agu, 168 n.
Agu-kak-rimi, 136, 204, 209
Ahab, 264 n., 304
Aharon, v. Aaron

Ahaz, 308
Ahi-tub, 284
Ai (goddess), 66, 74, 114, 224
Ai (god) 112, 114, 143, 218 *n*., 222, 224
Ai-da'ama, 218 *n*.
Ai-daggama, 218
Ai-kalabu, 112 ff.
Ai-kamaru, 113
Ailat, 191, (*v*. *also* Elat) 194
Ai-rammu, 112
Ai-rishat, 74
Ajalon, 229
Akbar, 111
Akharru, *v*. Amurru
Akhi- (Names with), 83
Akhi-ezer, 298
Akhi-hud, 298
Akhi-kariba, 84
Akhi-milki, 217, 221 *n*.
Akhi-ra', 298
Akhi-ram, 217
Akibu, 83, 110, 274
Akkad, 36 ff., 148, 185
Akrân, 299 *and n*.
Aku, 73
Aku-dainu, 73
Akur-ul-anna, 121
A'lam, 204
Alasia (Cyprus), 245
Alexander (the Great), 133
-'ali, 84
Al-kheresh, 238
Allah, 290
Almâku-hu, 80, 117 *and n*.
Alman, 204
Amalek, 148, 235, 240, 241, 244
-amara, 84
Amariah, 286
Amarna, *v*. Tel-el-Amarna
Amartu, 171
Amat-Istar, 188
Amaziah, 319 *n*.
Amen-em-hâît, 51
Amenôthes, 32, 154, 213
'ami-da, 81
Amîl-Bel, 61
Amlâtu, 211
Amlilatu, 211

'Amm, 48, 300
ammatu, 192 *n*.
'Ammi- (Arab.), 83 (Hebr.), 91
Ammi-amara, 84
  ,, -anisa, 84
Ammi-Baal, 217, 222 *n*.
  ,, -dhara'a, 84
  ,, -el, 90, 298
  ,, -hud, 98, 298
  ,, -kariba, 84
  ,, -nadab, 90, 95 *n*., 298
  ,, -sadugga, 88
  ,, -sami'a, 84, 248
  ,, -satana, 78, 93 *and n*., 95 *n*., 107 ff., 130
  ,, -shaddai, 109, 298.
  ,, -shapaka, 84
  ,, -tsaduka, 84, 90, 246, 248
  ,, -yada'a, 84
  ,, -yapi'a, 84
  ,, -yathu'a, 84
  ,, -zaduga, 68, 75, 89, 92 *n*., 93 *and n*.
Ammon, 48, 148, 201, 221 *n*., 237, 271
Ammu-ladin, 91
Ammu-nira, 217, 222 *n*. 228
Ammu-rabi, 105, 192
Ammu-rapaltu, 192
Amorites, 34 *n*, 57, 148, 171, 245 (*v*. also Martu).
Amos, 14 f.
Amraphel, 43, 93, 124, 147, 192 f.
Ammi-anshi, 49, 51
Amu, 47, 52
Amukkan, 211
-amur, 141 *n*.
Amur-Ashir, 141 *n*.
Amur-ila, 67
Amurri, 34 *n*., 57
Amur-Samas, 141 *n*.
'An, 257
Anab, 262
Ana-pani-ili, 72
Anat, 218, 219, 222
An-Baal, 71*n*.
Anbay (Nebo), 80, 116, 273 *n*.
'Aner, 149, 150, 158
-anisa, 84

An-Karih, 78, 79 *and n*.
Anshan, 37, 170
Anu, 66, 167, 175
Anu-bani, 62 *n*.
Anubis, 281
Anunit, 66, 184
-apika, 84
Apil-Bel, 121, 181 *n*.
Apil-Ea, 121
Apil-ili-shu, 73
Apil-Sin, 68, 72 *n*., 93, 103
Apir, 234
Apiru, *v*. Epri
Arabia, 34 f., 40
Arabia, East, 234 *n*., 268
Arabic, 202, 226, 304 *n*.
Arad-Elali, 115
Arad-Nirgal, 72
Arad-Ramman, 72
Arad-Sin, 169
Aram-Naharaim, 204
Aramaeans, 201 ff., 220
Aramäic, 54 f., 201, 202
Araru, 262
Arba, *v*. Kirjath Arba
-Ardat, 232 *n*.
Ari, 222
Ari-el, 222
Arioch, v. Eri-Aku
Arîsh (Wady el-), 236, 242, 251 *n*., 255 f.
Arka, 234
Arman, 205
Arôer, 262
Arpakeshad, 210 *and n*., 256, 292 ff.
Arrapach, 295 f.
Arvad, 217, 245
-asaph, 107 *n*., 217
Ashdod, 217, 221
Asher, 226 (*v. also* Asser)
Asherah, 218, 221
-ashir, 142
Ashir (god), 141 *n*.
Ashir-emuki, 141 *n*.
Ashir-tayar, 141 *n*.
Ashkelon, 221, 228, 264
Ashnunnak, 168
Ashtar-Kamosh, 273
Ashtaroth, *v*. Astaroth

Ashteroth-Karnaim, 148, 272, 273
Ashupi-ilu, 142 *n*.
Ashur (Assyra), 141 *n*., 144, 237
A'shûr, 247, 249, 250, 322 f.
Ashur (in S. Palestine), 237, 238, 243, 244, 252, 260, 263, *and n*., 313, 315
Ashur-Ai, 143
Ashur-bani, 141 *n*.
Ashurim, 236, 238
Ashur-imîti, 141 *n*.
Ashur-ishtakal, 141 *n*.
Ashur-rabi, 141 *n*.
Asser, 226 *and n*., 233, 234, 235 f., 238 *n*., 264, 265
Assur, *v*. Ashur
Assur-bani-pal, 194
Assur-bel-kala, 194 *and n*., 253
Assur-dan, 139
Assur-natsir-pal, 194 *n*., 219
Assyria, 30
Assyrians, 139 ff.
Assyriology, 29 f.
Astar, 222 (*v*. Athtar)
Astarte, 115 *n*., 195, 219, 222 f., 303
Astarti (City of), 262
Asurbanipal, *v*. Assurb.
Atar-ilu, 142
Athtar, 79 ff., 116, 247, 322
Atonement, Day of, 280
Aum, 80
-awwas, 81
Ayab, 261
Ayin, 230
azala, 278
Azanum, 111
-'azar, 111, 293
Az-azel, 278
Azi-baal, 217
azkarah, 277 f.
Azri-Yau, 319
-'azza, 81
Azzan, 299

Baal, 115 *n*., 217, 218, 222 f., 223 f., 286, 302 f.
an-Baal, 79 *n*.
ha-Baal, 296 *n*.

INDEX

pa-Baal, 296 n.
Baal-khanûnu, 217
Baal-maher, 219 n.
Baaloth, 273 n.
Baal-ram, 219 n.
Baal-samemi, 195
Baal-shaphat, 219
Baal-tsapuna, 253, 254
Baal-zabubi, 253
Baal-zephon, 253 f.
Ba-Anah, 272 n.
Ba-Asa, 272 n
Babylon (Babel), 162, 181, 184 f., 187 ff.
Babylonia, 30 f., 268
Babylonian Pantheon, 62 ff.
Bahrein, 211, 247 n., 272 f., 313 (v. also "Country of the Sea")
Ba'ilat Tsapuna, 254 n.
Baiti-ilâni, 194
Balaam, v. Bileam
Balâh, 248
Balak, 193
-bali, -balu, 71, 141 n.
Bamoth, 285
-bani, v. Anu-bani, Ashurbani, etc.
Bani-Sin, 72
bar, 208 n.
Barakish, 248 n.
Bared, 242
Barnaki, 300
Barnea (Kadesh), 148
Barsip, 35
Bashan, 148, 240, 243, 272
Basmat, 269 n.
Batsish, 234 n.
Ba'u, 65
Bausan, 320
Be-dad, 220 n., 272 n.
Beel-yada', 302, 303
Beerot, 228
Beersheba, 226, 242, 243
Be-eshterah, 272
Beirut, 228
Bel, 58, 62 f., 65 (= Ramman) 108, 144, 167, 175, 181, 181 n., 218, 219
Bela, 162, 193 196 (P. N.), 152, 220 n.

Bel-Ai, 143
Bel-Harran-shadûa, 108
Beli-ishmeanni, 73
-bel-kala, 194
Bel-kapkapu, 140
Bel-nadin-apli, 130
Bel-shadûa, 108
Bel-shimia, 128 f.
Benaiah, 303
Benjamin, 261 n.
Be'or, 152
Berdan, 242 n.
Berosus, 133, 136
Beth-Tsur, 318
Bethel, 194, 202, 295, 318
Bethuel, 297 n.
Be-zal-el, 301
Bi-Athtar, 79, 220 n., 273
Bikhishi, 261 f.
Bildad, 156
Bileam (Balaam), 26, 91, 152, 220 n., 243 ff., 289
Bi-mahali-Uzza, 237
Bi-mehal, 238 n.
Bin-inima, 261
Bir-tsur, 319
Birtu, 206
Bit-Amukkan, 211
Bit-Khabbâtu, 187
Bit-Saggil, 184 f.
Bit-Sha'alli, 211
Bit-Yakin, 211 n.
Bit-Zidda, v. Ezidda
Bodi-el, 203
Borsippa, 182, 183, 209, 323 f.
"Brook of Egypt," v. Arish
Bubastis, 260
Budi-Baal, 217
Budi-ilu, 203
Bukki, 299
Bulala, 205 n.
Burnaburiash, 59, 123, 133, 136, 137
Bur-Ramman, 73
Bur-Sin, 37
Byblos, v. Gebal

Caesarea, 140
Cambyses, 78, 248 n.

INDEX

Canaan, 264
Canaanite, 92 f., 119, 155, 215 f., 221, 273 f., 286, 302 ff.
Caphtor, 205
Cappadocian Tablets, 141 ff.
Carchemish, 203, 245
Cassia (Laurus), 317
-chadd, 314
Chaldaeans, 210 f., 259 *n*.
Chalup-tree, 35
Chamranu, 206
Charîlu, 206, 207
Cheber, 232, 238 *n*., 258 *n*.
Chedor-la omer, *v*. Kudur-lagamar
Chindaru, 206
Chodollogomor, 147 *n*.
Covenant, Book of the, 10, 20
Cyprus, 245 and *n*.
Cyrus, 248 *n*., 259 *n*.

-da'ama, 218 *n*.
Da'am-melek, 218 *n*.
-dad, 298
Dadi- (Names with), 84
Dadi-kariba, 84
Dagan-takala, 218
-daïnu, 73
Damascus, 212, 219, 268
Damgal-nunna, 65
-damik, 73 f., 102 *n*.
Damki-ili-shu, 121
Damku (god), 67 (P. N.), 102 *n*.
Damunu, 206, 211
-dan, 139, 298
Daphne, 252
Darius, 259 *n*.
Darkness (Land of), 35 *n*., 182, 183
Date-palm, 34, 317
David, 287, 303
Dawasir, 313
-dayan, 219
Debir, 221 *n*.
Decalogue, 20, 26
Dedan (Tidanu), 34, 236 ff., 270, 271
Dennaba, 220 *n*.
Descent of Ishtar into Hell, 64

Deuteronomy, 4, 10, 11, 282 ff., 288 *n*.
dhakar, 278
-dhamara, 84
-dhara'a, 81, 84
-dharaha, 81
Dhar'i-kariba, 84
Dhimri- (Names with), 81
Dhimri-ali, 84
„ -kariba, 84
„ -yada'a, 84
Dhu-Alam, 318 *n*.
Dhu-r-Rumma *for* er-Rumma (*v*. Rumma)
Dhu-Samway, 322
Dinhabah, 220 *n*.
Dintir (Babylon), 187 f.
Dor, 234
Dothan, 232 *n*.
Dul-mach, 179
Dunib, 220 *n*.
Dun-pa-uddu, 63
Duplicate passages in the O. T., 19 f.
Dur-ili, 170, 177, 186
Dur-mach-ilâni, 184 ff.
dûru (in personal names), 186 *n*.
Dzapgan, 246

Ea, 62, 64 f. (= Sin), 106, 167
Ea-gamil, 124
Ea-ma-la-ilu, 98 *n*.
Ebed, 303 *n*.
Ebed-Baal, 303 *n*.
Eber, 96, 244 ff., 256 f., 322 ff.
Eber ha-nahar, 251 f., 254 ff., 323 f.
Ebiasaph, 107 *n*.
Ebir-nâri, 195, 254 ff., 323 ff.
Ebsha'a, 52
Ebyatar, 107 *n*.
Eden, 313
Edom, 112, 148, 152, 201 f., 225, 235, 237, 261 f., 320
Eglon, 221 *n*.
Egypt, 227, 237, 245, 247, 250
Egyptian, Loanwords, 291 f., 295
ekhnome, 281
Eki, 105, 192 (Babylon), 187 ff.
Eki-rapaltu, 105, 192

332 INDEX

Ekron, 240, 253
El, 223, 297 *n.*, 302
Elali, 115, 142
Elali-bani, 115
Elam, 37 f., 40, 159, 169, 175, 181 f., 185, 207, 234, 292
Elamite, P. N., 59
Elani, 142
Elat, 196 (*v. also* Ailat)
El-eazar, 111, 293
El-Elyon, *v.* Elyon
Eli-ab, 298
Eli-dad, 298
Eli-ezer, 111, 118 *n.*, 297 *n.*
Eli-Shama, 298
Eli-tsaphan, 299
Eli-tsur, 298
Eliyada, 302, 303
Eliyasaph, 298
el-Oela, 77, 271, 276
Ellasar (Larsa), 147
Elmodad, 111
Elohist, 9, 308 *n.*
El-Pa'ran, 194, 197
El-Shaddai, *v.* Shaddai
Elyon, 150 ff., 154 ff., 223
Emim, 148
Emi-zaduga, 107 *n.*
Emu (= Ammu), 91, 107 *n.*, 156
-emuki, 73, 141 *n.*
Emutbal, *v.* Yamutbal
En-anab, 262
Enan, 299
Engedi, 148
En-mishpat, 148, 255
Ennam-Ai, 141 *n.*
Ennam-Ashir, 141 *n.*
Ennam-Sin, 141 *n.*
En-nun-dagalla, 105, 180 f., 183
Enun, 105
Ephah, 236
ephah (measure), 293
Eponymous Rulers, 143, 144
Epri, 257 f.
Erech, 121 *n.*, 128, 167, 175
Eri-Aku, *v.* Iri-Aku
Eri-Aku (Arioch, Ri-Aku), 40 f., 69, 147, 159, 166, 167 ff., 184 ff., 189, 203

Eridu, 167
er-Rumma (Wady), 313, 314 *n.*
E-saggil, *v.* Bit-Saggil
Esarhaddon, 255, 300
Esau, 201, 261
Eshcol, 149, 150, 158
Eshru, 260
Ethnological Table, 95
Ezekiel, 279, 282 ff.
-ezer, 115, 298
E-zidda, 182
Ezra, 14, 23, 279, 300

Faishân, 315
fanaka, 300 *n.*
Feminine names, 319, 320
Fetishism, 28, 290

Gadanum, 111
Gadatas, 24
Gaddi, 299
Gaddi-el, 298
Gamaru, 142
Gambulu, 206, 211
-gamil, 73, 121
Gamli-el, 298
gam-tree, 317
Gamunu, 111
Gari, 262 f.
Garia, 142
Gath, 229 *n.*, 232, 241
Gaww, 318 and *n.*
Gawwat, 318
Gaza, 221, 225, 236, 237, 243 f. 250 ff., 268, 271, 320
Gazri, 229, *v. also* Gezer
Gebal, 155, 217, 219, 228, 245 *n.*
Geihan, 315
Gelam, 241
Gemalli, 299
Gerar, 242 *n.*
Ger-Ashtoreth, 219
Ger-melek, 219
Gesem, 225 *n.*
Geshur, 240 ff.
Gezer, 220, 221, 229, 231, 241 *n.*, 264
ghaliyat, ghalwa, 277
Ghanna, 63 *and n.*

INDEX

Gibeon, 225
Gibil, 65
Gibil-gamis, 39, 128
Gideon, 269
Gikhon [Gihon], 313, 315
Gilead, 269
Gillo, 241
Gimil-Ea, 62
Gimil-ili, 67
Gimil-Samas, 62
Gimil-Sin, 37, 237
Gimti, 229
Gimti (Ginti)-Kirmil, 229, 261
gin (Measure), 291 *n*.
Gir, 208
Giri-dadi, 219
Girra-la-gamil, 105, 179 *n*. (*v. also* Urra-la-g)
Girsu, 208 f.
Gishban, 205 *and n*.
Gishdubar (Nimrod), 35, 39, 128
Gishgalla, 105
Goi, 147, 184, 204, 208 *n*., 318 *n*.
Goshen, 125, 214, 225 ff., 235, 257, 260
Gosom, 225
Gu, 208 *n*.
Gubin, 35
Gudea, 34 ff., 198, 237
Gula, 63 *and n*., 65, 194
Gul-ki-shar, 121, 126, 129 f.
Gumânatu, 111
Gurruda, 193
Gushgin-banda, 65
Guti, 204, 208 *n*., 317, 318 *n*.

ha-Baal, 296 *n*.
Hadad, 219, 220 *and n*.
Hadır, 262
Hadramaut, 76, 77, 79, 268, 272, 317, 318 *n*., 320 *n*.
Hagar, 242, 259
-hail, 319
Halfan, 322
Ham, 48
Hama-Atht, 79, 246
-hamaya, 319
Hami-tal, 321
Hammamât, 257

Hanakitess, 321
Hanni-baal, 217
Hanni-el, 298
Haran (Harran), 72, 108, 147, 202, 204, 209
Harim, 318, 320, 321
Hasor, 231
Hauhum, 221 *n*.
Haupi-Atht, 79
Haupi-ilu, 79
hawaya, hawah, 100, 114
hayah, 100
Hazezon-Tamar, 148
Hebrew, 95, 96, 100, 118, 215 f., 228, 274 f., 286 *n*., 304 *n*.
Hebrews, 95, 229 ff., 256 ff.
Hebron, 149, 158, 202, 221 *n*., 229 *n*., 231 f., 242
Helal, 115
Helam, 204
Heroopolis, 257 *n*.
Heru-sha, 47
Hiddekel, *v*. Khiddekel
hilâl, 115
Hin (measure), 291
Hiram, 217
Hittites, 155, 245 *n*., 264 (*v. also* Khattu and Kheta)
Hoham, 221 *n*.
Holiness, Law of, 10
Horam, 221 *n*., 231
Horites, 148, 261 f.
Horus, 281
Hosea, 11, 16
-hûd (from yehûd), 298
Hyksos, 43

Ibishu, 91, 107 *n*.
Ibla, 34
Ibni-ilu, 62
Ibr naharan, 247, 248 ff., 322 ff.
Ibri, 230 f., 256 f., 323
Ibshi-na-ilu, 99, 100 *n*.
-idinam, 73
Ichabod, 115
I-ezer, 115
Igur-kapkapu, 140
Ikib-ilu, 142
-ikisham, 73

334 INDEX

Ikun-ka-ilu, 99
Ilâli, 115
-ilat, 79
Ili-'amida, 81
,,-awwas, 81
,,-'azza, 81
,,-dhara'a, 81
,,-dharaha, 81
,,-emuki, 141 n.
,,-hail, 319, 320
,,-ishtıkal, 141 n.
,,-kariba, 81 n.
,,-ma-amur, 141 n.
,,-ma-nabata, 81
,,-padaya, 81
,,-rabbi, 81
,,-radsawa, 81
,,-rapa'a, 81
,,-sa'ada, 81
,,-sami'a, 81
,,- hara'a, 82
,,-sharraha, 82
,,-wahaba, 81
,,-yada'a, 81
,,-yapi'a, 81, 248, 250
,,-yasu'a, 249
,,-za'ada, 81
-illat-su, 73
Ilsu, 249
Ilu-abi, 98
Ilu-amar, 143
Ilu-ashir, 203
Ilu-bani, 62, 67, 141
Ilu-damık, 74, 102 n.
Ilu-ishme-khani, 71
Ilu-ma, 127
Ilu-ma-Gishdubba, 128
Ilu-ma-ilu, 121, 127
Ilu-milki, 142
Ilu-na, 107
Ilu-ni, 67
Ilu-rabi, 106, 207
Ilu-shu-abu-shu, 73
Imgur-Sin, 72
-imiti, 141 n.
Imperfect Forms, 59 f.
-imuki, v -emuki
Incense, 270, 271
Incense, Altar of, 277

Ine-Tutu, 181
Ingi, 36
Ingi (Ki-Ingi), 36
Ini-Malik, 61
Ini-Sin, 37
I-noam, I-nuam, 218 n, 264
Ipik-ili-na, 107
-irigam, 73
Irikatta, 234
Irishti-Ai, 72
Irsu, 249
-irtsiti, 98 and n.
Isaac, 201, 242
Ishai, 115
Ishbaal, 219
Ishbak, 236
Ishbi-Nirgal, 61
Ish-ki-bal, 121, 130
-ishmeanni, 73
-ishmi, 73
Ishmael, 118 n., 270, 297 n.
Ishmaelues, 201, 269
Ishmi-dagan, 61, 140 n.
Ishmi-Sin, 73
Ishnunna, 168
-ishtakal, 141
Ishtar, 63 64, 65, 74, 166, 194
Ishtar-lamazi, 141 n.
Isimanai, 195 n.
Isir'il, 258, 264
ismid, 52 n.
Israel, 228, 257, 297 n.
Istar-umma-sha, 74
I-tagama, 218
I-takkama, 218
Ithamar, 115
ithmid, 52 n.
Itti-nibi, 121
Izebel, 115

*Jacob, 109, 118 n., 125, 132, 201 ff.
Jacob-el, 110 n., 294
Jebus, 199
Jehoiada, 303
Jehonathan [Jonathan], 303
Jehoshaphat, 223, 299, 303
Jehovah, 100 n.
Jehovist, 9, 2 8, 307 and n.

* For other words usually spelt with J see under Y.

INDEX 335

Jeremiah, 16
Jericho, 49, 231
Jeroboam, 91
Jerub-baal, 302
Jerusalem, 149, 153, 199 f., 229, 230; *v. also* Salem
Jeshurun, 305
Jethro, 276, 279 f., 289
Joab, 303
Joash, 303
Job, 261
Jobaal, 303 *n.*
Jof, 314
Jokhebed, 115
Jokshan, 236, 270
Joktan, 96
Jonah, 144
Joram, 112
Jordan, 193, 254
Jordan, Region East of, 271 f., 323
Joseph, 111 *n*, 114 *n.*, 132, 269
Joshua, 221, 223, 225, 231, 302
Jotham, 303
Judah, 242 (*v. also* Yehuda)
Judge of the dead, 73
Junbula, 206 *n.*

-ka-, 298
Kabadh, 78
-kabod, 115
Kabri, 206 (for Kibri)
kadesh, 113
Kadesh (Barnea), 148, 162, 191, 225, 243.
Kain, 242, 243
Kainan, 256
-kalabu, 112
kalabu, 113
Kaldu, 210 f.
Kaleb, 299, 306
Kâlu, 196
kamaru, 112
Kambyses, *v.* Cambyses
Kamosh, 273
Kapasi, 155 *n.*
Kardu, 210 f.
Karduniash (Babylonia), 187, 210
-kariba, 81, 84
Ķariba-ilu, 82

Kariba-ilu Watar, 78, 320
Karmel, 226, 229, 241
Karnaim, 148, 272
Karnak, 260, 265
Karnâvu, 247, 272
Kashdim, 210, 247 *n.*
Kashdu, 210 f.
Kashi, 38 f.
Kassite, P. N., 59, 104
Kassites, 38, 136 f., 234, 293
Katabanians, 48, 76 f., 272, 229 *n.*
-kebed, 115
Kedar, 207, 237, 270, 271
kedeshah, 113
Kedor-laomer, *v.* Kudurlagamar
Keft, 155 *n.*
Keîlah, 229, 232, 260
Kelakh, 238
keleb, 113
Keleb-elim, 114
Kemuel, 297 *n.*
Kenites, 243 f.
Keshad, 210, 292 ff., 295
Ketsiah, 269
Keturah, 269
Keturies, 201
Khabbâtu, 187 *n.*, 230
Khabirai, 234
Khabiri, 155, 230 ff., 235, 236, 264
Khakhum, 34
Khali- (Names with), 83
Khali-amara, 84
" -ilu, 207
" -kariba, 84
" -wakula, 84
" -yada'a, 84
Khami-tal, 321
Khammu-rabi, 41, 44, 69, 88, 92, 95, 103 f., 118 ff., 144 *n.*, 164, 172 ff., 179, 183, 192 f., 259
Khammu-rabi dynasty, 68 f. (*v. also* Khammu-rabi)
Khamu-niri, 217 *n.*
Khana, *v.* Ghanna
-khani, 71
Khani-rabbat, 187
knanûn, 217
Khanûnu, 221 *n.*
Khapini, 262

Khapir, 234
Khar, 262 n., 265
Kharbi-shipak, 234
Kharshu-bâ-naimat, 238
khatta'at (Sin-offering), 321
Khâtu, 37
Khavila [Havilah], 238, 239, 247 n., 313, 315
Khavîlân, 247
Khayani, 262
Khayappa, 236 n.
Khebron, v. Hebron
Kheta, 245, 264
Khid-Dekel, 314 f.
Khini-Anabi, 262
Khnûm-hotpû, 52
khoshen, 280 ff.
Khumbaba, 40
Khusha, 115
-ki-, 141
Kibri, 207 f.
kiddah, 317 n.
Ki-Ingi, v. Ingi
Kilti, 229
-kima-, 71, 185
Kimashu, 34, 38, 183
kimmatu, 106
Kimta-rapashtu, 88
Kimtu-kittu, 88
Kimtu-rapaltu, 105, 183
Kingi, v. Ingi
Kir, 205 ff., 208, 211
Kirjath Arba, 229 n., 232 f.
Kirmil, 229
Kishar, 33, 37, 57
Kish-ili, 73
Kittim, 245 n.
kittu, 71, 88
Kode, 245
kohen, 17
komer, 113
Kubburu, 111
Kudur-dugmal, v. Kudur-lagamar
Kudur-lagamar, 40 f., 147 f., 164, 171 ff., 178 ff., 193
Kudur-mabug, 40 f., 57, 159, 166 f., 175 f., 177
Kudur-nankhundi, 159

Kudur-nuggamar, v. Kudur-lagamar
Kudurra, 234
kummu, 106
Kurigalzu, 136
Kush, 39, 314 and n.
Kushites, 39 f.
Kuti, 245

Labaya, 229, 232 n., 232, 266
Labdudu, 206
Lachish, 220, 221, 228, 231
Ladanum, 269
-ladin, 91
Lagamal, 44, 159
Lagamar, 44, 159, 173
Lahai Roi, 207, 242
-lamazi, 141
Lamga, 117 n.
Larsa, 40, 159, 162 n., 165 f., 168, 177 f. ; v. also Ellasar
Lât, 79
lavi'u, lavi'at, 276, 320 n.
Leba'oth, 232 (not Leba'oth)
Lebbakh-tree, 35
leshem, 281, 291
Letushim, 236
Le'ummim, 236
Levi, 233, 266 f., 277
Levite priestesses, 320 n.
Levites, 277, 282 ff.
Libnat, 241
-libshi, 99
Libyans, 264 f.
Li'itâu, 206
-liki, 73
-litsi, 99
Lot, 146 f., 148
Luchuatu, 206 f.
Lugal-banda, 65
Luhai-Atht, 207
lummû, 106
Lycians, 265

-ma- (in Arab. P. N.), 82
Ma-'ân, 76 f. (v. also Minaeans), 247, 270, 271
Madal, 262
Madga, 193

INDEX 337

Madhai, 247 *and n.*
Ma'di-, 83 ff., 143
Ma'di-kariba, 84, 248
Magan, 34, 76 *n.*, 271
-magir, 73
-mahali-, 238
-maher, 219
Ma'în, 76 *and n.*
Maïr, 194, 196
Makhdi, 143
Makhnûbi-ilu, 111
Makhnûzu, 111
Makrûb, 76, 113
Malagi, 193, 195, 196, 253
Malgi, Malgu, 193, 196, 253
malgû, 193
Malik (God), 61
„ erroneous reading for Ai, 112 *n.*
-Malik, 61, 320
Malikhu, 206
maliku, 230
Malkâ, 193
Malkiel, 233, 258 *n.*
Mamlu-Ea, 121
Mamre, 149, 150, 157
Manda-tribes, 181
Mannu-balu-ili, 71
Mannu-shanin-Samas, 70, 141 *n.*
Manum-bali-Ashir, 141 *n.*
„ -balu-ili, 141 *n.*
„ „ -Ishtar, 141 *n.*
„ ki-Ashur, 151 *n.*
Ma'on, 76 *n.*, 225, 271
Maphlitat, 238
Mar'ash, 37, 212
mârat irtsiti, 98 *n.*
Marduk, 63, 144, 185
Marduk-Ai, 143
Marduk-akhi-irba, 234
Marduk-shadûa, 108
Marduk-taiar, 141 *n.*
margu, 193 (for murgu)
Margûla, 321
Mar-irtsiti, 98
Mar-Istar, 73
Markhashi, 37
Mar-Simani, 195 *n.*
Martu (god), 57, 72

Martu (West, Countries of the, Amorite-land), 34, 57 f., 166, 170 f., 194 *n.*, 223, 237
„ -bani-ameli, 70
Mash, 34, 35, 183
Mashkhuru, 142
Massaean, 112
Matan-Addi, 218
Matred, 262
Mattan, 217
Mattan-Baal, 217, 219
Mauk, 169 *n.*
Mautebah, 319 *n.*
Mavuk, 169 *n.*
Mazanum, 111
Mazoy, 250 *n.*
Medan, 236, 238
Media, 248 *n.*
Medina, 271
Mehdeba, 262 *n.*, 274
Mehetab-el, 262
Melakh, 196
Melam-kurkurra, 121
Melam-matâti, 121
Melchior, 217
Melchi-zedek, 146, 149 ff., 190, 289
-melek, 218 *n.*, 221
Melk-kart, 221
Melukhkha, 34
Memphis, 254 *n.*, 280
Mentu, Menti, 47, 260
Mephaat, 272
Merib-Baal, 302
Merodach, *v.* Marduk
— baladan, 211 *n.*
Mesa, 273 f.
mesdemet, 52 f.
Meshriki, 323
Mesopotamia, 252, 255 f., 323 ff.
Metre, 182, 310 f.
Mê-Turnat, 205
Me-zahab, 262 *and n.*
Midian, 236, 247 *n.*, 249 *n.*, 270, 276 f., 279, 319, 320 *n.*
Midianites, 269, 319 *n.*
Mi-ka-el, 398
-mikhir, 219
Milam-, *v.* Melam

22

INDEX

Milgia, 193, 195
milk (King), 217, 221, 230
-milki, 217
Milki-ashapa, 217
Milki-el, 229, 231 f.
Milki-ramu, 142
Milki-uri, 217
Milkom, 221 n.
Milkura, 217
-milkut, 217
Minaean, 76 n., 90, 100 f., 115, 246 ff., 268 ff., 319
Mînephtah, 122, 244, 258, 264 f.
Minkhah, 321 n.
Mi-sha-el, 298
Mish-ki, 182
Mishpat, 148, 299
Mishtu, 261 f.
Mitanni, 155 and n.
Mitinti, 221
Mitsr, 237 (v. also Egypt)
Mi-ur-urra, 166
Moab, 148, 201, 237, 271, 272 f.
-modad, 111
Monotheism, 74
Moreh, 171 n.
Moses, 114, 161, 199, 223, 224, 275 ff., 291, 305
Motab, 319
Muabbit-kissati, 121, 126
-muballit, 73
Mûdadi, 75, 111
-mudi, 73
mukarrib, 76
-munna', 300 n.
Muraggila, 321
murgu, 193
Mutabil, 170
Mut-Addi, 218, 219, 261
Mutsrân, 246, 248, 270, 276

-na (suffix), 60, 107 f., 111
Nab'al, 79 n.
-nabata, 81
Nabataeans, 206 n., 319 n.
Nabati, 142, 207
Nabatu, 206 f.
Nabi-Sin, 72
Nabium, v. Nabu

Nabonassar, 133
Nabonidus, 123, 164
Nabti- (names with), 83, 207
Nabti-ali, 84
,, -kariba, 84
,, -yapi'a, 84
Nabu (Nabium, Nebo), 40, 63, 80 103, 181
Nabu-kima-abi-shariâni, 185
-nadab, 90
-nadiba, 84
-nadin, 129
nahar, 251, 254
Naharim, Naharin, 155, 204, 220 n.
Nahor, 210
-na'imat, 238
nakhal Mitsrayim, 255
Nakhshon, 299
Nakrah, 78 ana n.
Name of Yahveh, 87
Names of three elements, 70 f.
Naram-Sin, xiii., n. 61
nâru, 250
Nash'i- (names with), 83
Nash'i-kariba, 84
Nashk, 78
-natan, 303
Natan-Addu, 218, 219
Natanum, 82
Natiyan, 319
-natsir, 73
Natunu, 75, 111
Nebayoth, 206 n., 270, 273
Nebo, v. Nabu
Nebo (Mt.), 273, 274, 285
Nebuchadnezzar I., 129
,, II., 259 and n.
neder, 321
Negeb, 242, 252
Nehemiah, 23, 300
-ner, 217 n.
Nergal, v. Nirgal
neshem, 281
Nethan-el, 298
-ni (suffix), 60
Nimrod, v. Gishdubar and Gibil-gamis
Nina (goddess), v. Ghanna, Gula
Nindar, 66, 144

INDEX 339

Nindar-Ai, 143
Ningal, 64, 116
Ningirshu, 67
Nin-gish-zidda, 66
Nin-lilla, 66
Nin-mar, 116
Ninni, 65
Nin-shagh, 167
Nippur, 166, 167
-nira, v. Ammu-nira
Nirgal, 63, 144, 156
Nirgal-Ai, 143
Nisaba, 64
Nisin, 36, 140 n., 162 n., 167 f.
-no'am, 218 n.
-nu (suffix), 60
Nuffar [Niffer], 166 n.
Nun (Hebr.), 299
Nun, 62
Nunia, 299
Nun-magh, 166
-nur, 70
Nûr Bel, The, 37 f., 57
Nur-ili-shu, 72
Nur-Ramman, 62, 177 n.
Nur-Samas, 72
Nur-Sin, 72
Nusku, 40, 63, 65

Oedem, 49
el-Oela, 77, 271, 276
Og, 243
olah, 277
Ophir, 234 n.
Opis, 173 n., 205
-or, -uri, 217
Orthography, 274 f.
Othniel, 297 n.

pa (Arabic), 98 n.
 ,, (Eg. article), 293
pa-Baal, 296 n.
pa-bil-sag, 63
Padan, 205
Padan-Aram, 202, 204 f.
-padaya, 81
Pa'ish, 262
Pakes, Pakesem, 225 n.
pakhad (cf. Gen. xxxi. 42), 300 n.

Paknu, 129 n.
Pa-la-Samas, 98 n.
Palti, 298
Palti-el, 298
Pan-ki, 205 n.
Pannaku, 300 n.
Paradise, 313 ff.
Pa'ran, El, 148
Parnak, 300
Parsu, 248 n.
Pasagga, 63
Pedah-tsur, 298
Pe'ish, 261
Pekod, 206 n.
Peleg, 96
Pelusium, 252, 253
Penê, Baal, 115 n.
Persia, 248 n.
Pesakh, 291 f.
peshet, pesht, 291
Pethor, 220 n.
Phakus, 225 n.
Philistines, 205, 240, 244, 256
Phinehas, 284, 291, 294
Phoenician, 215, 220, 274 ; v. also Canaanite
Phoen. alphabet, 75, 274, 275 n.
Phoenicians, 265
Pidia, 228
Pikinnu, 129 n.
Piknanum, 129 n.
-pilakh, 73
Pilakh Ashur, 141 n.
Pir'am, 221 n.
Pir'i-Ai, 73
Pir'u, 221 n.
Pishon, 313, 315
pishtah, 291
-pi-shu, 71
pîtu, 291 n.
Planet-gods, 62 f.
Potiphar, 291
Priestly Code, 9 f., 14, 16 f., 26, 277 ff., 304 n., 307, 308 n.
Psalms of Penitence, 312 f. and n.
Pu-Addi, 218
Pukûdu, 206
Pulasati, 244
Pungunu-ilu, 129

340 INDEX

Puti-el, 291, 293
-putram, 73

Rabbat-Ammon, 187
Rabbâtu, 185, 187
-rabbi, 81
Rabbi-Atht, 207 *n.*
Rabbi-nadiba, 84
-rabi, 140
Rabi-Addi, 218
Rabî'at, 207 *n.*
Rabi-ilu, 207 f.
-radsawa, 81, 319, 320
Ragaz (metre), 311
Ragmat, 247
-ram, 217
Ramman, 57, 62, 65 (= Bel), 73, 218
Ramman-rimeni, 73
Ramses (Land of), 228 *n.*
Ramses II., 125 *and n.*, 228, 231, 235
„ III., 231, 244 f., 249
„ IV., 257
-rapa'a, 81
Raphi, Raphia, 251 *n.*, 254, 324
Raphua, 299
Rapiku, 206
Reguel, 276
Rehoboth, 220 *n.*
Rephaim, 148
Resen, 140 *n.*
Resheph, 219
Re'u, 206 *n.*
Rhyme, 311 *n.*
Ri-Aku, *v.* Eri-Aku
Rib-Addi, 49, 155, 218, 219 *and n.*, 228, 245 *n.*
Ridâ', 247, 248 *and n.*
-rimeni, 73
Rim-Sin, 169
-rishat, 74
Riyâm, 250
-riyam, 84, 101
Rubuti, 229, 232 f.
Rubu'u, 206
Rummulûtu, 206
Ru'ua, 206

-sa'ada, 81
Sa'ada-Wadd, 79
Saba, 76, 236, 247, 318 *n.*
Sabaean Deities, 79
„ Inscriptions, 76 f.
Sabaeans, 247 *n.*
Sabîtu, 35
Sâbu, 35 *n.*, 38
Sa'd, 246, 248, 270
Sa'd-Lât, 79
Sa'du-ilat, 79
Sa'du-Wadd, 79
Sagas, 208, 228
Saihan, 315
Saklus, 265
Salem, 149, 152, 199
Salmanasar I., 203
„ II., 264 *n.*
Sam'al, 219, 243 *n.*, 319
Samas, 64, 74, 144
Samas-abi, 98
Samas-abuni, 73
Samas-Ai, 143
Samas-bani, 73, 141 *n.*
Samas-ilu-ka-ni, 72 *n.*
Samas-mudi, 73
Samas-natsir, 73
Samas-natsir-apli, 70
Samas-nur-mâte, 70
Samas-rabi, 141 *n.*
Samas-shar-kitti, 71
Samas-taïru, 73
Samas-ushur, *v.* Ud-ushur
-sami'a, 82, 84
Samsi-Ramman, 140 f.
Samsu-iluna, 60, 68, 89, 91, 102, 107, 317
Samsu-riâmi, 102
Samsu-satana, 68, 102, 110 f.
Samuel, 99, 304, 306 (*v. also* Shemu-el)
Sapati-baal, 217, 219
Sapin-mat-nukurti, 121, 130
Sapiya, 211
Sar, 239 *n.*
Saragîti, 206
Sardinians, 265 (*v. also* Shirdana)
Sargon, xiii., *n.* 198
Sargon (of Assyria), 195 *n.*, 236 *n.*

sata, satu, 107
-sata-na, 107 ff.
Script, Hebrew, 273 f.
Sea, Country of the, 128, 129, 181, 183, 211, 272 *n.*, 313
Sea, Peoples of the, 244 f., 264
Sebam, 272
se'eh, 280 *n.*
Seïr, 148, 229 *n.*, 260
Sela, 239
Semites (Divisions of the), 51 f.
senhem, 291
Serug, 207
Seti (Sethet, Suti), 50, 208 f., 209 *n.*
„ (Pharaoh), 226 *n.*, 235
Setnekht, 249
-sha-, 298
Sha'asu, 208, 230 *n.*
Shaddai, 109, 114, 223, 300, 305
shadû, 108
-shadûa, 108, 142
Shadû-Ai, 143
Shadûnu, 109
Shaggan, 205 *n.*
Shalim (god), 67
·shama', 298
Sha-Martu, 72, 94 *n.*
Shamashâtu, 273 *n.*
Sha'mat, 247
Sham-Baal, 219
Shamsum, 80
Shamu-Addu, 218
-shanin, 70, 141 *n.*
-shapaka, 84, 319
shaphat, 299 *n.*
-shaphat, 219, 223
Shaphat, 299
Shapia, 211
Shapi-Bel, 211
-shara'a, 82
-sharraha, 82
sharru, 150 *n.*
Sharru-Ai, 143
sharru dannu, 154 ff.
Shasu, 208
Shattrel-Hai, 207 f.
Sha'ul, 220 *n.*
. Shaveh, 150 *n.*

-shawwara, 319
Sheba' (Saba), 236
Shegû, 311
Shelah, 256
Shelomi, 299
Shelumi-el, 298
Shem, 295
Shem (= Yahveh), 87, 115 *n.*
Shem-baal, 115 *n.*
Shemîda, 94
Shemu-el, 93, 98, 298
Shem-zebel, 115 *and n.*
Shephat-iah, 303
sheti (Hebr.), 291
Shibam, 272
Shikhor, 240 f.
-shimi, 73
-shimia, 128
Shinar, 147
Shiphtan, 299
Shipti-Addu, 218, 219
Shirdana (Sardinians), 265
Shîri, 229, 261
Shuah (Sukhi), 236
Shu Ardat, 232 *and n.*
Shubaru, 208 *n.*
Shuhite, country, 156, 203, 323 (*v. also* Shuah)
Shum-Addi, 218
Shumi-abia, 99 *n.*
Shum-irtsiti, 98
Shumma-ilu-la-ilia, 70
shumu (son), 98 f.
Shumu-abi, 68, 97 f., 129 (*v. also* Sumu-abi)
Shumu-libshi, 99
Shumu-litsi, 99
shur, 239
Shûr (Land of = Ashûr), 238, 239, 241
Shûr (Wilderness of), 235, 240
Shussha, 116
Shusshi, 121
Shu-Tatna, 232 *n.*
Shu-Thelah, 232 *n.*
Sichor, *v.* Shikhor
Siddim, 148, 151, 162
Sidon, 217, 228
Simeon, 266

Simti-shilkhak, 166
Simurru, 38
Sin (moon-god), 62, 64 f. (= Ea), 71, 73, 116, 273, 318 *n*.
Sin (Wilderness of), 273
Sin-abushu, 73
Sinai, 273
Sin-akham-idinam, 71
Sinâtu, 273 *n*.
Sin-bani, 62
Sin-gamil, 73
Sin-idinam, 73, 172 ff., 176, 177 *n*.
Sin-ikisham, 73
Sin-illat-su, 73
Sin-imiti, 141 *n*.
Sin-imuki, 73
Sin-iragam, 73
Sin-kalama-idi, 70
Sin-liki, 73
Sin-magir, 73, 131
Sin-muballit, 68, 73, 93, 103, 112, 167, 177
Sin-nadin-shumi, 71
Sin-offering, 321
Sin-pilakh, 73, 141 *n*.
Sin-putram, 73
Sin-rimene, 73
Sin-rimenishi, 73
Sin-shadûni, 109
Sin-shimi, 73
Sinûhît, 49 ff.
Sirgulla, 33 ff.
Sirham, 314
Sir'il, 264 *n*.
Sisku, 121 *n*.
Sitriyara, 222 *n*.
Snofruî, 47
Sodom, 146, 148, 149, 156, 157
sol'am, 291
Solomon, 251 f., 287, 304
Stars, names of, 297 *n*., 298
Stibium, 52, 269
Styrax, 269
Su, 208
Su'aid, 321
Subar, 208
Subartu, 208 *n*.
Subsalla, 34
Sugalia, 142

Sugir, 208 f.
Sumaida, 84, 317 (*v. also* Sumîda')
Sumer, 36 ff., 147, 181
Sumerian, 166, 307, 312
Sumerian Personal names, 61, 67 f.
Sumerians, 291, 293 *n*.
Sumhu- (names with), 84 ff., 98 f., 101
Sumhu-ali, 84
„   -amara, 84
,,   -apika, 84
,,   -kariba, 84
„   -riâm, 84, 101
,,   -watara, 84
,,   -yada'a, 84, 98
„   -yapi'a, 84, 99
Sumîda'a, 99
Sumu-abi, 75, 93 (*v. also* Shumuabi)
Sumu-hu, *v.* Sumhu
Sumu-la-ilu, 68, 91, 93, 98 f.
Sumu-su-amina, 102
Suri, 208
Sutet, 208
Suti, 50, 208 f., 228
Syria, 208, 259

Tadua, 261
Tagi, 232 *and n*.
Tahpanhes, 251 *n*., 252
-takala, 218
-takkama, 218
-tal, 321
Ta'lab, 80
Tamar, 148
-tamar, 115
tamîd, 17, 277
Tammuz, 67
Tamna', 272
Tana, 49 f.
Tanit (goddess = She of Tana?), 115 *n*.
Tashmit, 64
-tayar, 73, 141 *n*.
Teima, 212
Telam, 241
Tel el-Amarna, 32 f., 45, 155, 199, 208, 213 ff., 260, 308
Tel el-Kebir, 239
Tel Sifr, 167, 175

INDEX

Teman, 237
Tenu, v. Tana
terûmah, 17
Thapsacus, 251
Thauban, 321
-thelah, 232 n.
Thummim, 281
Thutmosis, 295
Tid'al, 147, 184 ; v. also Tudkhul
Tidanum, 34, 237
Tidnu, 237
Tiglathpileser I., 139, 203
,, III., 212, 219, 236 n., 253
Tigris, 314
Tihâma, 272 n.
Timna', 272
Tiphsah, 251 and n., 324
-tirshi, 231
To'i, 232 n.
torah, 17 n.
Totemism, 28
Tsab-ban, 205
tsadak, 95 n.
tsaduk, tsaduka, 84, 216
Tsaduku, 83
tsal, 300
tsaphan, 298, 299
Tsaphon-Baal, 299
Tsebaoth, 103
Tsel-Baal, 221 n.
Tsidki- (names with), 83
Tsidki-ilu, 142
Tsidki-Yahu, 83 n.
Tsil-Bel, 221 n.
Tsili-Istar, 141 n., 300 n.
Tsinnah, Tsinnat, 273
Tsophar [Zophar]. 249 n.
Tsur (Name for God), 86, 300, 318 f.
Tsuri-addan, 319, 321
Tsuri-addana, 319
Tsuri-el, 298, 319 n.
Tsuri-shaddai, 298
Tubba'i-, 83
Tubba'i-kariba, 84
Tudkhul (Tid'al), 43, 147, 184 f., 318 n.
Tukulti-Nindar, 194 n.

Tumilat, 239, 257 n.
turgudis, 184 and n.
Turnat, 205
Tushur, 234
Tutu, 181 n.
Tyre, 196 n., 217, 228, 253
Tyrrhenians, 265

Ubulu, 206
Ud-ban, 205
Udda-im-tigga, 167
Udumu, 262 f.
Ud-ushshuru, 234 n.
Ur, 36, 56, 71, 147, 162 n., 166 f., 209 ff., 237, 292 ff.
,, later kings of, 66 f., 104 n., 209 n.
Ur- (names with), 66 f., 70
-uri, v. -or
Uriah, 303
Urim, 281
Urra-gamil, 179 n.
Urra-la-gamil, 179 n.
Ursu, 34
Uru-azag, 121 n.
Uruk (Erech), 121 n., 128, 167
Uru-ki (moon-god), 62, 166
Uru-ku, 121, 126 ff.
Uru-milki, 217
Uru-salim, 154, 199 f.
Ur-ziguruvas, 168 n.
Ushtanni, 259 n.
-ushur, 234 n.
Usir-tasen, 51
Uzza, 116, 238, 278

Wadd, 79 f., 220, 276
Waddada-ilu, 82
Waga' (Wagg), 271
-wahaba, 81
Wahbu-ili, 82
-wakula, 84
Walig, 246
Wall of Egypt, 239 and n.
Warawa-ilu, 82
-watara, 84
Watar-il, 143
Water wheels, 227 n.
West, Countries of the, v. Martu

Western Semites, 53 f.
Western Semitic Alphabet, 75
Widâdu-il, 82
Wir'i- (names with), 84
Wir'i-amara, 84

Ya, 112, 144
Ya'a, 49
Yabishi, 262
Ya-bitiri, 218 *n.*
Yabni-ilu, 220
-yada, 99, 236 *n.*, 302, 303
-yada'a, 81, 84
Yada'a-, *v.* Yadi'a-
Yadhkur-ilu, 82
Yadhmur-malik, 320
Yadi'a-abu, 84, 317 f.
Yadi'a-ilu, 84, 317 f.
Yadi'a-sumhu, 84, 317
Yadikhabu, 318
Yadikhu, 75
Yah, 114, 143, 223 f., 303
Yahir, 78
Yahmi-ilu, 79, 82
Yahrak, 78
Yahram-ilu, 82
Yahu, 223
Yahveh, 9, 100, 114, 223 f., 303 f.
,, Tsebaoth, 103
Ya-kalabu, 112
Ya-kamaru, 114
Yakbar-ilu, 111, 207
Yakhir, 217
Yakhziru, 111
Yakin, 211 *n.*
Yakubu, 201 *n.*
Yamlik, 60, 301 *n.*
Yamnat, 247
Yamutbal, 166, 168, 170, 174 ff.
Yan'am, 221, 261
Yankhamu, 221
Yanuam, Yanoam, 218 *n.*
Yapa-Addu, 218
Yapa'i, 220
Yapakhi, 220, 231
Yapakhi-Addu, 218
Yaphia, 231
Yaphlet, 238 *n.*, 299, 301 *n.*
-yapi'a, 81, 84

Yapi'ân, 246, 272 *n.*
Yapi'u, 83, 220
Yapti-Addu, 220
,, -Khada, 220
Ya'qub-ilu, 95, 201 *n.*
Yara, 222
Yarbi-ilu, 60, 106, 110
Yarkhamu, 111
Yarmuth, 221 *n.*
Yashap-el, 110 *n.*, 294
Yashub, 110 *n.*
Yashup-ilu, 75, 82, 95
Yashûpu, 82, 110
Yashuya, 262
Yasma'-ilu, 82
Yasumûnu, 195 *and n.*, 253
-yathar, 283
Yathil, 248
Yathimat, 272
Yathi'u, Yathu'u, 83, 248
Yathrib, 271
-yathu'a, 84
Yatu'a, 207
Ya'zar-ilu, 111
Yedia-el, 317
Yeho, 223, 303
Yeho-addan, 319 *n.*, 320
Yehuda, 298
Yemama, 271, 318
Yerahmeel, 242, 297 *n.*
Yerimôt, 261
Yeshimon, 195 *n.*, 253
Yeshimoth, 272
Yir'i-ah, 83 *n.*
Yishai, 115
Yish'i, 92 *n.*, 301 *n.*
Yishiari, 222
Yith'i- (names with), 83
Yith'i-amara, 83
,, -kariba, 84
,, -yapi'a, 84
Yo, 303
Yuawwis-ilu, 82

-za'ada, 81, 84
Zabium, Zabu, 68, 93, 101, 102
Zadok, 284 f.
-zahab, 262
Zaidu-ili, 82

INDEX 345

Zakkalu, 234, 244
Zakunum, 111
Zal-munna, 301 n.
Zal-pak-had, 301 n.
Zanik-pi-shu-Shamas, 71
Zaphon, 253
Zapsha, Zapshali, 37
Zar, 239 and n.
Zar-ki, 262
Zayyada-ilu, 82
zebel, 115
zereth, 291
Zereth, 262

Zeruiah, 303
Zili-Ishtar, 141 n.
Zimran, 236
Zimri, 83 n., 299
Zimrida, 83 n., 220, 228 and n., 231
Zimri-rabi, 75, 83 n., 111
Zinjerli, 212, 243 n., 319
Zi-shamimi, 232 n.
Zi-tatna, 232 n.
Zitri-yara, 222 n.
Zoar, 162, 193
Zuzim, 148

LIST OF AUTHORS REFERRED TO

Amiaud, 35
Arnold, Will. R., 66 *and n*.
Astruc, 8

Baxter, 15
Bezold, 326 *n*.
Bleek, 7
Bondi, 291

Chabas, 257
Cheyne, 292 *n*., 295 f.
Cornill, 3

Dangin, *v*. Thureau
Delattre, 214 *n*.
Delitzsch, Franz, 310, 312 *n*.
Delitzsch, Friedr., 56, 120, 122, 141, 160 *n*., 206, 208 *n*., 300
Dillmann, 15, 20 f., 202, 308 *n*.

Ebers, 237 *n*., 257
Erman, 49 *n*., 280 *n*.
Euting, 212, 271, 276
Ewald, 7

Fries, ix.

Georges, 8 *n*.
Glaser, 38, 48, 76, 77, 78, 80, 90, 99, 206 *and n*., 237, 240, 241 *and n*., 246, 247 *n*., 248, 249, 250 *n*., 260 *n*., 270, 272 *n*., 277 *n*., 292 *n*., 313 f., 317 *n*., 322 ff.
Golenischeff, 141 *n*.
Graf, 7, 13, 26
Green, 18, 19
Gunkel, 182, 308 *n*., 309, 310

Guthe, 15 *n*.
Gutschmid, 133

Halévy, 121
Haynes, 166 *n*.
Hilprecht, 38 *n*., 97, 104, 120, 121 *n*., 122, 123, 128 *n*., 129, 166 *n*., 172, 234 *n*.
Holzinger, 21 *n*.
Hupfeld, 7

Jastrow, 258 *n*.
Jensen, 209 *n*., 234 *n*.
Justi, 6 f.

Kautzsch, 15 *n*., 21
Kittel, 20 *n*.
Klostermann, 9 *n*., 10, 13 *n*., 19, 243 *n*., 251
Kosters, 23
Kuenen, 7, 164

Lagarde, 242 *n*.
Lagrange, 172
Luschan, 212

Maspero, 49 *n*., 120
Meissner, 69, 97, 98 *n*., 99 *n*.
Meyer, Ed., 22 ff., 160. 164
Mordtmann, 274 *n*., 276 *n*., 317 *n*.
Müller, D. H., 243 *n*., 312 *n*.
Müller, W. Max, 46 *n*., 47, 209 *n*., 219 *n*., 226 *n*., 240 *n*., 254 *n*., 255 *n*.

Nestle, v.
Niebuhr, Carl, 120, 122
Nöldeke, 7 *n*., 159, 198

Oppert, 120

Peiser, 112, 120, 124, 128, 132 ff., 142
Perles, 312 *n.*
Peters, 166 *n.*
Petrie, 257
Pinches, 43, 88 f., 94, 104, 105, 112, 121, 143, 172, 179, 182, 194
Pognon, 89

Rawlinson, H., 159
Revillout, 131
Reuss, 7, 13, 26

Sarzec, 34
Sayce, 18, 41 *n.*, 89 ff., 171 *n.*
Scheil, 38 *n.*, 44, 111, 172 ff., 234 *n.*, 317
Schmidt, Nath., 258 *n.*
Schrader, 112 *n.*

Smith, G., 160
Spartoli, 179
Stade, 2, 7 *n.*
Strassmaier, 69

Thureau-Dangin, 237 *n.*

Vatke, 7, 13

Wellhausen, 2, 3, 4. 5, 6, 10, 13, 26, 27, 164. 198 f., 223, 284, 288 *n.*, 296 f., 300, 308, 316
Wette, 7
Winckler, 92 *n.*, 97, 120, 122, 123, 128, 133, 144 *n.*, 189, 214, 230 *n.*, 261, 262 *n.*, 325 *n.*

Zenner, 312 *n.*
Zimmern, 182, 214 *n.*, 229 *n.*, 308 *n.*, 310 *and n.*

LIST OF BIBLICAL PASSAGES REFERRED TO

Genesis ii. 10–14, 263 n., 313 ff.
x. 22–24, 256, 292, 295
x. 26, 111
x. 27, 314
xi. 10, 292, 295
xi. ff., 256
xi. 19, 206 n.
xi. 21, 207
xi. 31, 325
xiv. 43 f., 158 ff., 193, 196
xiv. 16–24, 146 ff., 156 f.
xvi. 7, 242
xvi. 12, 238
xvi. 14, 207 n., 242
xvii. 1, 109
xvii. 5, 275
xx. 1, 242
xxii. 22, 210, 293 n.
xxiv. 62, 242
xxv. 269
xxv. 3, 238
xxv. 8, 243
xxv. 11, 242
xxv. 18, 238, 315
xxxv. 7, 194
xxxv. 11, 109
xxxv. 27–29, 202
xxxvi. 220 n., 261 f., 272
xxxvi. 11, 249 n.
xxxvii. 269
xlvi. 17, 233 n., 258 n.
xlvii. 11, 228 n.
xlix. 266
Exodus i. 13, 227
iii. 14, 101
vi. 18, 233
vi. 22, 298

Exodus vi. 25, 293
xii. 14, 291
xii. 38, 257, 267 n.
xiv. 6, 265 n.
xvi. 15, 274 n.
xviii. 12, 276
xviii. 19 ff., 276
xix. 15, 321 n.
xx. 24, 287
xxviii. 17–20, 281
xxviii. 30, 281
xxx. 1 ff., 277
xxxi. 2, 300
Leviticus ii. 9, 277
ii. 16, 277
vi. 19, 321
xvi. 278
Numbers i. 297 ff.
iii. 30, 298
vi. 25, 72
vii. 297 ff.
xiii. 297 ff., 301
xxi. 20, 272
xxiv. 20, 246
xxiv. 21–24, 243
xxv. 14, 299
xxv. 15, 319 n.
xxvi. 24, 110 n.
xxvi. 32, 99
xxvi. 36, 232 n.
xxvi. 45, 233 n.
xxxiv. 297 n.
xxxiv. 20, 98
Deuteronomy ii. 12, 261
xi. 10, 227
xvii. 12, 284
xviii. 1–8, 284

BIBLICAL PASSAGES REFERRED TO

Deuteronomy xviii. 6 ff., 282
  xx. 2, 287
  xxiii. 17, 113
  xxvi. 5, 201
  xxviii. 49 f , 244
  xxviii. 68, 11, 263 f.
  xxxii. 4, 318
  xxxiii. 266
  xxxiv. 5-7, 285
Joshua x. 3, 221
  x. 33, 221
  x. 41, 225
  xi. 16, 225
  xiii. 2, 240
  xiii. 19, 262
  xiii. 24, 253 n.
  xiii. 27, 253
  xv. 3, 262
  xv. 24, 241
  xv. 27, 242
  xv. 51, 225, 241
  xvi. 3, 238 n.
  xix. 26, 241
  xxiv. 2 f., 254 n., 325
  xxiv. 14 f., 256 n.
Judges ii. 11, 303
  iii. 6, 303
  viii. 24, 269
  ix. 26, 303 n.
  x. 12, 249, 270
1 Samuel ii. 2, 318
  xiv. 3, 284
  xv. 7, 239
  xxvii. 8, 240 f.
  xxvii. 10, 242, 244 n.
  xxx. 29, 244
2 Samuel ii. 9, 240
  viii. 9, 232 n.
  x. 16, 204, 254 n., 322
  xv. 37, 154
  xxii. 318

1 Kings iv. 21, 251, 254
  iv. 23, 252
  iv. 24, 252, 325
  xiv. 15, 254 n.
2 Kings xiv. 2, 319 n.
1 Chronicles i. ff., 301 n.
  i. 17-24, 292
  i. 36, 249 n.
  iv. 34, 101
  vii. 2, 98
  vii. 31, 233 n.
  vii. 32 f., 238 n.
2 Chronicles xiv. 314 n.
Job i. 15, 17, 247 n.
  ii. 11, 249
Psalms xviii. 318
  xxviii. 1, 71 n.
  xxxvii. 7, 71 n.
  l. 31, 71 n.
  lxxxi. 6, 111 n.
  lxxxix. 14, 310
  xci. 1, 310
  cx. 4, 152
Isaiah xiv. 12, 115
  xxii. 6, 205
Jeremiah vii. 22 ff., 15, 16
  xliii. 7, 251 n.
Ezekiel xxiii. 23, 206 n.
  xl. 3, 285
  xliv. 9 ff., 283
Daniel x. 4, 314
Hosea i. 9, 101 n.
  viii. 12, 16
  viii. 13, 11
  ix. 3, 11, 263 f.
Amos v. 25, 15
  ix. 7, 205
Habakkuk ii. 20, 71 n.
Acts vii. 42, 15
Hebrews v. 10, 146
  vii. 1-3, 152

WORKS ON

Bible Study and the "Higher Criticism."

For Sale By

E. & J. B. YOUNG & CO. Cooper Union, Fourth Avenue, New York

The Hebrew Monarchy

A Commentary, with a harmony of the Parallel Texts and Extracts from the Prophetical Books. By ANDREW WOOD, M.A. With an Introduction by the late Rev. R. PAYNE SMITH, D.D. Small 4to, cloth, gilt edges, $7.50.

This important Commentary is unique. It exhibits the History of the Hebrew Monarchy in a connected narrative, with everything necessary for its elucidation.

"It makes what are merely dry bones in ordinary commentaries live before us."—*The Scotsman.*

The Bible in the Light of To-Day

By CHARLES CROSLEGH, D.D., author of "Christianity Judged by Its Fruits." 12mo, cloth, pp. 518. $3.00.

This volume indicates the lines on which it is possible to hold the Bible to the divine, and at the same time to accept without misgiving, nay, to welcome with gratefulness, whatever light the increase of human knowledge may be able to throw upon it.

The Primitive Hebrew Records in the Light of Modern Research

By W. ST. CHAD BOSCAWEN. With numerous illustrations. 8vo, cloth, $2.00.

"In this work I have placed before my readers the Babylonian and Assyrian versions of those traditions which are found in the early chapters of Genesis, and such comparisons are instituted as seemed to me to be within the range of fair criticism; and I have endeavored to conduct this inquiry in as unbiased a manner as possible."—*From Preface.*

Our Bible and the Ancient Manuscripts

Being a History of the Text and its Translations. By FREDERIC J. KENYON. Illustrated with 26 facsimiles. 8vo, cloth, red edges, $2.00.

The present volume deals solely with the Bible's external history, the transmission of the sacred text.

The "Higher Criticism" and the Verdict of the Monuments

By the Rev. A. H. SAYCE. Fifth Edition. 590 pp., 8vo, cloth, $3.00.

A work on the "Higher Criticism," rich in archæological information, showing the actual testimony which recent discoveries are giving to the antiquity and historical character of the Old Testament. It is readable, thorough, and timely.

You Need a Bible and You Should Have the Best.

THE VARIORUM BIBLE

From the Celebrated Press of EYRE & SPOTTISWOODE, London,

IS THE MOST COMPLETE AND PERFECT.

It is issued *with or without Teachers' Aids* and can be had with the "*Variorum Apocrypha*," edited by Rev. C. J. BALL.

HEAR WHAT THOSE CAPABLE OF JUDGING SAY OF IT:

PROF. PELOUBET in his *Quarterly Notes* says: "The most complete and perfect Bible for teachers and pastors in existence."

PROF. EZRA ABBOTT says: ". . . . very far in advance of any of its rivals."

REV. ALVAH HOVEY says: "The amount of knowledge which it puts within the student's reach is extraordinary."

WHY IT IS THE BEST:

BECAUSE it CONTAINS MORE VALUABLE INFORMATION as to the Text than all the other Teacher's Bibles put together.

BECAUSE ON THE SAME PAGE AS THE TEXT are the very best results of Biblical Criticism and Scholarship, and the Evidence for and against the Revised Version.

BECAUSE the AUTHORITIES ARE QUOTED in each case, except where a general agreement is acknowledged.

BECAUSE the Articles in the "Aids" are written by the ABLEST AND MOST EMINENT SCHOLARS, and are CONDENSED and RELIABLE.

ITS ADVANTAGES:

1. It contains a collection of Notes vastly superior to any that can be found in any other volume.
2. THE GENERAL READER unacquainted with the Hebrew and Greek languages, is enabled to arrive at a *truer*, *fuller* and *deeper* meaning of the text than he could obtain from any other work.
3. THE TEACHER will find the use of the Variorum footnotes of the utmost value in the preparation of lessons.
4. THE BIBLE STUDENT will find a more careful selection of critical data and authorities than is elsewhere accessible.

The book is printed from Bourgeois type on both "thin white" and "India" paper. Size 9¼x6¼ inches. Styles of binding, with prices, as follows:

WITH THE TEACHER'S AIDS

No. 2801.	White Paper.	French Morocco. Divinity Circuit, leather lined	$7.50
No. 2803.	White Paper.	Persian Morocco. Divinity Circuit, leather lined	9.00
No. 2804.	White Paper.	As 2803, with Apocrypha added	11.00
No. 2805.	White Paper.	Genuine Levant. Divinity Circuit, calf lined	12.00
No. 2857.	"India" Paper.	Best Levant. Divinity Circuit, kid lined	15.00
No. 2858.	"India" Paper.	As 2857, with Apocrypha added	18.00

WITHOUT TEACHER'S AIDS

No. 2240.	White Paper.	Grained cloth, red edges	4.50
No. 2233.	"India" Paper.	Turkey Morocco	8.00
No. 2235.	"India" Paper.	Best Levant. Divinity Circuit, kid lined	12.00
No. 2236.	"India" Paper.	As 2235 interleaved throughout for MS. Notes	15.50
No. 2237.	"India" Paper.	As 2235, with Apocrypha, but *not* interleaved	15.00

A full descriptive circular free on application.

E. & J. B. YOUNG & CO., Cooper Union, New York

www.ingramcontent.com/pod-product-compliance
Lightning Source LLC
Chambersburg PA
CBHW020314240426
43673CB00039B/802